SPECIAL EDUCATIONAL NEEDS AND ACCESS TO JUSTICE

The Role of the Special Educational Needs Tribunal

SPECIAL EDUCATIONAL NEEDS AND ACCESS TO JUSTICE

The Role of the Special Educational Needs Tribunal

Neville Harris
Professor of Law
Liverpool John Moores University

JORDANS
1997

Published by
Jordan Publishing Limited
21 St Thomas Street
Bristol BS1 6JS

British Library Cataloguing-in-Publication Data
A catalogue record for this book is available from the British Library.

ISBN 0 85308 407 6

Typeset by Mendip Communications Ltd, Frome
Printed in Great Britain by Biddles Ltd, Guildford and King's Lynn

FOREWORD

The special educational needs tribunal first set up under the Education Act 1993 is a radical innovation in several different ways.

In the field of education, it was the first national tribunal completely independent of the education authorities, with a national President, lawyer chairs, linked to the ordinary legal system through an appeal to the High Court on points of law.

In the field of welfare services, it was probably the first judicial body (in England at least) to have power to specify the services which must be provided for a particular individual. If a court makes a care order, giving a local social services authority parental responsibility for a child, it cannot direct the authority where to place the child or what services they must provide for him. If a Mental Health Review Tribunal is considering whether to discharge a patient from hospital, it cannot direct the health or social services authorities exactly what services they must provide for him if he is discharged. If a person is in need of community care services, there is no tribunal which can direct the authorities exactly what services must be arranged.

Yet the special educational needs tribunal can tell local education authorities, not only that they must assess a child's needs, or maintain a statement of his needs, but also what that statement must contain. Parents often succeed in getting the school they want named in the statement. Resources are, of course, a relevant factor. But, as Professor Harris has found, the tribunal tends to concentrate more on what resources it is reasonable to devote to the particular child, rather than how the provision for that child fits into the overall pattern of services for children with special needs within the authority's area.

So the justice which this tribunal makes available to parents and their children is indeed a very special kind of justice. By and large, Professor Harris has found that the tribunal is doing a very good job. On the whole, both sides think that it is independent and unbiased. Parents generally feel that they are put at their ease and able to have their say. Any complaints are more about the practical problems of travelling, venues, and pressure of time than about the substance of what is done.

The one big question is whether the child himself should have an independent voice in his own education. Everyone else may be trying to do their best for him. But in every other area of dispute about a child's upbringing, there is a formal requirement to discover the child's views and give due consideration to them, having regard to his age and understanding. Education looms very large in any child's life. Hopefully, he spends a great deal of his waking hours in some form of educational activity. It is curious that a system which is so radical in other respects has been slower than others to recognise his independent status.

All of this is thoroughly explored in Professor Harris's fascinating study. The Nuffield Foundation was glad to have helped this to happen, as it neatly combined three of our long-standing interests, in education, child law and access to justice.

Brenda Hale
High Court Judge
Nuffield Foundation Trustee

PREFACE

The field of special educational needs is one of the most important in our education system. At least one in five children has 'learning difficulties' – perhaps as many as two million children altogether. Since the introduction of the Education Act 1981, the principle of 'partnership' between parents, on the one hand, and schools and local education authorities, on the other, has been promoted as being essential to ensure that children's needs are properly identified and catered for, so that children with special educational needs are helped to develop their full potential. But special educational provision is generally more expensive than ordinary, mainstream, education. Furthermore, parents and professionals do not always agree on what is best for the child. Disputes therefore arise.

Parental participation in decisions concerning their child's special educational needs has been reinforced by important rights, which were strengthened under the Education Act 1993 (now consolidated in the Education Act 1996). These rights include the right to take a dispute to the Special Educational Needs Tribunal (SENT). The SENT was established in September 1994 and heard its first case in January 1995. Since then, nearly 1,500 cases have been decided by the tribunal and the rate at which parents have been appealing has been steadily increasing. Ministers promised that the SENT would provide a speedy, fair and accessible means of redress. Unlike the appeal arrangements which it replaced, it would be completely independent, have lawyer chairs, be governed by strict rules of procedure (which would include time-limits to prevent delays) and make decisions which are binding on the parties. There are some, including the Council on Tribunals, who have raised the question whether the SENT ought not to be the model for other education appeal arrangements – notably those concerning exclusion appeals.

In order to assess the SENT's success in meeting the objectives set for it and its contribution to access to justice in the field of education, the author embarked on a comprehensive and independent study of the tribunal, with the full co-operation of the SENT President and Secretariat. This book seeks to provide a detailed account and analysis of the findings of this research, showing how the tribunal works and highlighting its strengths and weaknesses. I hope that the contents will be of interest to all those who have an involvement with the field of special educational needs – whether as members of the tribunal, legal advisers, voluntary organisations, befrienders, teachers, school governors, educational psychologists, parents, and so on – and academics with an interest in child law and/or public law. The House of Commons Education Select Committee (as it then was) has expressed an interest in the findings (Session 1995–96, Second Report, *Special Educational Needs: The Working of the Code of Practice and the Tribunal* (1996), HC 205, para 9) and this book also aims to inform the wider policy debate on the arrangements governing special educational needs set in place under Part III of the 1993 Act. The book covers developments up to and including 24 January 1997.

In the course of the research, many people assisted in one way or another and I wish to acknowledge my indebtedness to them.

I must record my particular thanks to Helen Whittaker, who was the research assistant to the project, and to Irene Dyson, who rendered secretarial assistance.

The co-operation of the SENT President and Secretary was of critical importance, and I am particularly grateful to Trevor Aldridge QC (the President), Jessica Saraga (the Secretary) and Alison Henry for their assistance and interest in the project.

A large number of voluntary organisations, lawyers and local education authority officers, together with a substantial majority of the chairs and lay members of the tribunal, gave up some of their time to complete questionnaires and/or discuss the SENT. I also express my gratitude to them.

The research would not have been possible without the financial assistance of the Nuffield Foundation. I would also like to record my thanks to the Education Law Association (ELAS) for additional support.

Finally, I acknowledge with thanks the support of Martin West and Mollie Dickenson of Jordans in ensuring speedy publication of the research findings embodied herein.

Neville Harris
School of Law,
Social Work & Social Policy,
Liverpool John Moores University
January 1997

CONTENTS

TABLE OF CASES

References in the right-hand column are to page numbers.

TABLE OF STATUTES

References in the right-hand columns are to page numbers.

TABLE OF STATUTORY INSTRUMENTS

References in the right-hand column are to page numbers.

TABLE OF CODES OF PRACTICE ETC

References in the right-hand column are to page numbers.

TABLE OF ABBREVIATIONS

DFE	Department for Education
DFEE	Department for Education and Employment
ELAS	Education Law Association
ELR	Education Law Reports
GEST	Grants for Education Support and Training
IPSEA	Independent Panel for Special Educational Advice
LEA	local education authority
SEN	special educational needs
SEN Regs	Education (Special Educational Needs) Regulations 1994
SENT	Special Educational Needs Tribunal
SENT Regs	Special Educational Needs Tribunal Regulations 1995
1993 Act	Education Act 1993
1996 Act	Education Act 1996

SCHEDULE OF TABLES

Chapter 1

INTRODUCTION

1.1 THE SPECIAL EDUCATIONAL NEEDS TRIBUNAL – THE BROAD PICTURE

The Special Educational Needs Tribunal (SENT) hears appeals brought by parents against various categories of decision by local education authorities (LEAs)[1] concerning the assessment of, and provision to meet, special educational needs, which affect approximately one in five school children.[2] It is a very important tribunal for a number of reasons. It is the first education tribunal which is required to have a lawyer chair and which is governed by detailed rules of procedure. It is also the first *national* education tribunal; it is centrally administered and it operates under the overall control of a national President.[3] It also has a power to issue binding rulings, but at the same time it is part of the first education appeal system to provide for a right of further appeal to the High Court (on a point of law). This book is based on the first comprehensive independent study of the tribunal, which was conducted by the author with the support of a grant from the Nuffield Foundation together with financial support from the Education Law Association.

The SENT is intended to provide an accessible and effective means of resolving disputes between parents and LEAs over special educational needs matters. Many of the disputes concern the question whether a child

---

1 The six grounds and the statutory provisions which contain them are summarised in Chapter 10, at **10.2**. This field has its own terminology, and terms such as 'assessment' and 'statements' are explained below at **1.2**. SENT statistics for 1995–96 (supplied to the author by the SENT and now contained in T. Aldridge QC, *Special Educational Needs Tribunal, Annual Report 1995/96* (SENT, 1996), p 9) show that the overwhelming majority of appeals are related to statements of special educational needs: 37% of appeals were against the contents of the statement, 12.5% in respect of the school named in the statement and 16% against a refusal to make a statement. Just over 24% were concerned with the LEA's refusal to assess the child.

2 Various categories of special educational need are involved. Of the appeals brought in 1995–96, nearly 40% concerned 'specific learning difficulties' (including general literacy problems and dyslexia), 11% moderate learning difficulties, 8% speech and language difficulties and 7% emotional and behavioural difficulties (SENT statistics supplied to the author and now presented in T. Aldridge QC, *Special Educational Needs Tribunal, Annual Report 1995/96* (SENT, 1996), p 14).

3 Trevor Aldridge QC.

should be the subject of a statement of special educational needs and, if so, what kind of provision to meet the child's needs should be specified in the statement. Often at issue is the question of placement – in other words, the school which the child should attend. The choice of school will in many cases have considerable cost implications for the LEA concerned, and the tribunal may have to weigh the cost against a number of other factors in making its important decision concerning the child's education. Thus the amount of detail in this book is a reflection not only of the amount of evidence which was compiled in conducting the study, including information and views emanating from parents and a large number of others working in the field,[4] but also the complexity of the issues which confront this important tribunal.

Redress of grievance in respect of a whole range of administrative decisions by public bodies has become a matter of much interest and concern among academics and 'consumers' of public services alike. The massive changes to the education system and its legal framework over the past decade and a half have produced enormous opportunities for parents to challenge decisions affecting their children's education and to call providers of education to account. The particular significance of the SENT is that it represents the first attempt, in the education sphere, to establish an independent judicial body modelled along classic tribunal lines, where particular attention is given to accessibility and relative informality. Pressure is mounting to reform, along similar lines, the adjudication system concerned with other areas of education decision-making, such as school admissions and permanent exclusions from school. The SENT is thus seen as a model for the possible future development of education tribunals. Not surprisingly, therefore, there is considerable interest in its record in meeting its objectives of providing a fair, impartial, accessible and reasonably speedy avenue of redress for parents.

Reference was made above to the complexity of the issues in many special educational needs disputes. It should be appreciated that parents often have very strong feelings about the kind of regime which will best meet the needs of their children with learning difficulties. Their perspective of their child's needs and how they can best be catered for within the education system is often very different from that of the LEA, which, in addition to

---

4 Many different groups of people are involved in this field: children, parents, LEA officers, lay and lawyer members of the SENT, voluntary organisations, legal advisers and advocates, and – as witnesses or providers of specialist reports – teachers, health and welfare workers, psychologists and other experts.

having statutory responsibilities towards such a child, will have not only the needs of many other children to consider but also the limits to the resources at the LEA's disposal. It is not at all surprising that conflict arises. Despite the emphasis on 'partnership' between parents and schools/LEAs which has been promoted since the Education Act 1981 and given further impetus by the 1993 Act and the Code of Practice, the combination of continuing resource constraints on LEAs and increased expectations by parents, fostered in particular by the *Parent's Charter*, the DFEE's *Special Educational Needs: A Guide for Parents*[5] and the developing culture of education 'rights', mean that dispute resolution will have increasing importance. The number of appeals to the SENT to date has been several times greater than the number of appeals which were dealt with by local appeal committees and the Secretary of State under the previous arrangements.[6] Everyone working in the field confidently expects that number to continue to increase, although perhaps not so rapidly, for the foreseeable future.

Partly as a result of the way the legislation has been constructed and partly because of the very technical nature of diagnoses and definitions of learning difficulty, the SENT is faced with a challenging task. It not only has to apply the law accurately and fairly, which is not easy in such a rapidly developing field, it also has to make fine judgments about the needs of children, and the provision required to meet them, which will have crucial long-term effects as regards the children's intellectual, social and, in some cases, physical development as well as their academic attainment. The SENT has also to conform to expectations about a modern adjudication system: that it should minimise delays and provide a 'good service', which in this context means one which is, inter alia, accessible to parents whilst at the same time efficient. The objectives of the legislation which established the SENT were that it should provide an effective means of access to justice for parents, by operating 'a new system that is quick, simple, impartial and independent; a system in which informality is the key'[7] and one which is 'friendly' to parents.[8] Meeting these objectives depends, amongst other things, on establishing an effective organisational structure for the administration of appeals, fair

---

5 There are separate publications in Wales: *Education: A Charter for Parents in Wales* and *Special Educational Needs: A Guide for Parents in Wales*, both published by the Welsh Office.

6 See Chapter 2.

7 Hansard, HL, Vol 545, col 567, per Baroness Blatch, Minister of State.

8 *Official Report*, Standing Committee E, col 1168, 28 January 1993, per Mr T. Boswell MP, Minister of State.

and efficient procedures at all stages and an appropriately qualified tribunal membership. It also involves responding in particular to the needs of parents as they pursue their appeal through an unfamiliar judicial process.

There are, of course, limits to the assistance which an independent and impartial system can provide to one party. Parents make a choice about whether to appeal to the SENT and the onus on presenting the grounds for their appeal rests with them. If the LEA defends the case, the parents will also have to take responsibility for assembling any additional evidence that they believe supports their position on the issues under dispute. Although the tribunal may aim to deal with the matter in as inquisitorial a manner as possible, the appeal involves a dispute between two parties who may have diametrically opposing views; those views need to be heard properly and an opportunity given to the parties to question each other.

The hearing and the process leading to it inevitably assume an adversarial character at times. This means that despite the tribunal's efforts in asking the questions which have not been asked by the parties, and despite the tenacity and determination of many parents, the successful preparation and presentation of the parents' case will often require outside assistance. Voluntary organisations and lawyers offering specialist legal expertise have already developed a substantial involvement in this field. Their involvement is also important in helping parents cope with the nerves and apprehension which often afflict them when they attend the hearing, after what is likely to have been a considerable period of waiting (generally in excess of four months). Nevertheless, the system must be capable of doing its best for unaided parents, without prejudicing the tribunal's impartiality.

To many interested in a process designed to ensure that the best possible arrangements, within the scope that the law allows, are made for children with special educational needs, the emphasis on the rights and opportunities of parents in the above discussion, rather than on the rights of the child, may seem a little strange. After all, in the era of the Children Act 1989 and UN Convention on the Rights of the Child, which seek to put the child's interests and welfare to the fore (indeed, to make them 'paramount', in the case of the 1989 Act) in any decisions concerning his or her upbringing, support and other matters, and under which parental rights are perceived as merely a facet of parental responsibility to do what is best for the child, it seems inappropriate to speak of parents' rights in such absolute and exclusive terms. Unfortunately, the development of a 'consumer' culture in the field of education has depended in large part on the promotion of parental rights of choice, information, representation and redress, while the independent interests of children have generally not been recognised via specific children's rights in this area.[9] As Bainham has put it:

> 'We have, for example, the *parent's* charter ... *parental* choice of school ... *parent* governors ..., the *parental* right of withdrawal from religious education and collective worship ... the *parent's* ... right to withdraw his or her child from sex education ... [T]he effect of domestic educational policy of recent years has been to eclipse children's rights in stark contrast to the eclipse of parental rights elsewhere'.[10]

In the field of special educational needs, the position of parents as exclusive appellants against LEA decisions (which obviously raises problems for children in local authority care who have no parents to act as advocates[11]) under the legislation was confirmed last year by the Court of Appeal, which held that a child cannot be a party to the appeal before the SENT or any further appeal to the High Court.[12] The child is left merely with the possibility of his or her views being taken into account – due regard being had for the age and understanding of the child concerned – as recommended by the Code of Practice.[13]

Lord Campbell of Alloway's Education (Special Educational Needs) Bill, which (at the time of writing) is currently before Parliament, would, if enacted, extend an independent right of appeal to the child (so that either the parent or the child would be able to appeal). According to Lord Campbell, children need an independent right of appeal to the SENT because they may have no support from their parents; or the parents may have lost interest or patience in them; or relationships between parents and child may have simply broken down; or the child (especially the older child) may disagree with the parents (particularly where the parents are

---

9 For further discussion, see N. Harris, *Law and Education: Regulation, Consumerism and the Education System* (Sweet & Maxwell, 1993), pp 19–22.

10 A. Bainham, 'Sex education: a family lawyer's perspective', in N. Harris (ed) *Children, Sex Education and the Law* (National Children's Bureau, 1996), 30.

11 See J. Timms, *Children's Representation. A Practitioner's Guide* (Sweet & Maxwell, 1995), pp 429–430; S. Oliver and L. Austen, *Special Educational Needs and the Law* (Jordans, 1996), pp 95–97.

12 *S v Special Educational Needs Tribunal and the City of Westminster* [1996] ELR 228, CA. Note that in *Fairpo v Humberside County Council* [1997] 1 All ER 183, Laws J held that a foster parent with whom a child has been placed by a local authority is a 'parent' for the purposes of the Education Acts and thus has a right of appeal against a decision of the SENT.

13 Paragraph 1.120.

not the natural parents, as is often the case).[14] The Bill does not have Government support, however. The Minister, Lord Henley, has argued that there could be problems, for example if the child and parent disagreed, and that the present legislative provisions work satisfactorily:

> 'The approach of the tribunal that we have created under the 1993 Act to encourage various ways of hearing the child's views is the appropriate, right, proper and sensible way to tackle this matter. To place the weight of the statutory involvement on the child is not the right approach.'[15]

The involvement of children in the special educational needs appeal process is discussed further in later chapters.

Special educational needs is a very specialist field with its own distinct practices and procedures. Nevertheless, the attempt, in line with the Warnock recommendations[16] and the requirements of the Education Acts 1981 and 1993, to maximise the participation of children with special educational needs in mainstream schools (the principle of 'integration', now often referred to as 'inclusion'), has raised the profile of the field. The law on special educational needs is now one of the most important areas of education law, and one which has an impact on the whole of the education system. Because provision to meet special educational needs has considerable financial implications for schools and LEAs, and because at the same time parental demands that children with special educational needs should be properly catered for, the scope for conflict is considerable, as noted above. Special educational needs disputes are among the most hotly contested in the education field. The SENT is at the forefront of attempts to provide an effective dispute resolution mechanism and it warrants close attention.

1.2 SPECIAL EDUCATIONAL NEEDS: AN INTRODUCTION TO THE LEGAL FRAMEWORK

A detailed account of the law relating to special educational needs is outside the scope of this book.[17] Nevertheless, key aspects of the basic

---

14 Hansard, HL, Vol 575, cols 253–254, 29 October 1996.
15 Ibid, col 1155, 11 December 1996.
16 *Special Educational Needs*, Cmnd 7212 (HMSO, 1978).
17 See further S. Oliver and L. Austen, *Special Educational Needs and the Law* (Jordans, 1996); J. Friel, *Children with Special Needs – Assessment, Law and Practice, Caught in the Acts* (3rd edn) (Jessica Kingsley, 1995); and N. Harris, *The Law Relating to Schools* (2nd edn) (Tolley, 1995), Ch 9.

framework are outlined below, as some knowledge of the substantive issues in the field is necessary in order to understand the nature of the decisions which the SENT has to make.

The legislation applies to children with 'special educational needs' (SEN). The law states that a child (defined as a school pupil aged below 19[18]) has SEN if he 'has a learning difficulty which calls for special educational provision to be made for him'.[19] A child has a 'learning difficulty' in any one of three sets of circumstances:

'(a) he has a significantly greater difficulty in learning than the majority of children his age,
 (b) he has disability which either prevents or hinders him from making use of the educational facilities of a kind generally provided for children of his age in schools within the area of the local education authority, or
 (c) he is under the age of five years and is, or would be if special educational provision were not made for him, likely to fall within paragraphs (a) or (b) when over that age.'[20]

Thus to fall within the scope of the legislation, a child must have a learning difficulty within the terms of (a), (b) or (c) above and that difficulty must require special educational provision to be made for him.[21] 'Special educational provision' means provision which is additional to or different from the provision made 'generally' for pupils of the child's age in the LEA's non-special schools or in grant-maintained schools in the area.[22] In the case of a child aged under two, any educational provision needed would be classed as special educational provision.[23] There is a duty, resting primarily with LEAs, to ensure that 'best endeavours' are used to ensure that children with SEN receive the special educational provision their needs call for.[24] LEAs must also make the child's needs known to those who are likely to teach him or her.[25]

---

18 1996 Act, s 312(5).
19 Ibid, s 312(1). See also sub-s (3).
20 Ibid, s 312(2).
21 See, for example, *R v Hampshire Education Authority ex parte J* (1985) 84 LGR 547 (dyslexia can give rise to 'learning difficulty'); *R v Lancashire County Council ex parte CM* [1989] 2 FLR 279 (speech therapy can amount to special educational provision), disapproving *R v Oxfordshire Education Authority ex parte W* (1986) *The Times*, 20 November; *R v London Borough of Lambeth ex parte MBM* [1995] ELR 374 at 382 (a lift in a school, needed by a disabled pupil, would not amount to educational provision).
22 1996 Act, s 312(4)(a). See further *ex parte J*, op cit.
23 Ibid, s 312(4)(b).
24 Ibid, s 317(1)(a).
25 Ibid, s 317(1)(b).

In broad terms, LEAs and schools have a duty to ensure that children with special educational needs are educated in mainstream schools.[26] This embodies the key principle of 'integration' or 'inclusion' which was a cornerstone of the Warnock reforms. This duty is not, however, unqualified. In particular, educating a child in an ordinary school must be compatible with: (i) his receiving the special educational provision he needs; (ii) efficient education for the pupils with whom he or she would be educated; and (iii) the efficient use of resources.[27] Furthermore, educating a child at the school must not be 'incompatible with the wishes of his parent'.[28] This does not, however, give the parents a veto over the decision, because the LEA must still decide on the provision which will meet the child's needs, whether in a mainstream school or not.[29] If the child is educated in a mainstream school, the school and the LEA must ensure that, subject to the same conditions ((i)–(iii) above), he or she 'engages in the activities of the school together with children who do not have special educational needs'. The same conditions apply where the parent selects a school which he or she wishes to be named in a statement of special educational needs (see below).

LEAs have a duty to exercise their powers with a view to ensuring that pupils with SEN are identified. In practice, and in accordance with the provisions of the *Code of Practice on the Identification and Assessment of Special Educational Needs* (the Code of Practice),[30] day-to-day responsibility for identifying children with SEN rests with teachers, although health authorities and trusts will often also identify such children and, where they do, must bring them to the attention of the LEA.[31]

Appeals under the 1996 Act are concerned with formal assessment or statementing (see below). Formal assessment, whether at the request of the parent or at the instigation of a governing body of a grant-maintained school or the LEA, will only occur if the LEA considers that the child has,

---

26 1996 Act, s 316. In any event, LEAs (and in some cases, funding authorities) have a duty to ensure that schools in an area are sufficient in number, character and equipment to provide 'appropriate education' for all pupils; in respect of this duty, LEAs must take account of 'the need for securing that special educational provision is made for pupils who have special educational needs': 1996 Act, s 14(1)–(3) and (6).

27 Ibid, s 316(2).

28 Ibid, s 316(1).

29 See *S v Special Educational Needs Tribunal and the City of Westminster* [1996] ELR 102 at 113–114, per Latham J.

30 DFE (1994) Part 2. See, for example, para 2:71.

31 1996 Act, s 332.

or probably has, SEN *and* it is 'necessary ... to determine the special educational provision' which the child's special educational need(s) call(s) for.[32] In other cases, there will be no more than informal assessment carried out at school in up to three school-based stages.[33] A parent has a right of appeal to the SENT where the LEA decides not to carry out a formal assessment (including a further assessment).[34] Once the LEA serves notice of its intention to conduct a formal assessment, the parent may make representations within a prescribed period (of at least 29 days). The LEA must make an assessment if, having taken account of the representations and any submissions made to it, it remains of the opinion that the child's needs are such that it should 'determine' the special educational provision that should be made. When an LEA 'determines' the provision, it describes it, along with the child's various needs, in a 'statement' (see below).

The procedure involved in carrying out the formal assessment is prescribed by the Act and regulations.[35] The assessment must, for example, normally be carried out within ten weeks and must involve a range of professional inputs (or 'advice'). The parent's and the child's views should normally be taken into account.[36] The child will normally be examined, and the parent has a right to be present.[37] The LEA has a duty to inform the parent of its decision following assessment, together, in most cases, with its reasons.[38]

The LEA has a duty to prepare a 'statement' in respect of the child if, having carried out the formal assessment, it considers that it is 'necessary' to determine the special educational provision which is required for the child in the light of his or her learning difficulties.[39] The contents of the statement must be in the prescribed form (set out in 'parts') and contain the prescribed information.[40] The statement will cover the child's SEN (Part 2), the special educational provision which is required (Part 3), the

---

32 1996 Act, ss 323, 328, 329 and 331.
33 See the Code of Practice, op cit, para 1:4 for a summary. A considerable proportion of the Code is concerned with the school-based stages of assessment.
34 1996 Act, ss 328 and 329: see Chapter 10.
35 Ibid, Sch 26; Education (Special Educational Needs) Regulations 1994, SI 1994/ 1047, regs 6–9.
36 Education (Special Educational Needs) Regulations 1994, op cit, reg 10; Code of Practice, paras 3:100–3:102 and 3:120.
37 1996 Act, Sch 26 para 4.
38 Ibid, ss 321(4), 328 and 329.
39 Ibid, s 324(1).
40 Ibid, s 324(2)–(4); the Education (Special Educational Needs) Regulations 1994, op cit, Sch, Part B.

'placement' (the name or type of school which the child should attend or the means by which the child will receive education otherwise than at school) (Part 4), non-educational needs (Part 5) and non-educational provision (Part 6).[41] The various pieces of professional advice on which the main part of the statement is based must be appended.[42]

The legislation has always distinguished between children with SEN per se and children whose SEN are such that a statement spelling out the provision that they need is required.[43] However, there has been an understandable reluctance to include in the legislation a more specific definition of the circumstances when a statement should be made: under the 1981 Act, the LEA had to be 'of the opinion' that a statement should be made, whereas, as noted above, the 1996 Act provides for a test of necessity, while still leaving the decision to the LEA's discretion. The Code of Practice offers detailed guidance, but in essence it often comes down to the question whether the provision the child requires can, *in the opinion of the LEA*, be met from the resources normally allocated to mainstream schools in the area. According to the Code,[44] only if adequate provision could not be made from the school's own resources should provision be specified in a statement.

In many LEAs, decisions regarding special educational provision, including placement, may be heavily coloured by policy considerations, such as a policy of allocating resources and making statements in accordance with, inter alia, bands of intelligence scores or of funding provision almost exclusively in the LEA's own schools. Such policies are unlawful if they are too inflexible and fetter discretion, or if they are based on irrelevant considerations. To date, however, several LEAs have survived legal challenges to their SEN policies.[45] Thus it is not surprising that many parents appeal to the SENT over a decision by the LEA not to make a statement[46] and that at issue is the question of resources.

---

41 The degree of specificity required in relation to these contents of the statement was considered in *R v Secretary of State for Education and Science ex parte E* [1992] 1 FLR 377 CA; *Re L* [1994] ELR 16 CA; *R v Hereford and Worcester County Council ex parte P* [1992] 2 FLR 207; *R v London Borough of Hackney ex parte GC* [1995] ELR 144 QBD; [1996] ELR 142 CA.

42 Education (Special Educational Needs) Regulations 1994, op cit, Sch, Part B. See also *R v Mid-Glamorgan County Council ex parte B* [1995] ELR 168 QBD.

43 See *R v Secretary of State for Education and Science ex parte Lashford* [1988] 1 FLR 72.

44 Op cit, Part 4.

45 See, for example, *R v London Borough of Newham ex parte R* [1995] ELR 156, QBD; *R v Cumbria County Council ex parte NB* [1996] ELR 65, QBD.

46 1996 Act, s 325. See Tables 22A and 22B in Chapter 10.

Parents can also appeal to the SENT against the description in the statement of the LEA's assessment of the child's SEN, against the provision specified in the statement or against a decision by the LEA not to name a school in the statement.[47] They may also appeal against a decision to cease to maintain a statement.[48]

The 1993 Act introduced a new right for parents to select a school to be named in the statement. When, following the assessment, the LEA prepares a draft statement, it may not name a school in it. Instead, the parent has to be given an opportunity to choose a school to be named. If the LEA proceeds to make a statement,[49] it must include the name of the school selected by the parent unless the school is 'unsuitable' having regard to the child's age, ability or aptitude or to his special educational needs, or unless the attendance of the child at the school would not be compatible with the provision of efficient education for other children who attend or with the efficient use of resources.[50] Where an independent school is named in a statement, that fact does not automatically mean that the LEA will be liable to meet the fees; such liability might only arise if, inter alia, the naming of the particular school in the statement was necessary in the light of the child's specific educational needs.[51] As noted above, the parent can appeal against a decision by the LEA not to name a school in the statement.

If the LEA has decided to make a statement it must normally prepare it within eight weeks from the date on which a copy of the draft statement is served on the parents.[52] Once a statement is maintained by the LEA, it must ensure that the provision specified in the statement is made for the child unless the child's parent has made 'suitable arrangements'.[53]

---

47 1996 Act, s 326.

48 Ibid, Sch 27 para 11. A pending appeal to the SENT does not operate as a stay to the cessation of a statement: *R v Oxfordshire County Council ex parte Roast* [1996] ELR 381, QBD.

49 The fact that the LEA makes a draft does not bind it to make a statement: see *R v Isle of Wight County Council ex parte RS and AS* [1993] 1 FLR 634, CA.

50 1996 Act, Sch 27 para 3.

51 *R v London Borough of Hackney ex parte GC* [1996] ELR 142, CA; *Staffordshire County Council v J and J* [1996] ELR 418, QBD.

52 1996 Act, Sch 27 para 5; Education (Special Educational Needs) Regulations 1994, SI 1994/1407, reg 14(2).

53 1996 Act, s 324(5)(a). See *R v Governors of the Hasmonean High School ex parte N and E* [1994] ELR 343, CA; *R v London Borough of Hackney ex parte GC* [1995] ELR 144, QBD.

Furthermore, the head teacher of any maintained school named in the statement must admit the child to the school.[54]

Statements have to be reviewed by the LEA at least once every 12 months[55] or if there is a formal assessment. The statement may be amended by the LEA or, in respect of the school named, at the request of the parent. If the parent disagrees with the LEA or if his or her request is turned down, she/he may appeal to the SENT.[56] Wherever the right of appeal against a decision arises in the legislation, there is duty on the LEA to inform the parent of that right when notifying him or her of the decision.

(Note that the Education (Special Educational Needs) Bill (referred to above) would not only enable a child to appeal to the SENT but would also require the child to be informed of various matters (for example, a proposal to amend a statement) and to receive a copy of a proposed statement.)

1.3   THE STRUCTURE OF THE REST OF THE BOOK

The remainder of the book is primarily concerned with presenting and discussing the findings of the author's research into the SENT. The research covered the first 20 months of the tribunal's operation, which began on 1 September 1994.

Chapter 2 explains the background to the SENT and outlines some of the questions its development raises.

Chapter 3 describes the methodologies employed in attempting to assess the SENT's effectiveness in providing access to justice.

Chapter 4 explores the structure of the SENT. It focuses on the appointment, qualifications and experience of chairs and lay members of the tribunal and aspects of their role and training. It also discusses the SENT Secretariat and charts its development and growth.

Chapter 5 is concerned with the ways in which LEAs have been affected by the introduction of the SENT, in particular the new system's impact

---

54 1996 Act, s 324(5)(b) and (6).

55 Beginning with the date on which the assessment was carried out or the date of the previous review. See also the Education (Special Educational Needs) Regulations 1994, op cit, regs 15–17.

56 1996 Act, s 326 and Sch 27 paras 8 and 10.

on their workload and on the likelihood of settlement of disputes. It also looks at the provision of information by LEAs to parents.

Chapter 6 explores in detail the steps taken by the tribunal and by appellants (whose socio-economic profile is surveyed) in preparation for an appeal. This includes discussion of procedural matters, including standard forms and letters used by the tribunal and rules relating to notice and discovery, and also of the burden of work falling on tribunal members. Also considered are the waiting time between lodging an appeal and the hearing before the tribunal and the assembling of evidence, including independent expert reports.

Chapter 7 focuses on tribunal venues and facilities, providing, in particular, an objective assessment (based on empirical observation) of the use of hotels for SENT hearings.

Chapter 8 looks at the role of representation before the SENT and, in particular, at who is providing it and the extent to which they are trained to do so. The effectiveness of representation is also assessed. The evidence presented includes parents' views on the value of representation.

Chapter 9 examines the hearing itself, in some depth. It presents evidence on the views of the parties on the way they were treated and the extent of their participation in the hearing, the involvement of children in hearings, and the kind of procedure followed.

Chapter 10 focuses on the decision of the tribunal. It explores such issues as the possibility of bias in decision-making, the provision of reasons for decisions and the use of the right of further appeal to the High Court on a point of law.

Chapter 11 presents some conclusions and recommendations for reform.

The author intends to continue to monitor the SENT and welcomes comments on its operation.

Chapter 2

THE EVOLUTION OF THE SPECIAL EDUCATIONAL NEEDS TRIBUNAL

2.1   INTRODUCTION

The law on special educational needs is now contained in the Education Act 1996[1] – a consolidation measure incorporating the Education Act 1993, Part III. The 1993 Act introduced important reforms in this field, including a new *Code of Practice on the Identification and Assessment of Special Educational Needs.*[2] One of the aims of the reforms was to improve the opportunities for parents to influence decisions concerning their children's education. The introduction of the SENT was one of the means of promoting parental rights. This reform established an important new appeal mechanism for parents, in place of the bifurcated system which operated under the Education Act 1981. The changes to the appeal arrangements under the 1993 Act, introduced in 1994,[3] were in some ways the most significant of all of the reforms to the law on special educational needs previously contained in the Education Act 1981. With the exception of the new Code of Practice, other elements of the legislation tended for the most part to develop and improve on the framework proposed in the Warnock Report[4] and enshrined in the 1981 Act.

This chapter examines the historical background to the reform of the SEN appeal system in order to explain both the deficiencies in the previous arrangements which the new system is intended to remedy and the questions arising from the establishment of the SENT.

2.2   THE EDUCATION ACT 1981

The Education Act 1981 set out a new legal definition of special educational needs – with reference to the concept of 'learning difficulty' rather than categories of disability and educational 'sub-normality' which prevailed under previous legislation (principally the Education Act 1944). It also enshrined in law fundamental principles on such matters as

---

1 Part IV of the 1996 Act, which came into effect on 1 November 1996.
2 DFE, 1994.
3 The SENT came into existence on 1 September 1994.
4 *Special Educational Needs*, Cmnd 7212 (HMSO, 1978).

integration of children with special educational needs into mainstream schooling, partnership between schools, LEAs and parents and support for special educational provision. In these respects the 1981 Act was, as noted in Chapter 1, modelled on the recommendations of the Warnock Report,[5] which also made specific recommendations on teacher training, the curriculum, careers guidance and other matters.

Warnock placed considerable emphasis on the importance of the role of education authorities, but the Committee also believed that LEAs should be accountable to parents for their decisions. Thus, for example, the report recommended that parents should have ready access to the documents comprising the records of their own child, which subsequently came to be referred to as a statement of special educational needs, with its form prescribed by law.[6] Warnock also made recommendations for parents to have a right of appeal against a decision by an LEA to record or not to record their child as in need of special educational provision.[7] Appeal was to lie to the Secretary of State. At the time that this recommendation was made, parents' right of appeal to the Secretary of State (under s 34 of the Education Act 1944) was limited to cases where the authority's decision was that the child required special education.

When the Education Bill was before Parliament in 1980–81, it was clear that the Government had accepted the Committee's recommendation on the right of appeal; but it was equally clear that Ministers anticipated that appeals would be very much a matter of last resort. For example, Baroness Young explained in the House of Lords that she had 'every hope that the arrangements in the Bill for the involvement [of parents] throughout the assessment procedures will make recourse to an appeal . . . a very rare occurrence'.[8] Indeed, Ministers were confident that LEAs' decisions would be pragmatic in nature where SEN assessment and provision were concerned, so that there would be no need for parents to have a right of appeal against a refusal by the LEA to accede to their request for the assessment of their child's needs. If the LEA decided not to proceed with an assessment 'that would normally be because it has been persuaded by the representations of the parents. Therefore it is unnecessary to think of a right of appeal for the parents in that case'.[9]

---

5 *Special Educational Needs*, Cmnd 7212 (HMSO, 1978).
6 Ibid, para 4.70.
7 Ibid, para 4.74.
8 Hansard, HL, Vol 421, col 982, 23 June 1981.
9 Ibid, HL, Vol 423, col 999, 30 July 1981, per Baroness Young, Minister of State.

The 1981 Act provided for two separate grounds and routes of appeal:

(1) Under s 5 of the Act there was a right of appeal to the Secretary of State when the LEA, having made an assessment, considered that it was not required to determine that special educational provision should be made for a child. In other words, parents could appeal against a decision not to issue a statement of special educational needs.[10] On an appeal, the Secretary of State could, if he thought fit, direct the LEA to reconsider its decision.[11]

(2) Parents could appeal under s 8 against the special educational provision proposed in a statement following the first or any subsequent assessment of a child, or against any amendment of an existing statement by the LEA. Under this second ground, an appeal could involve a two-stage process. Initially, it lay to an appeal committee – this was in effect an extension of the role of the lay appeal committees established under the Education Act 1980 to deal with school admissions appeals, although frequently there was an attempt to ensure that a person or persons with experience of special educational needs was/were included on a panel. The committee's decisions on special educational needs appeals were not binding on LEAs. The committee could only confirm the provision specified in the statement or remit the case to the LEA for reconsideration in the light of the committee's recommendations.[12] The parent had a right of further appeal against the committee's decision, or against the LEA's decision on a remitted case. This further appeal lay to the Secretary of State, who could confirm, amend or order the cessation of a statement.[13]

In response to arguments that the right of appeal would be ineffective if an appeal committee's decision could not bind the LEA, the Government had argued that questions of special educational placement at a particular school, which were expected to be the principal issue in many appeals, were very different from those concerning placement at ordinary schools:

'Factors such as the availability of medical and other supporting services, the limited number of places available in any particular type of special school, and the limited variety of special needs for which any one school can provide

---

10 1981 Act, s 5(6).
11 Ibid, s 5(8).
12 Ibid, s 8(4) and (5).
13 Ibid, s 8(6) and (7). The Secretary of State's decision could only relate to provision *to be made* and could not, thus, have retrospective effect: *R v Secretary of State for Education and Science ex parte Davis* (1988) *The Guardian*, 12 December (QBD).

are crucial in special education. They make such cases far more complex than ordinary ones. That is why the appeals committee's view will not be binding.'[14]

It was also claimed that the role of the appeal committee would be rather different. In school admission appeals under the 1980 Act, 'the question to be resolved will be choice of school on grounds of parental preference', whereas in SEN appeals under the 1981 Act, 'the question is likely to be of how well the school or other provision proposed will match the needs of the child'.[15] The Government also acknowledged that the appeal committees' potential lack of expertise in the field of SEN might make it inappropriate for them to be the final arbiters:

'given the range and variety of complex issues which might conceivably be placed before them, we can never ensure that an appeal committee will be composed of the people with precisely the kind of expertise which may be required in each case to reach a definite decision.'[16]

Thus, the committee would have the power to refer the matter back to the LEA for further consideration in the light of the observations it had made. Parents would be able to make a further appeal to the Secretary of State who could confirm, amend or order the cessation of a statement.[17]

Attempts by the Opposition to secure an amendment to the Bill, to the effect that the appeal committee's decision would be binding on the LEA, were, therefore, resisted. Yet concern continued to be expressed that an appeal to the Secretary of State would not be particularly accessible to most parents: 'it demands great stamina, determination and persistence on the part of a parent who has already been through all the procedures first'.[18] In fact, the number of such appeals, although fairly small, increased almost year-on-year from 1984–1991, more than trebling over this period, as shown in Table 1.

---

14 Hansard, HC, Vol 998, col 33, 2 February 1981, per Mr M. Carlisle MP, Secretary of State.
15 Hansard, HL, Vol 421, col 982, 23 June 1981, per Baroness Young, Minister of State.
16 Ibid, Vol 423, col 899, 31 July 1981, per Baroness Young, Minister of State.
17 1981 Act, s 8(7).
18 Hansard, HL, Vol 421, col 1021, 23 June 1981, per Baroness Darcy de Knayth.

Table 1

Appeals to the Secretary of State under the Education Act 1981, 1984–1991

Grounds and route	1984	1985	1986	1987	1988	1989	1990	1991
Section 5	19	21	28	36	37	50	64	72
Section 8	20	28	36	33	36	49	42	78
Totals	39	49	64	69	74	99	106	146

Source: DFE Statistics supplied to the author.
Note: s 5 covered appeals against the LEA's decision not to make a statement, whilst s 8 appeals were further appeals following a local appeal committee's decision on a parent's appeal against provision proposed in a statement.

Appeals to the local appeal committees under the 1981 Act were not centrally monitored, other than via the Council on Tribunals' Annual Reports. It is not clear from these reports how many appeals were heard each year by local appeal committees. The author estimates, extrapolating from information given by a representative sample of LEAs, that there were 300–400 such appeals each year,[19] in addition to the 100 or so appeals which went to the Secretary of State, some half of which (those under s 8 of the Act) had been heard by local appeal committees first.

The case for reform

Calls for reform of the appeal arrangements under the 1981 Act were part of a general pattern of criticism of aspects of the legal regime.[20] Discussion in this book must concentrate on the appeal system, but it is important to note that there was evidence that the partnership arrangement with parents, which the architects of the 1981 legislation expected would lead to resolution of difficulties without recourse to the

---

19 A total of 71 LEAs provided information in response to a request for data concerning appeals under the 1981 Act between 1 April 1993 and 31 March 1994, or any other recent period of 12 months prior to the introduction of the SENT; there were 226 appeals lodged in total.

20 For an early critical review, see V. Hannon, 'The Education Act 1981: New Rights and Duties in Special Education' (1982) *Journal of Social Welfare Law* 275.

appeal system, was not working as well as had been expected.[21] Indeed, commentators highlight an increased resort by parents to redress mechanisms to resolve conflicts over special educational needs.[22]

Doubts about the capacity of all lay committees to perform a quasi-judicial role had been confirmed by Professor Kathleen Bell's report on supplementary benefit appeal tribunals, which highlighted various problems in these, almost exclusively, lay panels' conduct of hearings. The problems included ineffective weighing up of evidence, procedural irregularities and lack of adequate reasons for decisions.[23] Local education appeal committees gave rise to similar concerns,[24] along with continuing anxiety about their lack of independence.[25] Nevertheless, the publication of approved codes of practice on education appeals, coupled with an increasing amount of training, helped to ameliorate some of these problems.

Another problem was one of delayed justice. One of the major criticisms of the operation of the 1981 Act was that parents and children were faced with delays at all stages – assessments, statementing and appeals. So far as appeals were concerned, they involved 'a lengthy process and one which few parents undertake', with parents often having to wait six months or longer for a decision from the Secretary of State.[26] The Government acknowledged the problem and attributed the delay to increases in the number and complexity of appeals.[27] It was accepted by the DFE that the fact the appeal process in general operated slowly added to the anguish of

---

21 See, for example, House of Commons, Education, Science and the Arts Committee, Third Report, 1986/87, *Special Educational Needs: Implementation of the Education Act 1981*, Vol 1, HC201–1 (HMSO, 1987); and House of Commons Select Committee, Third Report, 1992/93, *Meeting of Special Educational Needs and Provision*, HC287-I (HMSO, 1993).

22 See, for example, S. Wolfendale, 'Policy and provision for children with special educational needs in the early years', in S. Riddell and S. Brown, *Special Educational Needs Policy in the 1990s* (Routledge, 1994), at pp 60–61.

23 K. Bell, *Research Study on Supplementary Benefit Appeal Tribunals. Review of Main Findings: Conclusions: Recommendations* (HMSO, 1975).

24 See Council on Tribunals, *Annual Report, 1986/87* (HMSO, 1987), paras 3.24–3.26; *Annual Report 1987/88* (HMSO, 1988), paras 2.34 and 2.41.

25 V. Hannon, op cit, refers to the committees as '"quasi-independent" since LEAs themselves not only nominate the membership, but may also have a majority of their own elected members on them' (at p 283).

26 Audit Commission/HMI, *Getting In On the Act – Provision for Pupils with Special Educational Needs – The National Picture* (HMSO, 1992), paras 37 and 133.

27 DFE, *Special Educational Needs: Access to the System – A Consultation Paper* (DFE, 1992), para 20.

parents and children and worked against the child's educational interests. Further concerns which had been raised, such as the fact that parents who appealed to the Secretary of State were not entitled to an oral hearing or to see the official advice on which the Secretary of State's decision was based, and that the decision was, in any event, often not binding on the LEA, were also acknowledged.[28]

It was announced that the Government had, therefore, decided that changes were required: 'the Government has concluded that the present statutory arrangements for appeals under the 1981 Act no longer meet parents' legitimate expectations of a clear, timely and effective means of redress for their grievances'.[29] The failure of the 1981 Act appeal arrangements to provide an effective avenue of redress for parents was reinforced by the increasing resort which parents had had to judicial review. It was reported that, in 1992, 120 applications for judicial review were made in SEN cases.[30] The Council on Tribunals commented that special educational needs issues had become increasingly contentious.[31] Most of the applications for judicial review were made on behalf of children, who qualified for legal aid.

2.3 PROPOSALS FOR A SPECIAL EDUCATIONAL NEEDS TRIBUNAL

The Government proposed the creation of an independent special educational needs tribunal (SENT), with a lawyer chair and two lay members with experience of special educational needs or local government, to hear appeals.[32] The SENT would have several advantages over the old system. First, it would be independent. Secondly, its decisions would be binding on the parties and on schools. Thirdly, it would operate on one tier, which would help to reduce delays. Ministers promised that the new appeals system would provide a speedy and effective forum for the resolution of disputes, and one which would be accessible. It would be 'friendly to parents and suitable for the swift prosecution of justice'.[33] These various objectives would be achieved or

28 DFE, *Special Educational Needs: Access to System – A Consultation Paper* (DFE, 1992), para 20.
29 Ibid, para 21.
30 *Times Educational Supplement*, 15 January 1993.
31 Council on Tribunals, *Annual Report, 1992/93* (HMSO, 1993), para 2.11.
32 DFE, *Special Educational Needs: Access to the System* (DFE, 1992), paras 23–27.
33 Hansard, HC Standing Committee E, cols 1181–1182, 28 January 1983, Mr T. Boswell MP, Under Secretary of State.

furthered by giving the tribunal a largely autonomous existence from the DFE, by requiring tribunals to consist of specialists (as noted above), by reinforcing the tribunal's independence by putting its operation under the supervision of a President, and by creating a unitary appeal system in place of the two-tier system which operated under the 1981 Act.

The Government did not propose that legal aid would be available for SENT hearings. It hoped that local 'concordats' might be agreed whereby LEAs would not normally bring lawyers to tribunal hearings if parents were not legally represented.[34] This is discussed further in Chapter 8. Appeal against the decision of a tribunal would lie to the High Court.

The jurisdiction of the tribunal would be wider than that of the appeal bodies under the 1981 Act. There would be six grounds of appeal altogether (parents would be able to appeal over refusal to assess or re-assess the child, over a decision to cease to maintain a statement of SEN and over the school named in the statement, in addition to the pre-existing grounds). As noted above, the decision of the tribunal would be binding, although the tribunal would have the power to remit to the LEA for reconsideration in the light of the tribunal's observations the question of whether a statement should be made.

It was estimated that the SENT would hear many more appeals once fully established. This increase would arise partly as a result of the widened grounds of appeal, but largely because of the tribunal's greater accessibility. In its first year (1 September 1994–31 August 1995) 1,170 appeals were registered by the SENT, but in its second year (1995–96) there were 1,622 – an increase of 39%.[35] The indications are that 1996–97 will see a further increase.[36] There have been many more appeals than were initially expected. The SENT's current case load 'is apparently in excess of three times the initial estimates'.[37]

---

34 DFE, *Special Educational Needs Tribunal – Consultation Paper on Draft Regulations and Rules of Procedure* (DFE, 1994), para 36.
35 SENT statistics provided to the author and now reported in T. Aldridge QC, *The Special Educational Needs Tribunal, Annual Report 1995/96* (SENT, 1996), p 7.
36 In September 1996, 199 appeals were registered, compared to 162 in September 1995. However, according to the SENT, this increase may in part reflect the fact that the speed of registration has improved.
37 Council on Tribunals, *Annual Report 1995/96* (HMSO, 1996), para 2.49.

2.4   THE SENT – QUESTIONS ARISING

As noted earlier, the reforms were introduced in 1994, under the Education Act 1993. The new system is described at length in later chapters.[38] At this point, however, it is important to consider some of the questions to which the establishment of the SENT gave rise and which formed part of the basis for the author's research.

Inevitably, with a new system, there were many unanswered questions, which could only be answered fully in the light of experience once the tribunal was in operation. Some of these questions are outlined below.

(1)   Given the detailed procedural rules, the lawyer chairmanship and the court-like powers which the tribunal would have (including powers to order 'discovery of documents' and 'awards of costs'), would the new system be as 'informal' as had been promised?[39] Indeed, to what extent would it be possible to ensure such informality whilst at the same time guaranteeing procedural fairness and efficiency?

(2)   How would the tribunals balance the interests of the individual child against the LEA's need to keep within the limits of its resources and to serve its wider policy goals?

(3)   Would the tribunals act independently, or would lay members with experience of working in LEAs be overly sympathetic to the LEA's position, as was believed to be the case under the old system?

(4)   How would the apparently presupposed sympathetic chairmanship of the tribunals, by lawyers, compensate for the absence of legal aid for parents who would be facing, in many cases, experienced LEA officers who would be conversant with the legislation?

(5)   How far would the elaborate procedural arrangements which would apply to appeals before tribunals present a barrier to unassisted parents who sought to challenge a decision of the LEA in their case?

(6)   How successfully would the appeals system be able to balance the need for proper preparation of evidence and exchanges of documentation, which could take a fairly lengthy period, as against the need for a swift resolution of the dispute, in the interests of the child concerned?

---

38   For a general overview of the SENT, as part of an analysis of Part III of the 1993 Act on special educational needs, provision and appeals, see J. Robinson, 'Special educational needs, the code and the new tribunal' (1996) 8(1) *Jnl Education and the Law* 39, and A.N. Khan, 'Provision for Special Educational Needs in Britain' (1995) 6(3) *Jnl Education and the Law* (Canada), 301.

39   See the doubts expressed in J. Rabinowicz and J. Friel, 'The New Tribunal, First Responses' (1994) 21(1) *British Journal of Special Education* 27.

The key question relating to the SENT, with which many of the above questions are concerned, was how effectively would it provide access to justice for parents and children? It was an important question to ask, because the SENT was already being held out as a potential model for the future development of education tribunals in general. Even before the author's research commenced in 1994, the Council on Tribunals was calling for school exclusion appeals to be brought within the jurisdiction of the SENT.[40] It has therefore been critically important to ensure that a clear picture is obtained of how the SENT has been matching up to the objectives set for it. The next chapter explains how the author conducted the research which has produced the findings reported and analysed in this book.

---

40 Council on Tribunals, *Annual Report, 1992/93* (HMSO, 1993), para 2.15. The SENT President's view is that exclusion cases are unsuitable for the SENT because they require a quick decision: see Council on Tribunals, *Annual Report, 1995/96* (HMSO, 1996), para 2.54.

Chapter 3

RESEARCHING THE SPECIAL EDUCATIONAL NEEDS TRIBUNAL

3.1 ACCESS TO JUSTICE

The starting point in many studies of tribunals is discussion of the Franks Committee's report published in 1957, which identified openness, fairness and impartiality as the three hallmarks of a good tribunal.[1] Today, it is not always accepted that tribunals should be open to the public (indeed, hearings of the SENT are generally held in private, open only to prescribed categories of persons). As regards the other characteristics – set in the modern context and taking account of the particular jurisdiction – the SENT should be independent, impartial, skilled, accessible and thorough in its approach, and should play an enabling role towards parents and children, whose views should be given due weight. The tribunal should also operate in such a way as to ensure that cases are concluded, and decisions issued, as speedily as possible, given the detrimental consequences of delay for children and their education.

Assessing the quality of decision-making is always difficult and might ultimately demand independent scrutiny of individual decisions, taking account of all of the evidence which was considered by the tribunal and, if it were possible, the factors which influenced the course of the hearing, such as the dynamics of presentation and witness examination, and the credibility of oral evidence. This is almost entirely impracticable for the purposes of most research studies. Nevertheless, it is entirely feasible to assess the quality of the various components of the tribunal – such as the qualifications and experience of members, their training and so on – and, by empirical observation, to examine the way in which hearings are conducted. Such methods have been used in studies of tribunals in the past[2] and have revealed insights into the opportunities for parties to present their evidence and about the role played by members and other participants – in particular, representatives. The picture can be built up

---

1 Committee on Administrative Tribunals and Inquiries (chair: Franks), Cmnd 218 (HMSO, 1957), para 42.
2 See, for example, R. Lister, *Justice for the Claimant*, Poverty Research Series No 4 (Child Poverty Action Group, 1974); H. Genn and Y. Genn, *The Effectiveness of Representation at Tribunals* (Lord Chancellor's Department, 1989); J. Baldwin, N. Wikeley and R. Young, *Judging Social Security* (Clarendon Press, 1992).

further by ascertaining the perceptions of those involved;[3] in the case of the SENT, they include parents, LEAs, chairmen and members of the tribunal, voluntary organisations and legal advisers and representatives.

It is a reasonable assumption that if the adjudication system in question is inherently fair, and operates fairly in practice, it will tend to produce a just result under the law – irrespective of whether the law itself is regarded as meeting widely held perceptions of social justice. But the system cannot be considered fair unless there is some certainty of effective access to it.

Access to justice is undoubtedly a very broad concept and, in assessing it, account must be taken of the particular type of jurisdiction involved. Thus, in the context of appeals by parents of children with learning difficulties, it is necessary, for example, to take account of the fact that many appellants will be unrepresented at the hearing and may not have had access to independent advice in connection with their appeal. It is also important to consider the position of the child within the SEN appeal process.

At the same time, there are qualities which represent common standards for *all* tribunals. These are premised on the basis that tribunal adjudication is intended to provide a more accessible (as regards informality and cost for litigants) alternative to the courts. Effective access to justice in the context of a public welfare dispute demands that cost, complexity, formality, inequality of the parties, delay, inconvenience of location, and other matters which could stand in its way, should be minimised; at the same time, all aspects of the appeal process should be as fair as possible. Impartiality is vital. It is also important to determine whether the decision actually produces an outcome sought by the tribunal. If the decision is not acted upon, the effectiveness of the appeal system is clearly undermined. There have, for example, been complaints that LEAs do not always implement the decision of the SENT (see Chapter 10 at **10.8**).

---

3 See ibid, and also R. Sainsbury, M. Hirst and D. Lawton, *Evaluation of Disability Living Allowance and Attendance Allowance*, DSS Research Report No 41 (HMSO, 1995), Ch 20 and R. Berthoud and A. Bryson, 'Social security appeals: what do claimants want?' (1997) 4(1) *Journal of Social Security Law* 17.

3.2 INDIVIDUAL ELEMENTS OF THE RESEARCH INTO THE SENT

Evaluation of the SENT involved two separate strands of research:

(1) Reviews of: the historical background; the legislation, case-law and guidance; and evidence from official reports and other surveys.
(2) A detailed empirical study.

Through the evidence compiled, a detailed picture of how the SENT has been operating, and its strengths and weaknesses, has emerged.

The reviews

The historical background
This was discussed in Chapter 2.

The evolving legal framework
The legislation has continued to evolve over the past two years. The most important development has been the amendment – indeed, replacement – of the SENT Regulations,[4] which govern procedure before, during and after tribunal hearings. Consolidation of Part III of the 1993 Act into the Education Act 1996[5] occurred just after the work was completed. (As noted in Chapter 2, the substance of the statutory provisions is unaltered.) There has also been a considerable amount of case law. Several of the important decisions which clarified issues under the 1981 Act are now of no more than historical interest and of little relevance to the new legal regime. But there has also been a large amount of litigation over matters arising under the 1993 Act; the leading cases are discussed in later chapters. It should be noted that judicial review has largely given way to appeals on a point of law under RSC Ords 55 and 56, as the courts have adopted a more or less consistent line on the exclusivity of the statutory procedure for resolving most SEN disputes.[6] Decisions of the SENT itself, although not binding precedents in later cases, have been summarised and published by the President of the SENT, in the form of

---

4 SI 1995/3113, which replaced SI 1994/1910.
5 The SEN provisions, including the structure and jurisdiction of the SENT, are in Part IV of the 1996 Act.
6 See, for example, *R v Special Educational Needs Tribunal ex parte F* [1995] ELR 213, where Popplewell J applied the exclusivity principle in the terms that it was laid down in *R v Chief Constable of Merseyside ex parte Calveley* [1986] QB 424 and *R v Secretary of State for the Home Department ex parte Swati* [1986] 1 WLR 477. Exception to this principle, the possibility of which the court confirmed, has been

Digests of Decisions, which are included (with the President's permission) in the *Education Law Reports*. The President has also issued Practice Statements and Guidance, which are discussed later in this book.

Published evidence on the SENT

The President published his first Annual Report, covering 1994/95, in November 1995. The report contained useful statistical information and frank discussion of the problems which arose in the first year of the tribunal's operation, plus the President's assessment of the degree of success achieved in resolving them. The second annual report, covering 1995/96, was published recently and, although succinct, provides similarly informative data and discussion.

Evidence from external sources about how the tribunal has been operating has also emerged at various times since 1994. Particularly valuable is the report by the House of Commons Education Select Committee (now part of a combined Education and Employment Committee) into the operation of both the Code of Practice and the SENT itself, published in February 1996.[7] All the major players in this field – including voluntary organisations, LEAs, academics and other interested parties – submitted evidence. Oral evidence from senior SENT personnel and selected voluntary organisations, was also taken by the Committee. The report and minutes of evidence were of considerable value to the research because of the range of views recorded on the early experience of the SENT. Among the evidence submitted to the Committee were the author's preliminary findings deriving from the survey of parents, which in fact proved to be the only major independent evidence at that time on parents' perceptions of the new system.[8] Other evidence came to light through a small number of articles in some of the specialist SEN journals and in the course of conferences and meetings (the researchers attended several organised by ELAS).

---

difficult to secure. *Swati* was applied to the same effect in another recent SEN appeal case, this time in the Court of Appeal: *R v Special Educational Needs Tribunal ex parte South Glamorgan County Council* [1996] ELR 326. See further Chapter 10 at **10.9**, 'Effect of appeal procedure on access to judicial review'.

7 House of Commons Education Committee, Second Report, 1995–96, *Special Educational Needs: The Working of the Code of Practice and the Tribunal*, HC 205 (HMSO, 1996).

8 The Select Committee drew particular attention to this evidence in its report: op cit, para 9.

The empirical study

The evidence derived from the reviews has been useful, but has merely supplemented the huge amount of data produced by the research project itself. Thus the evidence concerning the operation of the tribunal on which the author relies is principally that which was obtained via observation of 40 tribunal hearings and from separate questionnaire surveys of parents, LEAs, chairs and lay members of tribunals, voluntary organisations and lawyers. Both qualitative and quantitative data was obtained and is presented in later chapters. Qualitative data includes such matters as parents' perceptions of the degree of formality or informality of proceedings and tribunal chairs' views of the contribution to good decision-making made by the lay members. Quantitative data includes such matters as the numbers of persons present at tribunal hearings, the ages of chairs and members, the number of children who attended tribunal hearings, the average length of the hearings, and so on.

The survey of parents

The survey of parents aimed to ascertain parents' views on various issues, and in particular:

- the quality of the information provided to them by the tribunal on their rights of appeal and the procedure involved;
- whether they had had available to them the services of an adviser to help with the preliminary stages of the appeal, and, if so, the adviser's professional status and the quality of his or her advice and assistance;
- whether they were represented at the hearing, and, if so, the professional status of the representative and the level of the parents' satisfaction with his or her work;
- the extent of the parents' participation in the hearing;
- the nature of the hearing, the complexity of the language used, how well the parents were able to understand all of the discussion, the effectiveness of the procedure, how the tribunal treated the parents, and related issues;
- whether the child attended the hearing and, if so, whether he or she was asked to give his or her views;
- those features of the tribunal procedure which the parents felt to be particularly good or bad and those which differed from their prior expectation.

Parents were also asked to give any general comments about their experience in making an appeal to the SENT. They were also asked to state their occupation, and that of their partner, so that a simple social class analysis could be carried out.

The evidence which was produced by this survey proved, as anticipated, to be of particular importance to the research, because of the emphasis in the Government's policy in this area on parental rights and because of the established principle that effective parental participation in decision-making processes is critical to achieving an appropriate regime for the education of children with SEN.

The adoption by the SENT of a centralised, rather than a regionalised, administrative structure meant that appeal papers were being sent out from one point (and then two points, when the Darlington office opened) to the rest of the country. Following discussion which the author had with the SENT, it was decided that the most effective means of ensuring a widespread distribution of the parents' questionnaire would be to arrange for it to be sent out to parents with their copies of the appeal documents. The SENT President has shown a particular interest in the research and agreed to co-operate with this method of distribution.

Of 200 questionnaires which were distributed, 118 were completed and returned (by post). This represents a response rate of 60%, which is quite high for a survey of this kind, conducted in this manner. For example, in Hazel Genn and Yvette Genn's postal survey of appellants in their research into representation in certain other tribunals,[9] there was a much lower response rate.

Parents were invited to state their name and address if they were willing to be contacted further about the various issues raised in the questionnaire. A majority of parents (75%) gave this information and from this it was possible not only to carry out some follow-up interviews but also to construct a regional breakdown. Two-thirds of the parents who gave their address lived in the South of England (including London), with the remaining one-third living in the North and Midlands. The high proportion of respondents from London and the South is not surprising given the fact that this area is the largest in population terms and also has generated the highest proportion of appeals to date.[10]

---

9 *The Effectiveness of Representation at Tribunals* (Lord Chancellor's Department, 1989).

10 T. Aldridge QC, President, *The Special Educational Needs Tribunal, Annual Report 1994/95* (SENT, 1995), Appendix 1, and *Annual Report 1995/96* (SENT, 1996), Appendix 2, which show the number of appeals as a proportion of the school population in each English and Welsh LEA. The *Annual Report* has not adopted an entirely apt method of comparison arising from the correlation of data, because school populations vary as to the extent of SEN.

It would have been very difficult to conduct interviews of the children concerned and it is very unlikely that such interviews would have yielded very much to assist in an evaluation of the SENT, because so few children have attended SENT hearings. Nevertheless, the way that children's views on their education are dealt with under the new system and their status in SENT appeal cases are considered elsewhere in this book.

The survey of LEAs

LEAs have key legal responsibilities in respect of SEN and are one of the parties to an appeal to the SENT, so it was particularly important to conduct a survey of LEAs, looking at the way that they conduct their role and at their perceptions of the new appeal arrangements.

As noted in Chapter 1, LEAs are responsible for statutory assessment and statementing of children with SEN.[11] They also have a general duty to exercise their powers with a view to securing that they identify those of the children for whom they are responsible who have SEN and in respect of whom it is necessary for them to determine the special educational provision which any learning difficulty may call for.[12] For this purpose, the LEA is responsible for children registered at maintained, grant-maintained or grant-maintained special schools (or at another type of school but at the LEA's or the funding authority's[13] expense). It is also responsible for children who are registered pupils at other schools and children aged between two and school leaving age who are not registered pupils, who in either case have been brought to the LEA's attention as having, or probably having, SEN.[14] LEAs are responsible for ensuring that, in conformity with the Code of Practice and the 1996 Act, formal assessment of such a child is carried out in appropriate cases and that a decision is taken as to the appropriate provision for the child concerned.[15] Once such provision has been determined in a statement, the LEA will be under a duty to carry out a review of the statement every 12 months or at other prescribed intervals.[16]

---

11 1996 Act, ss 321, 324, 328 and 329.

12 Ibid, s 321.

13 There are two funding authorities, one for England (the Funding Agency for Schools) and one for Wales (the Schools Funding Council for Wales): see 1996 Act, ss 20 and 21.

14 1996 Act, s 321(3).

15 Ibid, ss 323 and 324, op cit.

16 Ibid, s 328 and the Education (Special Educational Needs) Regulations 1994, SI 1994/1047, regs 15 and 16.

Although the Code of Practice places considerable emphasis on school-based assessment and provision (stages 1–3), LEAs are responsible for all the critical decisions concerning the education of children with the greatest learning difficulties. The decisions which are subject to a right of appeal under the 1996 Act are all LEA decisions. It also has to be borne in mind that although maintained schools have control of their own budgets, which are determined with reference to, inter alia, the numbers of children at the school who have special educational needs, overall expenditure of resources on special educational provision continues to rest with the LEA. In many LEAs, an element of funding for school-based education will be controlled centrally in respect of pupils with statements.

The combined effect of these provisions is that LEAs have decision-making responsibilities in relation to needs and provision regarding individual children, in addition to having control over the resources within the authority to meet the needs of all children with statements. Consequently, LEAs will not only be party to appeals to the SENT, but can be expected to defend their decisions tenaciously, especially where granting the parents' wishes would involve increased costs.

The survey of LEAs aimed to discover not only officers' perceptions of the appeal process, including the conduct of tribunal hearings, but also the various ways in which LEAs staffed and organised their SEN appeals operation. Of particular interest was evidence on the impact of the new appeal system on LEAs' workloads and on their preparation for individual appeal cases. Were LEAs, for example, finding that it was necessary to prepare cases more thoroughly and to go to greater lengths to justify their decisions? LEAs were also asked about their policy concerning their use of legal representation at hearings.

One of the major criticisms of the local appeal arrangements under the 1981 Act was that the system was biased in favour of LEAs. There is no objective empirical evidence to confirm this view, but certain features of the old appeal system undoubtedly weakened its independence. For example, LEAs organised appeal committees and appointed members to them. One of the objectives of introducing the new appeal system under the 1993 Act was to establish more independent arrangements. LEAs were asked, therefore, about their views on the extent to which the new system had altered the balance in favour or against parents, as compared with the situation under the 1981 Act. They were also asked about whether the introduction of the new tribunal had made it more likely, or less likely, that disputes would be settled without recourse to an appeal hearing. The emphasis placed by the Code of Practice on 'partnership' and on school-based solutions to SEN problems promoted conciliation; but no one could be sure that this would work out in practice.

All 116 LEAs in England and Wales[17] were sent questionnaires, of which 80 were completed and returned – a response rate of just under 70%.

The survey of chairs and lay members

As indicated above, the quality of decision-making in tribunals clearly hinges principally on the capabilities and conscientiousness of the tribunal panel itself. The objective behind this part of the questionnaire survey was, therefore, to find out as much as possible about chairs' and lay members' attitudes and approach to their work on the tribunal, and their views on each other's performance. There was also an opportunity for the chairs and lay members to comment on the effectiveness of the training they had received.

Chairs had a rather different background to the lay members, being lawyers (mostly private practitioners) who would be familiar with quasi-judicial decision-making processes. The lay members lacked legal training and yet had previous experience and, in many cases, qualifications, in the field of special education and/or LEA administration. These differences were expected to produce a degree of divergence of opinion between each of the groups. The two categories – chairs and lay members – were therefore surveyed separately. Although many of the questions were common to both groups, there were several questions that were specific to each: for example, chairs were asked about the extent of their knowledge of the law on special educational needs and the extent to which such knowledge had proved important for the work.

The numbers of chairs and members of the SENT were not so large as to make it necessary to select a specific sample. Consequently, questionnaires were sent to *all* chairs and members, numbering, at that time, 32 chairs and 88 lay members. The questionnaires were in fact distributed by the SENT office. As with the other surveys, there was a very high response rate: 25 chairs (78%) and 66 lay members (75%) returned completed questionnaires.

The survey of lawyers and voluntary organisations involved in SENT appeals work

Lawyers and voluntary organisations working with SEN cases could offer the most objective view of the way in which tribunals were conducted of

---

17 The questionnaire was sent out shortly before a number of unitary authorities were introduced under the 1995 local government reforms.

all those who had had an involvement with them. Although it was anticipated that some of these bodies would, at the stage at which the research was being conducted, have been involved in relatively few cases, it was decided that their accounts of their experience would be useful in building up the overall picture. As anticipated, there was considerable variation in the number of cases with which each of the lawyers and voluntary organisations had been involved. Consequently, quite a number of them were unable to assist with the survey. However, over 20 replies were received, including responses from all the major voluntary organisations working in this field, which contained some of the most critical comments about the new tribunal. Of particular interest were the views on appeals procedure, tribunal venues and the conduct of hearings.

Observations of hearings

There is no express right under the SENT Regulations for researchers to attend hearings of the SENT (although Council on Tribunals members are permitted to attend so that they can monitor selected proceedings). Only if *both* parties to an appeal give written consent and if the chair agrees is it possible to attend the hearings for research (or other) purposes. Fortunately, many parents and LEAs gave permission for the author or his research assistant to attend their hearings, by signing and returning the consent slips which were sent out with appeal papers by the SENT office.

However, even where it had been agreed that the author or his assistant could attend a particular hearing, we were sometimes thwarted by the withdrawal of the appeal before it took place (withdrawal happened in approximately 1 in 5 SENT cases in 1994/95, rising to over 1 in 3 cases in 1995/96, according to SENT statistics[18]). Although initially it had been anticipated that it would be desirable to attend up to 70 hearings, it became apparent after about 30 observations that all of the main strengths or weaknesses had been uncovered and that further observations were unlikely to yield anything different; it was decided, therefore, that an observation of a total of 40 hearings would be sufficient to confirm the picture which had been built up and to ensure that a reasonably wide spread of tribunal venues was inspected. The first observation took place in London in March 1995 and the fortieth was in Chester in May 1996.

The observations revealed a great deal about the dynamics of hearings. It

---

18 T. Aldridge QC, *The Special Educational Needs Tribunal, Annual Report 1995/96* (SENT, 1996), p 7.

was found that chairs adopted quite different approaches to each other, although there was a fairly uniform attempt to make the proceedings as informal as possible. (In fact, many hearings were still fairly formal in certain respects.[19]) Careful note was taken of the running order, the length of the hearing, the number of people present, the ethnic backgrounds of the appellants, whether the child was in attendance, witness details, types of representative (if any), the nature of the appeal, and other matters. The visits for observations revealed the wide range of premises used for hearings: from the permanent suite of rooms at SENT HQ in London, to various grades of hotel.

The tribunal sits all over the country so that the hearing can be held somewhere which is convenient to the parents and the LEA. The consultation document said that the hearing would take place in a venue which was 'easily accessible to both the parents and the LEA . . . normally . . . within a few miles of the parents' home'.[20] The current tribunal guide states that the hearing will 'take place as near your home as we can arrange it', with London or South-East appeals to be held in London, where convenient.[21] As there is large population living within one hour's travelling time of London, a high proportion of appeals are heard at the SENT suite in Victoria Street. Not surprisingly, therefore, many of the observations took place there. The overall geographical spread of the hearings observed is shown in Table 2 below.

Table 2

Geographical spread of tribunal observations

Region	% of cases
The South (including London, Hampshire, Kent, Essex etc)	49%
Midlands (including Nottinghamshire, Staffordshire, Warwickshire and Birmingham)	11%
North East (including Hull, Newcastle, Barnsley and Leeds)	19%
North West (including Merseyside, Cheshire, Lancashire and Greater Manchester)	21%

---

19 See Chapter 9.
20 DFE, *Special Educational Needs Tribunal – Consultation Paper on Draft Regulations and Rules of Procedure* (DFE, 1994), para 21.
21 DFE, *Special Educational Needs Tribunal: How to Appeal* (DFE, 1994), p 12.

As it happens, this variation in the geographical spread does seem to reflect variations in the number of appeals registered against particular LEAs' decisions. The author was informed, for example, that the areas categorised in Table 2 as the Midlands have had significantly fewer appeals registered against them compared to, for example, the South. This variation to some extent reflects, in turn, differences in the proportion of school pupils who have special educational needs and statements,[22] although the higher number of appeals in London and the South may also reflect such factors as the greater availability of voluntary sector advice and support in these areas or, more speculatively, higher levels of LEA intransigence or possibly a stronger tradition of litigiousness among the population there.

3.3   TIME SCALE OF THE RESEARCH

The main part of the research was conducted between September 1994 and June 1996. The parent questionnaires were issued throughout 1995 and early 1996. The survey of chairs and members and LEAs took place in late 1995 and early 1996. The survey of lawyers and voluntary organisations took place between late 1995 and June 1996. Finally, as noted above, the 40 observations took place between March 1995 and May 1996. Updating of data, including legal developments, continued through to January 1997.

---

22 See, for example, Audit Commission/HMI, *Getting In On the Act – Provision for Pupils with Special Educational Needs – The National Picture* (HMSO, 1992).

Chapter 4

THE STRUCTURE OF THE SPECIAL EDUCATIONAL NEEDS TRIBUNAL

4.1 INTRODUCTION

This chapter discusses the structure and organisation of the SENT. It focuses, in particular, on the role of the President and the Secretariat and on the appointment, background, experience and other aspects of the tribunal membership – the chairs and lay members. Also examined are training and the changing administrative structure of the SENT.

The operation of the SENT is governed by a combination of law and managerial/administrative policy and practice. So far as the law is concerned, the SENT operates within a tight legal framework under the Education Act 1996 (to which all section numbers below refer) and the Special Educational Needs Tribunal Regulations 1995.[1] The tribunal's jurisdiction, powers, and constitution are prescribed under this legislation. Detailed provision as regards tribunal procedure is also laid down. The legislation further provides for the SENT to be under the supervision of the Council on Tribunals and for there to be a right of appeal against the decision of the SENT on a point of law to the High Court.[2]

Policy and practice have governed various aspects of the organisation and management of the SENT, and the role of the President within the SENT system, as each have been evolving since the tribunal's inception. As the workload of the tribunal has increased, so has the pressure on its administration. The tribunal has had to respond to the pressure by increasing its personnel and by reassignment of administrative tasks, where appropriate and where possible. The present organisation of the SENT is described below.

---

1 SI 1995/3113.
2 Part III of the 1993 Act in fact amended s 11 of the Tribunal and Inquiries Act 1992 to achieve this.

4.2 THE PRESIDENT AND THE SECRETARIAT

The SENT system as a whole is under the general direction of a President appointed by the Lord Chancellor.[3] The President must be a lawyer (the precise requirement is that he/she must have a 'seven-year general qualification' for the purposes of the Courts and Legal Services Act 1990 – basically, a barrister or solicitor with rights of audience in the High Court etc held for at least seven years).[4] The first President, and present office holder, is Trevor Aldridge QC. Many of the powers of the President are exercised on his behalf by the tribunal Secretary and other administrative staff. The President has no express power to delegate his powers to the Secretariat, but is implicitly empowered to authorise the Secretariat and other administrative staff to exercise some of his powers on his behalf in certain set circumstances. The Secretary is not mentioned in the 1996 Act, but is referred to extensively in the SENT Regulations, which provide that a function of the Secretary may be performed by another member of SENT staff who is authorised to perform it.[5]

The President has overall responsibility for establishing tribunals to hear appeals, for the times and places at which they sit,[6] for the selection of chairs and lay members to sit on each appeal[7] and for other procedural matters connected with the appeal. There is detailed discussion of procedural issues, including the powers and duties of the President and Secretary, in Chapter 6. The organisation of the SENT Secretariat, on the other hand, is discussed later in this chapter.

The Secretary of State, with the consent of the Treasury, is empowered to provide staff and accommodation, remuneration and allowances for the President and tribunal members, and to defray the expenses of the tribunal.[8] The Secretary of State is also empowered to pay allowances with regard to the attendance of persons at the tribunal.[9]

---

3 1996 Act, s 333(2).
4 Ibid, s 334(1).
5 Regulation 38.
6 Regulation 4.
7 Regulation 5.
8 1996 Act, ss 333(6) and 335.
9 Ibid, s 336(3).

4.3   THE APPOINTMENT OF CHAIRS AND LAY MEMBERS

Independence

One of the major strengths of the SENT is the independence of its membership, as compared with the local appeal committees which had jurisdiction under the Education Act 1981. As noted in Chapter 2, LEAs were responsible for appointments to those committees. In contrast, appointments to serve on the SENT as a chair or lay member are made by the Lord Chancellor, in the case of chairs, and by the Secretary of State, in the case of lay members.[10] There have been some suggestions that the local authority background of the majority of lay members of the SENT might make them biased in favour of LEAs, but this was not borne out by the research (see below).

Term of appointment

The initial appointment of chairs and lay members is for a term of one year. Chair appointments are subsequently renewed for either one year or three years. All members' re-appointments have been for three years. Further renewal is possible, indeed it is probably expected.[11]

Chairs or lay members may resign at any time.[12] However, in the first 18 months of the SENT, there was only one resignation (for personal reasons).

Qualifications and experience of chairs

To be eligible for appointment as a chair of the SENT, a person must be a lawyer with a seven-year general qualification (as in the case of the President).[13] In the first round of appointments, 32 chairs were appointed to the chairmen's panel. All appointments were made on a part-time basis. The main/most recent occupation of chairs appointed from 1 September 1994 is shown in Table 3 below.

---

10 1996 Act, s 333(3) and (4).
11 The 1996 Act provides that chairs and members are eligible for re-appointment: s 334(5)(b).
12 1996 Act, s 334(5)(a).
13 Ibid, s 334(1).

Table 3

*Present main career of chairs of the SENT appointed from
1 September 1994*

Occupation	Numbers	Percentage
Solicitor	17	71%
Barrister	4	17%
University administration	2	8%
Lecturer	1	4%

(n=24)

No specific reasons for having lawyer chairs of the SENT was given when
the legislation was proposed and progressed through Parliament.
Ministers merely referred to the proven standard format of tribunals,
including legal chairmanship. The general expectation is that lawyer
chairs will be able to deal more effectively than laypersons[14] with such
matters as adducing evidence, conducting proceedings fairly and dealing
with any complex points of law. Lawyer chairs are also expected to be
better suited to the task of writing up tribunal decisions.

Clearly, it would be hoped that SENT chairs would develop appropriate
expertise in the law of SEN, which is an area of growing complexity,
although one on which there are few experts.[15] Chairs were asked about
their knowledge of the law on SEN and, as shown in Table 4, just under
half of chairs rated their knowledge as 'good'.

---

14 On the experience of lay chairs of other tribunals, see Chapter 2.

15 There are few lawyers specialising in this field. Several practitioners with such
    expertise who were interviewed in the course of the research would have been well
    qualified to serve on the tribunal but preferred to concentrate on advocacy and
    leave adjudication to others.

Table 4

How chairs rated their knowledge of the law on SEN

Level of knowledge	Number of chairs	Percentage
Exceptionally good	0	0%
Good	12	48%
Adequate	11	44%
Fairly poor	2	8%
Exceptionally poor	0	0%

(n=25)

Given the fact that the survey was carried out after most chairs had sat on no more than 15 occasions, the level of self-assessed expertise seems broadly acceptable. By this time, chairs had attended only one or two days' training, on which approximately one-third of the time was spent on the law. It is to be anticipated that chairs' expertise will increase with experience, but further training will clearly be important and it will be necessary to ensure that chairs in particular are kept up to date with the developing case law. It should be stressed that the overwhelming majority of chairs in the survey acknowledged the importance of knowledge of the law on SEN for their SENT work (see Table 5).

Table 5

Chairs' views on the importance of knowledge of SEN law for SENT work

Level of importance	Number of chairs	Percentage
Extremely important	9	36%
Fairly important	5	20%
Important	9	36%
Not particularly important	2	8%
Not at all important	0	0%

(n=25)

In the light of the importance attached by chairs to knowledge of the law on SEN, a target for training must be to raise the proportion of chairs whose self-assessed knowledge of the law (as shown above in Table 4) is better than 'adequate'.

Turning to chairs' adjudicative experience, a significant number of chairs had past or current appointments as adjudicators with other tribunals, particularly those relating to social security, employment and mental health. The extent of this experience is shown in Table 6 below.

Table 6

Alternative adjudicative experience of SENT chairs

Adjudicative body	Number of chairs
Social security appeal tribunal	5
Child support appeal tribunal	2
Disability appeal tribunal	1
Rent assessment committee	2
Immigration assessment	1
Commissioner for income tax	1
Deputy district judge	2
Other education appeals	2
Health service committees	2
Legal Aid Board committee	1

Note: Two of the respondents sit on more than one tribunal/panel.

Despite many chairs' previous adjudicative experience, their experience of SEN was unsurprisingly rather more limited than that of the lay members (see below). A number of chairs had dealt with child care law or mental health law in practice; but very few had professional experience of working with the law on SEN. Nevertheless, many did have some indirect involvement with the SEN field in general. Several had worked as governors of special or mainstream schools and one was closely associated with a special needs charity. Furthermore, five of the 25 chairs who responded on this point had family experience of SEN. Many chairs also had a special interest in education in general. For example, seven of the chairs had current or previous experience as a school governor. Often, however, experience of SEN was indirect and distant.

Qualifications and experience of lay members

In 1994/95 there were 88 lay members; that number was later increased to 120.

Qualification for appointment as a lay member is prescribed by the SENT Regulations 1995, which state that a person may not be appointed as a member of the lay panel:

> 'unless the Secretary of State is satisfied that he has knowledge and experience in respect of—
> (a)   children with special educational needs; or
> (b)   local government.'[16]

A majority of the lay members in the survey had worked in local authority administration and also had previous experience either as teachers (of children with and/or without learning difficulties) or as educational psychologists. Only one-third of the lay members had not worked in local authority administration and, of them, the majority were either teachers (predominantly of children with learning difficulties) or educational psychologists. Only four of the lay members had experience which was confined to working in the voluntary sector, although 11 other lay members had worked in the voluntary sector in addition to having experience in local authority administration or teaching.[17]

Thus, what is clearly shown by the survey is the LEA background of a majority of SENT lay members, confirming what SENT statistics on the first 79 lay members appointed in England reveal. The SENT's figures show that 53 of the 79 (67%) lay members had what is described as 'local authority experience'. However, of the 13 recently appointed additional lay members (who were, therefore, not among the first 79), only six (46%) seemed to have such experience.

The preponderance of former LEA advisers or senior officers, confirmed by the survey findings, has been a particular criticism directed at the SENT, as noted above. The chief concern is that panel members with such a background are likely to be overly sympathetic to the problems confronting the LEA. Nevertheless, the evidence does not justify such a view (see **4.4** below) and, in any event, the tribunal has been keen to balance against this criticism the incontrovertible argument that persons sitting as lay members need to have appropriate experience of special educational needs and/or local government so that they have the expertise that the tribunal requires when making a decision in a case. Some commentators have, however, argued that the SENT should include

---

16 Regulation 3.
17 One chair in the survey believed that the description 'lay' member used by the SENT was inappropriate: 'They are not in my view "lay" members but bring very specialised knowledge and experience with them, which if properly used is of inestimable value' (also cited below).

persons whose experience of special educational needs is not merely professional. The Bolton Institute of Higher Education, in its evidence to the House of Commons Select Committee, put this argument succinctly: 'tribunals lack, what we call, the "scrutiny of ordinariness", where parents might have their concerns addressed by tribunals which include non-professionals'.[18]

Among lay members there was, not surprisingly, considerably less previous experience of adjudication work than among chairs. Nevertheless, nearly one in five respondents (13 out of 70 lay members) reported previous or current experience of acting in an adjudicative capacity including, in many cases, past experience as a member of a local appeal committee for SEN cases under the Education Act 1981.

Lay members' reasons for joining the SENT

Lay members were asked what had motivated them to become involved with the SENT. Clearly, some aspects of the overall character of the tribunal membership would be revealed by such responses. Ideally, those working in such a specialised field should have a strong commitment towards ensuring that, within the terms of the legislation and Code of Practice, and within practical limitations, the best possible arrangements are made to ameliorate the learning difficulties of children whose needs have come to the notice of an authority.

An overwhelming majority of the lay members said that they had previous experience of SEN and wished to put their experience to good use, especially following retirement. One or two had worked under the 1981 Act appeal system and had wished to be part of the new system because they believed it would be fairer. Although a small number mentioned the attractiveness of payment for undertaking the work,[19] altruism prevailed.

The following comments by lay members on their reason(s) for becoming a member of the SENT are drawn from a representative sample of the replies received (n=39):

- 'A wish to help ensure SEN are catered for as well as the legislation permits.'

---

18 House of Commons Education Committee, Second Report, 1995–96, *Special Educational Needs: The Working of the Code of Practice and the Tribunal*, HC 205 (HMSO, 1996) Minutes of Evidence and Appendices, Appendix 9.

19 The fee at the time for lay members was £119 per case; since April 1996 it has been increased to £140. Travel expenses are also reimbursed.

- 'Personal interest in success of tribunal; desire for continued involvement with SEN.'
- 'Considerable experience (25 years) working with SEN pupils, their parents, schools and relevant framework and a wish to continue in this field.'
- 'A wish to use my expertise following retirement.'
- 'An interest in SEN children and their difficulties. A knowledge of the shortcomings of the former appeals process. A worthwhile occupation in retirement. Some additional income.'
- 'As a retired education officer, to retain some link with education, but particularly to be part of a system offering a less formal, and more sympathetic, response to parents' concerns about their children.'
- 'Opportunity to put my skills and experience in SEN to good use. Opportunity to keep abreast of SEN issues and debates.'
- 'Having been involved with the former local appeals committees (as an expert witness), I felt that it was important that people with SEN experience volunteered to serve on the tribunal.'
- 'Twenty-one years as an educational psychologist, interested in attempting to match children's rights against the resources available to LEAs.'

Chairs' reasons for joining the SENT

Among the tribunal chairs in the survey, the motivation to become a chair of the SENT involved, for the majority, one or more of three principal factors: an interest in education and, in some cases, specifically SEN; a desire to pursue or develop a judicial career; and an interest in a professional activity offering something different to everyday legal practice. The following are representative comments:

- 'Professional development plus interest in education by virtue of being a long-standing school governor.'
- 'Prospect of a new experience and the opportunity to try a judicial role.'
- 'It is an area of the law in which I have always had interest and I was interested in joining a completely new tribunal at the outset.'
- 'I have been a solicitor in private practice for 12 years and I wanted a change, something very different with an element of "public service".'
- 'A desire to serve in a judicial capacity in an area which was of interest and I had some (indirect) experience.'

Chairs and lay members with disabilities

One lay member in the survey commented that 'many members have little experience of disability'. In fact, there is no requirement for members of the SENT to include persons with special educational needs themselves. Few such people have been recruited. Those that have include two of the lay members in the survey who reported that they were blind. One of them suggested that perhaps more people with special educational needs ought to be recruited to the tribunal. Clearly, provided they are capable of performing the role of tribunal chair or member, there is a strong argument for ensuring that there are a reasonable number of persons with special educational needs on the panels. Such an arrangement works quite successfully in the case of disability appeal tribunals (DATs), which are concerned with appeals relating to attendance allowance and disability living allowance. Under the legislation,[20] one of the 'wing' members of the DAT must be a person who is experienced in dealing with the needs of disabled persons: (a) in a professional or voluntary capacity; or (b) because they are themselves disabled.[21] There is no suggestion, in relation to those tribunals, that these members' disability makes them incapable of acting impartially. On the contrary, their disability provides them with an insight which is conducive to good decision-making in these cases.

In practice, although a majority of SENT lay members do have some professional experience of dealing with SEN, only a small minority of the membership have SEN themselves. The DFEE, with the support of the SENT President, has sought to recruit such persons to panels whenever possible, but there is a case for taking further steps to increase the number. However, where chairs are concerned, the Lord Chancellor's policy in relation to all tribunal chair appointments is to appoint the best candidate and not to discriminate positively in favour of persons with a disability.

Gender of chair and lay member panels

The gender profile of the chair and lay panels is very similar. SENT statistics, applicable to the first round of appointments, show that 36% of chairs and 38% of lay members were women. However, there has been an attempt, in relation to recent appointments, to increase the proportion of

---

20 Social Security Administration Act 1992, s 42(4).
21 As the other wing member is a medical practitioner, the disabled wing member must not be so qualified.

women members. Of 16 recently appointed additional chairs, six (37.5%) are male and 10 (62.5%) are female; and 50% of the recently appointed lay members are female.

Ages of chairs and lay members

There is quite a contrast in the age profiles of chairs and lay members respectively. According to the survey returns (which, it will be recalled, covered four-fifths of the membership), 80% of chairs were aged under 50, compared with just 32% of lay members. (SENT figures relating to the first 89 lay members show that 29% were under 50; the SENT has not had access to equivalent statistics for chairs (the information is held by the Lord Chancellor's Department, which has apparently refused to disclose it to the SENT), hence the need to rely on the survey data for a comparison.) Almost 25% of the lay members in the survey (and 19% of all lay members, according to SENT figures) were aged 60 or over. The oldest lay member was 69 on appointment.

This disparity perhaps reflects the different characteristics which are sought when recruiting to each of the separate panels. Where chairs are concerned, a legal qualification, legal experience and a commitment to SENT work will be prime factors. Work on the SENT will be less remunerative than much professional legal work,[22] and yet is very demanding. It is therefore likely to attract mid-career lawyers, who are looking for a new challenge. This was confirmed by many of the comments from chairs, reported above. Where lay members are concerned, however, professional (including voluntary work) experience of SEN or mainstream education seems to be a primary qualification for many. According to the survey, many lay members had 20, 30 or even 40 years' experience in the field of SEN. A significant number had retired from their posts in education (profiles of the first 89 lay members issued by the SENT reveal that 21% were retired); but, as noted above, they wanted to continue to work in this field and saw the tribunal as an ideal opportunity to put their experience to use. Obviously, therefore, lay members would tend to be older, as noted above.

Ethnicity of panels

As will be shown in Chapter 6, ethnic minorities appear to be under-represented among appellants. This is also true of tribunal members; the overwhelming majority are white (see Table 7).

---

22 Chairs are currently paid a fee of £253 per case, increased from £233 in April 1996. They also qualify for travel expenses.

Table 7

Ethnicity of SENT lay members in England

Ethnicity	Numbers	Percentage
White	73	92%
Black Caribbean	2	3%
Indian	2	3%
Middle Eastern	1	1%
North African	1	1%

(n=79)

Source: SENT statistics supplied by the Secretariat.
Note: Recently, a further 14 lay members were appointed, all of whom are white.

One explanation for this situation is that relatively few members of ethnic minorities have considerable professional experience of SEN. Nevertheless, there are disturbingly few non-white members of the SENT and greater efforts should be made to redress this problem.

4.4   CHAIRS' AND LAY MEMBERS' VIEWS ON EACH OTHER

Despite the different professional backgrounds of chairs and lay members, the evidence suggests that individual tribunals have been operating on a harmonious basis. In many of the hearings which were observed during the research, a 'team' approach was adopted, allowing the complementary skills and backgrounds of tribunal members to blend in a way which is particularly suitable for hearings of an inquisitorial nature.

A major contributing factor in the development of a harmonious, team approach has been the respect and generally high regard which chairs and members seem to have for each other (see below).

Lay members' views on the chairs of the tribunal

Although some lay members in the survey have found one or two chairs to be rather domineering and/or abrasive in manner, very high opinions of the overwhelming majority of chairs were expressed. The following comments are typical:

- 'excellent';
- 'I found chairs to be superb';
- 'I have generally been *very impressed*!';
- 'they have all been surprisingly good';
- 'very satisfactory on the whole'.

However, a significant minority commented that some chairs were far better than others:

- 'variable';
- 'from being professionally excellent to poor';
- 'I was not happy about . . . one chair and asked for the President to ensure I did not sit with him again and gave my reasons';
- 'extremely mixed'.

Despite these negative comments, the overall picture is one of praise from lay members for chairs' skill and efficiency, their relaxed and informal approach and their care in ensuring that lay members are able to participate effectively in the hearing:

- 'I have been very pleased by the professionalism of the chair persons and the way they have got the tribunal to work as a team.'
- 'Friendly to parents.'
- 'Good humour and appropriate sensitivity for the parents.'
- 'Caring and sensitive to the needs of both parties.'
- 'Chairs on the whole involve lay members effectively when education issues or resource issues are being discussed and seem to value the lay members' expertise equally when making a decision.'
- 'Courteous, easily understood by parents, capable of "leading" discussions with other lay members.'
- 'Managed to create an informal, relaxed atmosphere whilst maintaining an efficient and well ordered hearing.'
- 'I was concerned – and said so at interview – that lawyers as chair persons might prove to be *too* daunting for some parents. This has *not* been the case to date. Chair persons to date have been understanding, kindly and friendly – and very efficient.'
- 'Putting parties at ease, trying to avoid acrimony and eliciting evidence in an ordered way.'

Some members also commented that they found the chairs to be particularly knowledgeable on the law and practice. However, there were some lay members who found the opposite to be true. One, for example, referred to the 'limited knowledge base of many'.

There were other criticisms of some chairs. One member was dissatisfied that the chair with whom he had sat on two occasions had been late both times. Another commented that some chairs had 'obviously not prepared themselves adequately'. Some members felt that some of the chairs had tended to allow the hearing to progress too quickly – for example, one said that one or two chairs 'had been in a bit of a hurry'. Equally, there were some members who had the opposite criticism, describing the approach taken by some chairs as 'too laboured and pedantic' or referring to the fact that some had 'gone on too long'. A common observation, although not really a criticism, was the variation in approach and the lack of procedural consistency between different chairs. This is an important issue which is dealt with in Chapter 9.

The overall level of respect which members seem to have developed for the lawyer chairs of the SENT reinforces the argument that it was entirely appropriate to make it a requirement that the chair should be a lawyer. Nevertheless, the experience and knowledge of the lay members represents an equally vital component, as confirmed by the views expressed by chairs (see below).

Chairs' views on the lay members

When chairs were asked for their assessment of the lay members and their contribution to the adjudicative process, they were almost universal in their praise. Typically positive comments included:

- 'The members have brought experience and understanding.'
- 'Very knowledgeable.'
- 'Members have been excellent and made important contributions.'
- 'A very valuable contribution.'
- 'Indispensable.'
- 'Effective, well prepared and decisive.'
- '[Lay members] bring specialised knowledge and experience with them, which if properly used is of inestimable value.'

These comments demonstrate that precisely the qualities and background experience that it was hoped would combine well with the skills of lawyer chairs to provide a well-balanced and effective team have proved highly advantageous. It should be stressed, however, that a number of chairs found there to be some variation in the effectiveness of tribunal members. For example, one chair commented: 'I find the quality of lay members very mixed and their contribution and assistance to the whole process is very varied'. Another said: 'some have been excellent –

others not quite so good'. One of the specific criticisms of some lay members made by a number of chairs is that they are at times reluctant to participate in the proceedings. Several chairs commented that they had hoped that the lay members would play a more active role, such as by intervening and asking questions. One chair referred to the 'negligible participation' by some lay members, while another said that the one or two members had taken 'little or no part in the discussion at the hearing . . . they seemed to be there for the ride!'.

These criticisms aside, chairs (who are arguably in the best position to judge the matter) believe that most lay members are playing a very important role in the decision-making process.

Are lay members pro-LEA in their approach?

One final issue concerns the extent to which the majority of lay members' background in local government has in any way caused them to be pro-LEA and less impartial in their approach. Several lay members in the survey commented on the LEA background of some of their colleagues. One said that he had sat on two separate occasions with a colleague who was an educational psychologist in his own LEA and that this 'would not seem a very balanced panel (particularly as we were sitting in an adjoining authority)'. Another contrasted the position under the 1981 Act, where local appeal committees 'had "lay" members in the true sense, usually councillors with an interest in special education'.

Tribunal chairs are probably in the best position to judge whether there is any LEA bias among the lay members, because lay members' attitudes and prejudices may well only surface during the closed decision-making session. Despite the concerns expressed in some quarters about potential LEA-bias on the part of tribunal members who have a background of working for LEAs, this was not in fact borne out by the experience of the chairs with whom they had sat. One chair said that, whilst it was difficult to generalise, those members with previous local authority experience had, in fact, 'been very demanding and critical of LEA actions'. Another said that although a majority of the members with whom he had worked had a background of working for LEAs, he had found himself to be

> 'pleasantly surprised at the constructive criticism the lay members offered in private of the LEA's actions in individual cases . . . I have found them to be very fair minded and independently minded and certainly not "pro LEA" as was suggested in the recent BBC 2 TV series *Old School Ties*.'

When interviewed by the author, the SENT President also confirmed that he had come across little or no evidence of LEA-bias. Observations of hearings and, in some cases, the deliberations of the tribunal in the course of the research also confirmed a broad picture of neutrality, despite a possibly excessive sympathy for the LEA's position in a few cases. The question of bias is discussed further in Chapter 10.

4.5   HAVE THE RIGHT PEOPLE BEEN RECRUITED TO SENT PANELS?

It seems fair to conclude that the SENT has been successful in recruiting to the panels persons with appropriate skills and experience. The true test of chairs' and lay members' effectiveness lies, however, in the performance of their task. This is discussed in Chapters 9 and 10, which concentrate on the hearing and decision-making process. It is only this stage that, for example, the distorting effect, if any, of many years' LEA-based work experience on the judgement of a SENT member would be palpable, although chairs' opinions regarding the members (see above) would seem to reduce the likelihood of such a finding. Nevertheless, one can conclude at this stage that there is a highly motivated, keen and (in the light of the findings reported below) interested tribunal membership.

The above evidence should reassure the President and others, and help to confirm them in their view, that the constituent elements of the tribunal are appropriate.

4.6   CHAIRS' AND LAY MEMBERS' INTEREST IN THE WORK

Almost all of the chairs and lay members in the survey envisaged remaining on the SENT for the foreseeable future, and the most probable reason for that was the high level of interest that the work itself held for them. Only one of the lay members, and none of the chairs, had found the work to be less interesting than they had anticipated at the outset. In fact, many reported that the work had proved to be more interesting than they had thought would be the case (see Table 8 below).

Table 8

Extent of chairs' and members' interest in the work as compared with prior expectation

Level of interest	Number of chairs (C) and lay members (M)		Percentages	
	C	M	C	M
More interesting	8	31	32%	44%
As interesting	17	37	68%	54%
Less interesting	0	1	0%	1%
No response	0	1	0%	1%

Note: Figures for chairs (n=25); figures for lay members (n=70).

4.7   TRAINING OF CHAIRS AND LAY MEMBERS

Training of panels is now considered essential in almost all tribunal jurisdictions. It is often an explicit term of appointment to a tribunal that a member will participate in any training provided; and, in any event, those who refuse to be trained could be dismissed or face non-renewal of their appointment. Training has, not surprisingly, been given quite a high priority in the SENT. The President has said he sets 'great store by the value of training'.[23] Separate training is organised for members of the tribunal Secretariat and for chairs and lay members. (But note that only a limited number of the Secretariat staff have had disability awareness training.)

Chairs and lay members received joint initial training in September 1994. The training was organised on a regional basis, with two two-day sessions in Bolton and Reading. The sessions covered the legal and administrative frameworks, the Code of Practice and some aspects of the judicial task. Chairs received further training in March 1995, comprising one day's training in London, and there were further sessions for both chairs and members in November of that year, in Birmingham. Communications between tribunals and the parties to an appeal was one of the subjects

---

23 T. Aldridge QC, *Special Educational Needs Tribunal, Annual Report 1994/95* (SENT, 1995), p 20.

covered.[24] There was a further induction training conference for 30 new members in June 1996. A particular feature of that conference was the involvement of experienced SENT chairs and members in giving most of the presentations. This increased the practical orientation of the induction training, which included a mock tribunal. As in the earlier induction training programme, chairs and members received their training as a single group, although there were some separate sessions.

Although some changes have been made in response to trainees' suggestions (see below), the SENT President and Secretary envisage training continuing along similar lines in the future, although some localised activities are developing, with members based in the South East currently setting up their own training group meetings.

Chairs and lay members in the survey were asked to assess the quality and suitability of the training they had been given. (For the most part, their comments do not relate to the most recent training sessions.) The tribunal carries out its own evaluation and, clearly, one would expect chairs' and members' satisfaction with their training to increase as the training itself is improved in the light of experience. In fact, findings from our survey reveal that most chairs and lay members were satisfied with the quality of training provided and found it useful.

Table 9

Chairs' and lay members' assessment of the quality of training provided by the SENT

Quality of training	Number of chairs (C) and lay members (M)		Percentages	
	C	M	C	M
Exceptionally good	0	0	0%	0%
Good	14	22	56%	32%
Satisfactory	10	41	40%	58%
Quite unsatisfactory	1	7	4%	10%
Extremely poor	0	0	0%	0%

Note: Figures for chairs (n=25); figures for lay members (n=70).

---

24 See R. Brooke Ross, 'New Training Initiatives 1995/96' (1996) 3(2) *Tribunals* 15.

The figures in Table 9 show clearly that, whilst a majority of the chairs rated their training as 'good', the majority of members rated it as merely 'satisfactory'. However, at the time that the survey was conducted, chairs had received a second round of training whereas members had not. This may partially account for the disparity in satisfaction levels. (Indeed, some chairs commented specifically on the usefulness of the February 1995 training.) Another factor is that the majority of lay members have experience of education – in many cases as teachers themselves. Consequently, they may be expected to judge more critically the organisation of training and the various presentations made. Examples of specific comments are set out after Table 10 below, which shows how chairs and members rated their training in terms of its usefulness for their role.

Table 10

Chairs' and lay members' views on the usefulness of induction and training session(s) in preparing them for sitting on the SENT

Degree of usefulness	Number of chairs (C) and lay members (M)		Percentages	
	C	M	C	M
Exceptionally useful	7	6	28%	9%
Fairly useful	11	16	44%	24%
Useful	6	35	24%	51%
Not very useful	1	11	4%	16%
Of no use	0	0	0%	0%

Note: Figures for chairs (n=25); figures for lay members (n=68).

As in Table 9, there is a clear indication in Table 10 that lay members found the induction and training session(s) less useful than chairs. Indeed, only one chair out of 25, compared with 11 out of 68 (just under one in six) lay members, rated the induction and training sessions as 'not very useful'.

Although chairs in the survey were generally positive about the training received, a recurring criticism was that, at least initially, there was insufficient emphasis on the process of chairing a tribunal, and a couple of chairs commented that they would have liked the law to be covered in more depth. Many chairs had also wanted, and therefore welcomed, the separate training (ie separate from members' training) which they received in the second round. Several chairs felt that the relevance and usefulness of the training offered had improved after the first round; one commented that he was pleased that chairs' feedback to the President had been acted upon.

In general, and although more critical, members were satisfied with the training received, as noted above. Most found that it was useful to have the legal framework set out and for the general approach to adjudication of SEN disputes to be covered:

- 'It provided a necessary general base and method for approaching the cases.'
- 'It did provide a good framework for the analysis of case papers and the decision-making process.'

Several of the lay members felt that it had been useful to have received at least the initial training with the chairs, and some also explained that it had been helpful to have had an opportunity to meet with other members to see the range of experience and different perspectives which members were bringing to the tribunal.

There were, however, a number of criticisms. Some members said they would have liked more case material to aid discussion of practical approaches to problems. Role playing is often used in tribunal training, and many SENT members believed that their training sessions should make more use of it. The initial training did include a decision-making session. Several members found this to have been particularly helpful.

Many of the lay members who were only fairly satisfied with the initial training felt that it was probably as good as might have been expected and that training would probably have a more relevant focus in the future as it was developed in the light of the tribunal's experience.

4.8 LOCATION AND FREQUENCY OF SITTING

The SENT sits throughout the country. Consequently, tribunal chairs and members are recruited from various regions. Although it is expected that the majority of cases with which chairmen and members will be involved will have originated from their particular region, chairs and members will on occasion be asked to sit in other areas. Several provincial chairs, for example, have been asked to travel to London for a hearing. One of the advantages of this is that it facilitates monitoring of these chairs' conduct of cases by the President. Nevertheless, most sittings will take place in the particular region in which the chair or member is based. This has the advantage that the chairs and members will have 'some knowledge of the region' and that travelling time and costs will be kept to a minimum for all concerned.[25]

A few chairs in the survey commented critically on the geographical distribution of cases which they had been asked to chair. One commented that he was 'surprised' that he had yet to hear a case in his home county and was unhappy about this because of the considerable travelling time to some hearings. (He also commented that no allowance for travelling time was made in the fee for the work; in fact, he was mistaken about that, because travelling time is included in determining the number of hours absent from home, which forms the basis of the fee paid.) However, a few chairs acknowledged that it was important for chairs to sit in other regions in order to widen their experience. Chairs living in counties in which very few appeals tend to originate – such as Devon, Cornwall or Shropshire – will inevitably face a large number of journeys outside their county for SENT hearings.

In fact, chairs who indicated firmly that they were not willing to travel outside their area seemed to be granted an exemption from doing much travelling. One chair said that in his experience some chairs were 'not prepared to travel so they get all the easy access cases in Manchester or Liverpool'; this caused him to be 'concern[ed] about the general fairness to the body of chairmen and members being selected'. According to the SENT, the need to send chairs outside their area has arisen when all local panel members have been unavailable on a particular date. The SENT reported to the author that very few chairs refuse to travel outside their area. A majority of the out of region hearings on which chairs have been asked to sit have been in London. The recent increase in the number of chairs, including those who are London-based, is expected by the SENT to reduce considerably the need for out of region chairing. However, because a chair's local connection to an area often produces a conflict of interest in cases (which seems to be a common problem according to the SENT), he or she will not be able to sit locally in any event.

There were no comments from lay members about the geographical distribution of their hearings, which suggests that very few have been asked to travel outside their region. On the other hand, lay members were

---

25 DFE, *Special Educational Needs Tribunal – Consultation Paper on Draft Regulations and Rules of Procedure* (DFE, 1994), para 21.

concerned about the 'uneven requirement to sit' (as one member put it) as between different members. In their terms of appointment, lay members agree to sit for not less 20 nor more than 70 days per year. The Secretariat aims to allocate at least 24 days' work per year. Several members were, however, concerned that they had had relatively few sittings – less than they had anticipated. The surveys of both chairs and lay members were conducted simultaneously, and each reveal the wide disparity in the frequency of sitting referred to above (even allowing for the fact that not all questionnaires were completed on the same date); see Table 11 below.

Table 11

Number of cases assigned to chairs and lay members of the SENT by the date of the survey

Number of cases	Number of chairs (C) and lay members (M)		Percentages	
	C	M	C	M
5 or fewer	3	12	12%	17%
6–10	7	25	28%	37%
11–15	8	23	32%	32%
16–20	4	4	16%	6%
21 or more	3	5	12%	7%
No response	0	1	0%	1%

Note: Figures for chairs (n=25); figures for lay members (n=70).

Whilst it is clear that some chairs and members had sat on four or more times as many occasions than others, the majority of chairs and lay members had sat between 6–15 times. It has to be borne in mind that there have been more appeals in some regions than others, producing a disparity in the case-loads. On average, chairs had sat more or less as often as lay members. But far fewer lay members than chairs were sitting as frequently as they had anticipated when they were appointed. As shown in Table 12 below, 69% of lay members had expected to be called more frequently, as compared with 32% of chairs.

Table 12

Extent to which frequency of sitting matched anticipation of chairs and lay members when appointed

Anticipated frequency of sitting	Number of chairs (C) and lay members (M)		Percentages	
	C	M	C	M
More frequently	8	48	32%	69%
As frequently	15	19	60%	27%
Less frequently	2	3	8%	4%

4.9 ADMINISTRATIVE ORGANISATION OF THE SENT

The administrative structure of the SENT has evolved over the two-and-a-half years of its existence. Initially, the SENT Secretariat was staffed by just five full-time equivalent (FTE) officers. This total gradually increased but did not reach double figures until February 1995. Table 13 below shows the steady increase in the SENT's staffing levels, including the increased numbers of higher grade personnel within the Secretariat.

Several LEAs in the survey commented that because the SENT administration is centrally based, in London, it is too remote from many of the locations from which appeals originate and where the tribunal sits. An office has now been opened in Darlington, which has responsibility for all cases in the North of England, but there are still users of the SENT who believe that the introduction of further regional centres would be an improvement, particularly if those centres could also have permanent accommodation for tribunal hearings. Operating a number of regional centres would also obviate the need for the clerks to travel so far afield for hearings. Clerks often have to travel to the tribunal venue the day before the hearing and stay overnight for a morning start. This is obviously an expensive way of operating a tribunal system.

Reorganisation of administration has resulted in there being six higher executive officers as line managers with discrete areas of responsibility, working under the Secretary. The next tier down are mostly senior clerks who in turn are above clerks in the administrative structure.

Table 13

Special Educational Needs Tribunal staffing levels: September 1994–July 1996

Month and Year	Staff grade[a]					Total FTE[b]
	G7	HEO	EO	AO	AA	
Sep 1994	1	1	1	2	0	5
Oct 1994	1	1	1	3	0	6
Nov 1994	1	1	1	3	0	6
Dec 1994	1	1	1	5	0	8
Jan 1995	1	1	1	6	0	9
Feb 1995	1	1	1	6	1	10
Mar 1995	1	1	2	10	2	16
Apr 1995[c]	1	2	4	7	2	16
May 1995	1	2	4	6	2	15
Jun 1995	1	4	4	8	2	19
Jul 1995	1	4	4	11	2	22
Aug 1995	1	4	4	11	3	23
Sep 1995	1	4	5	10	3	23
Oct 1995	1	5	6	12	2	26
Nov 1995	1	5	6	12	3	27
Dec 1995	1	5	7	12	3	28
Jan 1996	1	5	7	13	3	29
Feb 1996	1	5	7	10	4	27
Mar 1996	1	5	7	12	3	28
Apr 1996	1	5	8	13	3	30
May 1996	1	5	8	13	3	30
Jun 1996	1	5	8	12	3	30
Jul 1996	1	6	9	14	3	33

Source: SENT

[a] G7 = Grade 7 (in this case, the Tribunal Secretary)
  HEO = Higher executive officer
  EO = Executive officer
  AO = Administrative officer
  AA = Administrative assistant

[b] This refers to 'full-time equivalent' staff numbers. Note that in addition to these numbers, there were, at any one time, up to six temporary staff recruited from an outside agency to provide administrative assistance.

[c] In April 1995, there was an increase in the numbers of EO and HEO staff and a reduction in the number of AO staff. This resulted from staff regrading.

The distinction in status between senior clerks and clerks is a reflection of the more onerous responsibilities of the former. The following explanation was offered by one of the HEOs:

> 'Both "clerks" and "senior clerks" attend tribunal hearings on an equal basis. The seniority of the "senior clerk" is reflected in responsibilities as far as casework is concerned. The senior clerk, for example, is responsible for: monitoring the team workload to ensure that all stages of the appeals process are dealt with within the designated time targets; checking the work of the clerk for accuracy, especially in terms of jurisdiction; undertaking more 'complex' areas of work relating to particular appeals (with referral to the Team Leader where necessary), for instance correspondence relating to proposed schools, requests for directions, applications to strike out an appeal, etc; referring cases to the Team Leader with advice, where appropriate.'

The size of the SENT administration is still fairly small compared with other tribunals. However, as the case-load grows then, despite the economies of scale, so must the size of its administration. The President regards the present structure as functioning well, but further changes cannot be ruled out as the SENT continues to evolve.

In general, all those who have had contact with the staff at the SENT office, and with clerks in attendance at tribunals, have praised their efficiency and courtesy. Many parents in the survey praised the helpfulness of SENT staff in response to their queries. Undoubtedly, this friendly approach on the part of the SENT staff has made a significant contribution to the accessibility of the SENT to parents.

Despite this favourable picture, however, there have been criticisms. Some voluntary organisations and LEAs have been critical of the way the appeal documents have been put together – on some occasions there have been missing papers – and have been dissatisfied with various unexplained delays or late notification of changes. Many of the difficulties appear to have stemmed from under-staffing, a problem which the President acknowledged in his Annual Report for 1994/95.[26] By the time the tribunal entered its second year, however, the staff total had more than quadrupled and a clear management structure was in place.[27] All the

---

26 T. Aldridge QC, *Special Educational Needs Tribunal, Annual Report 1994/95* (SENT, 1995), p 10: 'The staff was increased during the year to cope with the work, but it was hard for recruitment to keep pace with the demands'.

27 'Cheerful hard work overcame the problems' resulting from a large influx of new appeals work in the autumn of 1995: T. Aldridge QC, *Special Educational Needs Tribunal, Annual Report 1995/96* (SENT, 1996), p 20.

indications are that the administration of the SENT has improved considerably.

4.10 COMPLAINTS ARRANGEMENTS

To date, no formal arrangements have been introduced for the consideration of customer complaints about the operation of the SENT. The Secretariat and the President are conscious of this deficiency, one which is inconsistent with developments elsewhere in the civil justice system, and a formal complaints system is likely to be instituted in the reasonably near future. At present, complaints will be dealt with informally by the Secretariat and/or the President, as appropriate.

Chapter 5

ORGANISATION OF SPECIAL EDUCATIONAL NEEDS APPEAL WORK WITHIN LEAs

5.1 INTRODUCTION

The new legislative framework concerning special educational needs and provision, which came into operation in 1994, undoubtedly created additional work for LEAs. Although much of the burden arising from the new legislation and the Code of Practice has fallen on schools themselves, in the form of extra administration on assessing, recording and planning, coupled with the additional responsibilities of SEN co-ordinators (SENCOs), LEAs have also faced particular pressures.

For one thing, the legal responsibilities on LEAs have become more onerous. There are now, for example, strict time targets, laid down by the SEN Regulations, in which to carry out a formal statutory assessment (normally 10 weeks[1]). Furthermore, where the LEA decides to make a statement, it has a maximum of two weeks in which to prepare a draft and serve a copy on the parents concerned; the statement itself must be made within eight weeks of the date on which the copy of the proposed (draft) statement was served.[2] Part of the procedure also now involves giving the parents an opportunity to express a preference for a particular school to be named in the statement.[3]

Before these provisions were introduced, many LEAs had a very poor record in producing a statement within the target figure of six months. A large number of complaints about these delays were brought to the local government ombudsman and awards of compensation to parents were quite common.[4] There is evidence that matters have, however, improved since the statutory time-limits were introduced, although not by as much as might have been expected. On average, LEAs in England and Wales

---

1 See the Education (Special Educational Needs) Regulations 1994, SI 1994/1047, reg 11.
2 There are exceptions: see ibid, reg 14.
3 1996 Act, Sch 27 paras 3–6.
4 See the many local government ombudsman investigations cited in N. Harris, *Law and Education: Regulation, Consumerism and the Education System* (Sweet & Maxwell, 1993), p 243.

prepared only 25% of draft statements of SEN within six months, timed from the point at which the authority received a written request to carry out an assessment, in the year from 1 April 1993. The following year, 1994–95, however, that figure increased to 32%,[5] indicating that, despite an improvement, many LEAs have struggled to meet the statutory time-limits introduced in 1994, and some have failed. One-third of local authorities did no better, and some did worse, than in the previous year, in meeting the target for producing draft statements. The Audit Commission concluded that, despite the fact that nearly two-thirds of local authorities were performing better than in 1993–94, 'large numbers of councils are failing to provide a service within the target time for some of the most vulnerable children in society'.[6]

Welcoming the establishment of statutory time-limits for the completion of statements, after a year in which he investigated 26 SEN complaints against authorities, one of the local government ombudsmen recently has indicated that if a local authority fails to meet its deadlines 'it is likely that I shall find maladministration'.[7]

The burden on LEAs has also increased as a result of the implementation of the Code of Practice on SEN, as noted above. As the Association of County Councils and the Association of Metropolitan Authorities said in evidence to the House of Commons Education Select Committee: 'for LEAs there has been more paper work and meetings – attendance at Annual Reviews, Transition Plans, Multi-Disciplinary Assessments etc'.[8]

The effect of the introduction of the new appeal system per se on LEAs' workload and administrative arrangements had, in contrast to the above developments, not been fully documented and the author set out to investigate it. The author's research has aimed, therefore, to establish a clear picture of how LEAs have been affected by the new system. It was anticipated at the outset that, while relieved of the need to organise local appeal committees, at least in relation to special educational needs cases, LEAs would face the increased burden of complying with the rather

5 Audit Commission, *Local Authority Performance Indicators 1994/95* (HMSO, 1996), Vol 1, p 12.

6 Ibid, p 11.

7 The Commission for Local Administration in England, *Local Government Ombudsman Annual Report 1995/96* (CLE, 1996), p 9.

8 House of Commons Education Committee, Second Report, 1995–96, *Special Educational Needs: The Working of the Code of Practice and the Tribunal*, HC 205, (HMSO, 1996), Appendix 3, para 2.4.

onerous requirements concerning the preparation and presentation of an authority's case to the tribunal.

Authorities were also expected to face more appeals, and this has, of course, materialised.[9] In one sense, the increase in appeals work is a reflection of LEAs' increased involvement with statementing and special educational provision for children via additional support to them in mainstream schooling.[10] The number of statements maintained by LEAs has increased by two-thirds since 1986, with a 13% increase in 1995 alone.[11] Parents often want a statement to spell out in detail the provision that the child requires, especially where the child is being educated in a mainstream school, and they often appeal if the statement is, in their view, insufficiently prescriptive, as well as where no statement is issued or if they disagree in the first place that their child should be educated in a mainstream school. Further factors are likely to include the wider grounds of appeal, greater awareness of, and willingness to assert, appeal rights and greater optimism about the chances of success following the establishment of an independent tribunal with the power to make binding decisions.

The introduction of a new legal framework for special educational needs and provision, including appeals, has inevitably meant some reorganisation and restructuring of administration for LEAs. Not only has this involved some reassignment of staff to new tasks, but it has also meant that the new legal basis on which decisions are taken (plus the requirements of the Code of Practice which, although not legally binding, are matters which LEAs and others must take into account[12]) has had to be learnt and translated into appropriate practice. Accordingly, training has been needed. For the purposes of the present research, it has been necessary to concentrate the investigation on training for and in connection with appeals work.

This chapter reports the findings of the survey of LEAs which was conducted as part of the author's research. As noted in Chapter 3, approximately 70% of LEAs in England and Wales responded. The results confirm that the introduction of the new appeal arrangements has

---

9 See Chapter 2.

10 See J. Evans and I. Lunt, 'Special Educational Provision after LMS' (1993) 20 *British Journal of Special Education* 59.

11 N. Pyke, 'Expenditure time bomb fear over special help', *Times Educational Supplement*, 29 November 1996.

12 1996 Act, s 313.

had a significant impact on LEAs' workload and on the likelihood of a dispute being settled without a hearing. This chapter also assesses the provision of information on appeals by LEAs.

5.2　PREPARATION BY LEAs FOR THE INTRODUCTION OF THE SENT: INFORMATION AND TRAINING

The extent of preparation for the new appeals system varied enormously between LEAs in the survey. A majority of LEAs provided staff with information on the new legal regime governing appeals, but this was not always reinforced by arranging for staff to attend either in-house or externally organised training sessions. Altogether, staff handling appeals work in 19 (just under 24%) of authorities did not receive any training on the new appeal system. In many authorities, however, some form of training was provided. In 21 LEAs there was in-house training, and approximately 75% of the authorities who provided such training also made arrangements for at least some of the staff to attend regional or national training conferences or seminars. In 37 LEAs – comprising almost half (46%) of all the authorities in the survey – at least some staff were able to attend such external courses.

It was predictable that authorities would have decided upon different means of preparing themselves for the introduction of the new appeal arrangements. But it may be assumed from the above data that some authorities were far better prepared than others.

5.3　RESPONSIBILITY FOR SEN APPEALS WORK WITHIN LEAs

The increase in workload arising from appeals work was not uniform across LEAs. Although, by the time of the survey, the new appeal system had been in operation for over 12 months, some LEAs had had very few appeals (in a few cases none). Others had had more but did not feel that there was an established pattern. Consequently, most LEAs had not increased staffing levels.

Only a minority of LEAs had staff engaged full time in SEN appeals administrative work; and none of these had more than four such staff. Of the 69 LEAs who responded on this issue, only 19 in total had staff engaged full time in appeals work, including five LEAs who used a combination of full and part-time staff. Quite a number of LEAs (22% of those who responded) had only one person engaged part-time in SEN appeals work, while a further 12% used two persons part-time and another 12% used three persons part-time. The remainder of LEAs, 19 (28%) of those who responded, had four or more persons engaged part-time in the work.

The disparity between LEAs clearly reflects differences in their administrative structures but also in the SEN appeals workload – itself partly a reflection of disparities in the incidence of statementing across authorities.[13]

In a majority of LEAs, responsibility for SEN appeals submissions rests with the education, rather than the legal, department. Of the 79 LEAs in the survey, 66 (84%) said it was the exclusive responsibility of their education department, none said it was the sole responsibility of their legal department, and 13 (16%) said that the responsibility was a joint one between the departments. The relatively low level of involvement of legal departments was rather surprising, given the suggestion made by some commentators, when the new appeal system was first introduced, that parents would be likely to be intimidated by the fact that the various documents they would receive from the LEA at the outset of their appeal would have the legal department's name on them. That problem does seem to have materialised in authorities in which appeals work is handled by the legal department, if the comments by one of the voluntary organisations working in this field are anything to go by:

> '[T]he first time they (parents) get a response from the authority through the Tribunal that response would come to them under the heading of the legal services department of the authority. Now that parent was put into an extreme situation of anxiety and that particular authority has represented all its cases from its legal services department and that does seem to be

---

13 In 1992–93, the authority which had the highest proportion of statemented children was 100 times more likely to make a child the subject of a statement than in the authority with the lowest proportion: House of Commons Education Committee, Third Report, 1992–93, *Meeting Special Educational Needs: Statements of Needs and Provision*, HC 287–I (HMSO, 1993), para 33. The differences in appeal rates across LEAs are documented in T. Aldridge QC, *Special Educational Needs Tribunal, Annual Report 1994/95* (SENT, 1995) and *Annual Report 1995/96* (SENT, 1996), and in a special report by IPSEA: E. Andrews, *Representing parents at the Special Educational Needs Tribunal: An evaluation of the work of IPSEA's Free Representation Service* (IPSEA, 1996).

unsatisfactory ... [I]t was not a recommended thing, but nevertheless it has happened.'[14]

As indicated above, however, only a minority of LEAs claim to have involved their legal department in this work. LEAs' perception that SEN work is essentially an educational matter rather than a legal matter is reflected in the designation of officers to attend SENT hearings on behalf of the authority. In the overwhelming majority of authorities, according to the author's survey, the designated officer will be an education officer rather than a member of the legal department. Almost all authorities in the survey (74 out of 80 replies, or 92.5%) specifically designate an officer to attend SENT hearings to represent the authority, and of these, 90% are education officers and the remaining 10% are described as joint education and legal officers. Separate legal representation is also used by some LEAs. The extent to which this is done is discussed in Chapter 8.

5.4 IMPACT OF THE SENT ON WORKLOAD AND SETTLEMENT OF DISPUTES

Workload

There is no doubt that the introduction of the new appeal arrangements has increased LEAs' pressure of work. When asked whether, and to what extent, their SEN appeals workload had changed since the introduction of the SENT in September 1994, six out of ten LEAs said that the workload had increased by 50% or more, and nearly two in ten reported a smaller increase. Only 5% of LEAs reported any decrease in workload. The full range of responses is shown in Table 14 below.

Table 14

Percentage change in surveyed LEAs' SEN appeals work since September 1994

Workload change	Numbers	Percentage
Increased by 50% or more	46	60%
Increased by less than 50%	14	18%
More or less remain the same	13	17%
Decreased by less than 50%	1	1%
Decreased by 50% or more	3	4%

(n=77)

14 Mr T. Healy, Evidence to the House of Commons Education Committee (see footnote 8 above), Q21.

The overall increase in workload is partly the result of there being a larger number of appeals. Extrapolating from the estimates, given by surveyed LEAs, of the number of appeals going to local appeal committees under the 1981 Act,[15] it would appear that there were approximately 400 such appeals per annum, compared with nearly 1,200 appeals registered by the SENT in its first year. A further factor is the change in the legal framework governing SEN appeals work. In particular, the time-limits (see Chapter 6) set by the SENT Regulations 1995 (and previously under the 1994 version) mean that LEAs will in many cases be forced to respond more quickly than they might have done under the old system. However, the LEAs were evenly divided on the question of whether the new system was in practice causing them to react more speedily to an appeal. Either way, the time-limit of 20 days on LEA replies to parents' notices of appeal is now being applied more strictly, thereby increasing the pressure on LEAs to act expeditiously.

Although the SENT recognised that some latitude in interpreting the procedural time-limits was initially appropriate while LEAs were becoming accustomed to the new appeal system, the President has subsequently sought to tighten up on late replies. He issued a President's Statement on this matter in November 1995 and commented that 'the extra time which is taken in disposing of appeals, if late replies are accepted, cannot be justified'.[16] The Statement proposes that tribunals should be more strict in enforcing the procedural requirements. Thus, tribunals are now instructed that if the LEA fails to meet the time-limit the tribunal should determine the matter in the absence of the LEA's reply, with the LEA having no further part in the proceedings.[17] This means that the pressure on LEAs to prepare appeal documents quickly has no doubt increased. Although extensions of time are possible, the President has made it clear that these will be given only in 'exceptional circumstances'.[18]

Even if LEAs' views, taken as a whole, were equivocal as regards the impact of the new system on their speed of response, most LEAs agreed or agreed strongly that the new system meant more preparation and overall work per case. Of the 77 LEAs who responded, 51 (63%) agreed that LEAs now have to have more evidence to support their decision. An

---

15 See Chapter 2.
16 See President's Statement, *Prompt delivery of replies by local education authorities* [1996] ELR 281.
17 As per reg 14 of the SENT Regs 1995: see Chapter 6. This will also happen if the LEA states in writing that it does not resist the appeal.
18 See President's Statement, *Prompt delivery of replies by local education authorities* [1996] ELR 281.

overwhelming majority of LEAs also agreed that the new system has certainly increased the amount of work per appeal: 90% of LEAs agreed that this was the case, just under half of whom agreed strongly. Only 10% disagreed that individual cases involved more work under the new appeal system.

Several LEAs in the survey made specific comments on the increased workload, seeing it in negative terms. Some saw it as an unwarranted drain on their already limited resources:

- 'The work generated by the tribunal for LEAs would belie the statement that its introduction is resource neutral.'
- 'The cost of the system to LEAs is substantial and is diverting much time, energy and funding from enhancing the quality of life and education for special needs children.'
- '[I]t assumes unlimited LEA time and resources. It is a diversion which can be ill afforded.'

A similar view was given by another LEA, in evidence to the House of Commons Select Committee:

- 'There has been a significant increase in appeals compared with the previous arrangement . . . The workload involved in responding fully to so many cases over a short period has resulted in pressures on officers and less time for more productive, school-based work.'[19]

In some LEAs the increase in workload has been quite dramatic. For example, one Inner London borough noted that between 1990 and 1994 it had two appeals to the local appeals committee and one to the Secretary of State, whereas over a period of approximately 12 months from late 1994 as many as 29 appeals were lodged with the tribunal. Another, North-West authority, reported an increase in local appeals from three or four per year to 17. Other authorities reported similar increases. One LEA (Outer London borough) commented: 'we estimate that there is an additional week's work per month generated since the SEN tribunal was introduced'. A survey of 15 London boroughs, the full results of which are shortly to be published, has revealed that the case load has continued to grow rapidly in these areas: from a total of 15 per year to 49 in 1994/95

---

19 Harrow Education Services Committee, in evidence to the House of Commons Education Committee (1996) (see footnote 8 above), Minutes of Evidence and Appendices, Appendix 23.

and 114 last year, although with a wide variation between authorities.[20] This survey has also yielded information on the additional costs faced by some LEAs in preparing and presenting appeal cases – up to £150,000 per year in the case of one authority.

Impact on disputes

Is the new system more conducive to conciliation, so that settlement without a hearing is more likely than under previous arrangements, or does it promote conflict? If the latter were the case it would be unfortunate, as the system is intended to promote settlement wherever possible. Indeed, the tenor and content of the Code of Practice on SEN would suggest the former, as the Code aims to promote a pragmatic approach to dealing both with children's needs and disagreements over them. But the procedure leading up to an appeal hearing is formal and, in some respects, adversarial in character, so that in some respects conflict is more likely.

LEAs certainly consider that the new appeal system generally promotes an adversarial rather than a conciliatory atmosphere in disputes between LEAs and parents. Of the 77 LEAs who responded, 46 (60%) said that they agreed or strongly agreed with the view that the new system had meant a smaller likelihood than before of a dispute being settled without a hearing. However, a fairly sizeable minority (40%) thought that the new system had not made pre-hearing settlement of disputes less likely. LEAs' comments reinforce the message from these figures:

- 'A significant proportion of parents resort immediately [to appeal] if they suspect the LEA may not satisfy their requirements. Opportunities for negotiation and conciliation effectively disappear.'
- 'Pressure to meet the tribunal's deadlines in response to appeals does not give much scope for reconsideration or negotiation with parents or professionals beforehand.'
- '[T]he SEN tribunal "ups" the stakes and raises further conflict rather than being a mechanism for conciliation.'

LEAs on the whole believe that the advantages of the new system to parents encourage those parents who are in dispute with an LEA to take the matter to a hearing. Altogether, 50 out of 77 (65%) LEAs agreed or

---

20 The survey, which was commissioned by the Association of Metropolitan Authorities and the Association of County Councils, is reported in J. Gardiner, 'Rise in special needs drains council funds' (1997) *Times Educational Supplement* 17 January.

strongly agreed that parents were more likely to fight on to the bitter end.

Many of the London LEAs, in the recent survey discussed earlier, have called for the introduction of an independent mediation or conciliation service to minimise the number of disputes going to the tribunal. The fact that an increasing proportion of appeals are withdrawn prior to the hearing, often as a result of settlement of the dispute, would suggest that such a system might have reasonable prospects of success because it would facilitate negotiations between the parties. On the other hand, many appeals are the result of an impasse between the LEA and the parents, and it is unlikely that conciliation or mediation would help. Moreover, if the process were protracted, the consequences which might arise if negotiations broke down and the appeal proceeded to a hearing would be: (i) that parents who need or want to use legal assistance might face additional overall costs; and (ii) an extension of the overall period of time it would take for the dispute to be resolved. In any event, parents who did not have legal or lay assistance might be at a disadvantage in the mediation or conciliation process, compared with LEAs.

Overall impact

Overall, the impact of the new appeal arrangements on LEAs has been considerable. There has been a substantial increase in appeals work, both in the number of appeals (which many LEAs regard as the result of parents becoming more assertive and litigious) and in the amount of work each case entails. The fact that LEAs are having to work harder to justify their original decision and to respond more quickly to arguments presented by the parents, may be regarded as an important advance in the field of SEN. On the other hand, the pressures of increased workload on LEAs at a time of extreme financial restraint and cut-backs in manpower have exacerbated their difficulties. Indeed, in these circumstances it is perhaps unsurprising that time targets are not always being met.

5.5   PROVISION OF INFORMATION BY LEAs TO PARENTS

LEAs are obliged to provide information on appeal rights to parents. Whenever an LEA issues a decision to a parent, it must, if the parent has a right of appeal against the decision, notify him or her of that right.[21] The

---

21 See, for example, s 325 of the 1996 Act.

appeal must be received by the Secretary to the tribunal not later than the first working day after the expiry of two months from the date on which the LEA gave the parent notice that he or she could appeal.[22] The President of the SENT has expressed the view that it is unfortunate that LEAs are not required to inform parents of the time within which they have to appeal. He reports that 'in an appreciable number of cases the authority has either not notified the parents of their appeal rights or has not done so accurately'.[23] The fact that time starts to run from the date on which parents are notified of their right of appeal by the LEA means that, where this information is not provided, some parents will in effect 'lose their right to appeal'.[24] In any event, delays will be caused to the process of resolving the dispute between the LEA and the parents which, as the President comments, will often be 'unhelpful to the children involved'.[25]

Some parents in the survey commented that the LEA had provided them with very little information on their rights of appeal. In fact, the statutory requirements involve the provision of merely the most basic of information – on the existence of the right itself. Clearly, there is a case for going further than this. Some LEAs supply parents with a copy of the SENT guide on how to appeal, and it would be desirable for this to become standard practice.

5.6 CONCLUSION

Some LEAs have clearly been struggling to meet the new and more onerous demands placed upon them by the SENT appeals system since 1994. The fact that the SENT has replaced an existing appeal system has meant that officers are familiar with a quasi-judicial process; but the SENT is very different in character to the old system, and the procedural requirements (discussed at length in Chapter 6) are very prescriptive, whereas previously there were few rules. Most important of all, whilst the new system has not eliminated altogether the long-standing problem of delays (again discussed in the next chapter), the procedure operates to a series of deadlines. Failing to meet a time target can be fatal to the LEA's case and hugely expensive if, from the LEA's point of view, the case is lost. Some LEAs will have learned their lesson the hard way.

---

22 SENT Regs 1995, reg 7.
23 T. Aldridge QC, *Special Educational Needs Tribunal, Annual Report 1994/95* (SENT, 1995), p 11.
24 Ibid.
25 Ibid.

Chapter 6

THE PRE-HEARING STAGES OF AN APPEAL

6.1 INTRODUCTION

The period between lodging an appeal and the date of the hearing –
comprising the interlocutory stages – normally runs for between four to
six months. It is during this period, on which this chapter focuses, that
most of the documentation relating to the appeal, including written
evidence in the form of reports, is compiled and arrangements are made
for the attendance of witnesses and others at the tribunal. The
interlocutory period is an important one, especially in view of the fairly
strong possibility of a case being settled before it reaches a hearing. Last
year, over one-third of appeals were withdrawn (see below), either
because the parties settled or, in a small number of cases, because the
parents simply no longer wished to appeal.

Given this book's access to justice theme, this chapter necessarily focuses
on the experience of parents. For example, the chapter examines their
access to advice and information and their general state of preparedness
for the hearing of their case. However, there is also considerable
discussion of the work undertaken by the chairs and lay members of the
tribunal. For them, preparation in the period prior to the actual hearing of
an appeal should involve careful examination of the documentation and
any necessary background research. It was of particular interest to
discover how much time they generally spend preparing for an appeal
hearing and how the amount of work which is entailed has compared with
their prior expectations.

The chapter also explains the legal provisions governing the interlocutory
stages of an appeal, including the important powers of the tribunal and
President. It also evaluates the various standard forms used by the
tribunal, particularly from the user's perspective.

6.2 THE APPELLANTS AND THE CHILDREN

The survey of appellants revealed evidence on the social class and
ethnicity of those bringing appeals. Gender was also monitored, although
for reasons explained below the most interesting statistic on gender
concerned the children, a very high proportion of whom were boys.

Social class

Although a majority of children with special educational needs have parents who belong to social class groups C2–E (reflecting the pattern of social division across the population as a whole), the parents who responded to the author's survey comprised equal numbers of A–C1s and C2–Es. This could indicate that it is more likely that middle-class parents will pursue their dispute with the LEA to an appeal, which would be consistent with the conclusion from other research that, in the field of special educational needs, 'the wealth of parents and their ability to manipulate the system become the ultimate arbiter of a child's educational opportunities'.[1] However, it could also indicate that such parents are more likely to complete questionnaires sent out by researchers! It is, therefore, difficult to draw any firm conclusions from this finding; but it seems probable that middle-class parents are more likely than others to utilise the SENT.

Ethnicity

So far as race and ethnicity are concerned, the research suggests that racial and ethnic minorities are massively under-represented among appellants. In the 40 tribunal hearings which were observed, all of the parents were white. Although one explanation could be that racial and ethnic minorities are, perhaps for cultural reasons, unwilling to grant permission for observation of their hearings, a much more likely explanation is that they are simply not making much use of the appeal system. One Inner London authority in the survey commented that 'the tribunal should publish the ethnicity of appellants; our experience is 13 cases (three black pupils, ten white) which does not represent the ethnicity of [our borough]'. Another Inner London borough drew attention to 'a lack of appeals from our large Asian population'. In research conducted by IPSEA into the use of its services by a sample of 42 clients, all of these clients described themselves as 'white'.[2]

If ethnic minorities are neither bringing SEN appeals nor seeking the help

---

1 S. Riddell, S. Brown and J. Duffield, 'Conflicts of policies and models – the case of specific learning difficulties', in S. Riddell and S. Brown (eds), *Special Educational Needs Policy in the 1990s* (Routledge, 1994), 119. See also B. Knill and K. Humphreys, 'Parental preference and its impact upon a market force approach to special education' (1996) 23(1) *British Journal of Special Education*, 30, at p 33.

2 E. Andrews, *Representing parents at the Special Educational Needs Tribunal: An evaluation of the work of IPSEA's Free Representation Service* (IPSEA, March 1996), para 2.4.

of the voluntary sector bodies active in this field, it is a serious matter. It certainly raises questions about ways in which the existing efforts to cater for the needs of ethnic minorities (which include publication of the information booklet and appeal forms in languages other than English and providing translators at hearings) can be improved. This may, in fact, be part of a much larger issue of access to justice for members of ethnic minorities, which cannot be explored here.

Gender

It proved very difficult to confirm the gender profile of appellants as a whole since, in some cases, one parent will insert his/her name in the appeal form even though both parents would regard themselves as appellants. Where only one parent gives notice of appeal, the SENT would in fact normally regard only that parent as the appellant; but any parent of the child is entitled to attend the hearing (see Chapter 9 at **9.3**).

There were some interesting findings with regard to the gender of the children concerned.[3] The SENT specifically monitors the gender of the children, and in 1995/96 77% of the appeals brought to the SENT concerned boys – an almost identical gender breakdown to that revealed by the IPSEA survey (75%).[4] The observations conducted as part of the author's research revealed an even wider disparity: of 40 cases covered, only four concerned girls (10% of the sample).

It has not proved possible to compare these figures with those on the gender of pupils who have special educational needs, even pupils with statements, because the DFEE does not keep such information. Nevertheless, DFE statistics for 1994 reveal that 46,001 boys with statements attended special schools, compared with 32,251 girls. Clearly, boys are more likely to be diagnosed as having learning difficulties than girls, as recent research has confirmed,[4a] but perhaps not quite to the extent reflected in the disparity between appeal rates. However, in seeking an understanding of the cause of the disparity, account needs to be taken of the kinds of disabilities with which appeals are particularly likely to be involved. As the SENT President commented to the author:

---

3 As noted elsewhere in this book, the child is not a party to the proceedings before the SENT, nor a party to any appeal to the High Court: *S v Special Educational Needs Tribunal and the City of Westminster* [1996] ELR 228, CA.

4 SENT statistics supplied to the author. E. Andrews, *Representing parents at the Special Educational Needs Tribunal: An evaluation of the work of IPSEA's Free Representation Service* (IPSEA, March 1996), para 2.1.

4a D. Budge, 'Huge gender gap in special needs revealed' (1997) *Times Educational Supplement*, 24 January.

'the Tribunal's workload appears to be disproportionately (in relation to the incidence of other disabilities) concerned with dyslexia, and dyslexia is known to be more common amongst boys than girls, for genetic reasons. Hence, a preponderance of boys in the Tribunal's workload is to be expected.'

6.3   PARENTS: ACCESS TO INFORMATION AND ADVICE

Some parents who appeal to tribunals have access to, and seek, legal advice from lawyers. But it is well known that the involvement of the legal profession in most tribunal work is rather limited. Previous research reveals that both the availability and quality of legal advice from lawyers in the field of welfare law is uneven and generally poor.[5]

In the welfare field, and this includes education, other advice agencies play a key role, although the quality of the advice varies.[6] In relation to special educational needs, the voluntary sector bodies provide an extremely important advisory and support service to parents, especially in relation to specific fields of learning difficulty – dyslexia, hyperactivity, hearing deficiency and so on. Some voluntary organisations have also worked with LEAs in developing the 'named person' role, which was promoted following the implementation of the Education Act 1981.[7]

Under the relevant provisions, incorporated into the 1996 Act, when the LEA proposes to carry out an assessment of the child's needs the parent has to be informed of the name of an officer of the LEA from whom information can be obtained;[8] the Code of Practice refers to this person as the 'named LEA officer'. But when the LEA decides to make a statement of SEN and serves a copy on the parent, it must also inform the parent of 'the name of the person to whom he may apply for information and advice about the child's special educational needs';[9] this is the 'named person', and he or she should not be the same person who is the named LEA

---

5   E. Kempson, *Legal Advice and Assistance* (Policy Studies Institute, 1989); N. Harris, *Quality and Effectiveness in Welfare Benefits Work in Solicitors' Offices*, Research Study No 9, (The Law Society, 1991). Standards being set for franchised legal aid work ought, in theory, to secure some improvement in the future.

6   E. Kempson, op cit; J. Steele and G. Bull, *Fast, Friendly and Expert?* (Policy Studies Institute, 1996).

7   For background, see P. Russell, *Developing the role of the 'named person': Some implications for policy and practice* (Council for Disabled Children, 1995).

8   1996 Act, s 323(1)(c).

9   Ibid, Sch 27 para 6(b).

officer.[10] Indeed, the Code of Practice advises that the 'named person' should 'normally be independent of the LEA and may be someone from a voluntary organisation or parent partnership scheme'.[11]

Parent partnership schemes have been developed in many areas (the Council for Disabled Children is co-ordinating a national consortium of these schemes) with the support of GEST funding from the DFEE. It was reported to the House of Commons Select Committee in February 1996 that many local authorities were working with the voluntary sector in their parent partnership schemes to produce leaflets, videos, information for parents, and so on, although some parents found it very difficult to use the information without a degree of individual support.[12] The level of advice and support to parents which the schemes provide, at a local level, varies. In any event, many parent partnership workers have little experience of the appeals process itself. Voluntary bodies have assisted in the development of these schemes, although some have taken policy decisions not to assist, in response to what they perceive to be a lack of financial support by the DFEE. Indeed, not all voluntary bodies working in this field have the resources or expertise to assist parents with appeals. This position was confirmed by the survey of voluntary organisations conducted as part of this research. There are, however, a small number of highly expert and extremely active voluntary bodies who do provide substantial amounts of advice for parents in connection with appeals to the SENT as well as, in some cases, supplying 'befrienders' and representing parents at tribunal hearings. The role of representation is a very important topic in this research and is dealt with separately in Chapter 8.

Parents included in the survey were asked whether they had received independent advice at the preliminary stage of their appeal: 65% had and 35% had not. It is important to bear in mind, however, that parents who receive advice are more likely to proceed with an appeal. Thus, as the questionnaire was distributed to parents with the appeal papers for the

---

10 The Code of Practice (1994), at 4:73 comments that 'the role of the Named Person is not the same as that of the Named LEA Officer'.

11 Ibid, Glossary at p 128. See also para 4:73. LEAs themselves are required to inform parents of their right to appeal (see Chapter 5 at **5.5**), but they are under no statutory obligation to provide any further guidance on appeals.

12 House of Commons Education Committee, Second Report, 1995–96, *Special Educational Needs: The Working of the Code of Practice and the Tribunal*, HC 205 (HMSO, 1996) oral evidence of Dr P Russell, OBE, Director, Council for Disabled Children, Q20.

hearing, it was perhaps more likely to have reached parents who had been advised than those who had not. The actual proportion of all potential appellants who receive advice may be somewhat less than 65%.

There continues to be debate about the importance of legal advice in connection with appeals.[13] Some argue that voluntary organisations and advice agencies have considerable expertise in this field and that assistance from solicitors in private practice is unnecessary. In general, this is the line taken by the guide on appeals,[14] which informs parents that they can obtain help in connection with an appeal from voluntary organisations, parents' groups or the 'named person' and states that 'these people will usually be able to give all the help you need without your needing a solicitor'. The guide does, however, indicate that legal aid advice and assistance (via the Green Form) may be obtainable for a meeting with a solicitor for advice about how to prepare the case. The guide also mentions that local citizens' advice bureaux can provide the names of solicitors who participate in the Green Form scheme and who may have experience in educational matters. However, in the survey, one firm of solicitors in South Wales reported that, in their area, the Legal Aid Board had 'no understanding of [SEN] work whatsoever' and that as a result there were 'many problems in providing proper advice in steps up to the hearing'.

References in the procedural guide to 'representation' are somewhat scattered. There is mention of the parent's right to 'send' someone to the hearing to represent him/her and, on a later page, the right to 'bring' a solicitor or barrister to the hearing. Although representation at the SENT is not covered by the legal aid scheme, parents may be willing to pay for it or may be able to secure lay representation by a voluntary organisation. One parent commented: 'we only found our representative after all our appeal papers had gone in, and then only by accident; more information should be made available to parents on where to look for representatives . . .'. This issue is discussed further in Chapter 8.

As all those familiar with this field will confirm, the law on special educational needs has grown in complexity (particularly in the light of an increasing volume of case law). Although most cases turn on questions of fact and involve little if any discussion of points of law,[15] the preparation

---

13 This is discussed further in Chapter 8, in the context of the involvement of lawyers as representatives.

14 SENT, *Special Educational Needs Tribunal – How to Appeal* (SENT, 1994), pp 5–6.

15 For a useful discussion of this distinction, see *South Glamorgan CC v L and M* [1996] ELR 400, QBD.

of an appeal can be a task which demands the skills of a lawyer – including the ability to pick out and challenge disparities and conflicts in the evidence on which the LEA is relying.

The need for legal advice is, overall, played down in the guidance; but some parents felt it to be particularly important. Although parents in the survey were most likely to consult a voluntary organisation, a surprisingly large number had received professional assistance from a solicitor or barrister, in some cases provided on a *pro bono* basis: see Table 15.

Table 15

Source of independent advice for parents in the survey

Adviser used	Numbers	Percentage
Solicitor	20	13%
Barrister	19	12%
CAB	2	1%
Other voluntary organisations	43	27%
Friend or relative	11	7%
Other*	24	15%
None	40	25%

* Includes special needs teacher, independent special needs consultant and Parent Partnership worker.
Note: some parents indicated more than one source of advice.

The parents were also asked to rate the services of their adviser. Over 90% of parents gave a high rating, stating that their adviser knew their case circumstances thoroughly and/or fulfilled their expectations. Only a very tiny minority were not satisfied with the advice received. Most of the dissatisfied parents indicated that the advice given had not advanced their knowledge or understanding of the case. However, it should be stressed that only nine parents out of 76 who had received advice expressed dissatisfaction with it; and no single agency predominated among the sources of advice referred to in responses from the dissatisfied parents, although, proportionately speaking, the highest level of dissatisfaction was with the advice provided by friends or relatives rather than professionals.

Some LEAs commented that appeals brought by parents were 'frivolous' and others recommended that there should be some mechanism for filtering out hopeless cases. It can be argued that where parents receive advice on their case it is perhaps more likely that frivolous cases will not proceed to a hearing, because parents will receive, and in many cases act upon, advice that their appeal is doomed.

Finally, it should be noted that many parents said that they could not have coped without the advice they had received. Furthermore, many commented favourably on the helpful approach of the SENT officials, emphasising that the tribunal can and does provide very useful basic factual information to parents on procedural and other matters. Comments included the following:

- 'The staff of the Special Educational Needs Tribunal when [it was] requested provided helpful advice and promptly returned telephone calls or correspondence.'
- 'Everybody concerned with the tribunal ... was very helpful.'
- 'We found the staff in London very helpful and felt supported by them as the appeal went through its various stages.'

The tribunal's information guide[16]

For many parents the only guidance which they will receive is a copy of the SENT booklet. This guide is 25 pages long, and the last 16 pages comprise the names and addresses of relevant government departments and voluntary and other organisations from whom further assistance can be obtained. The guide is written in plain English in the form of questions and answers. It has attracted a 'crystal mark' for its clarity from the Plain English Campaign. The SENT President regards the guide as important in promoting the accessibility of the tribunal.[17]

For a 'consumer' view of the guide, parents in the survey were asked whether they found the information easy to understand, helpful, difficult to understand or confusing. None of the parents regarded the information as 'confusing' and only six said that it was difficult to understand. All of the other parents described it as either easy to understand (55% of respondents) and/or helpful (63% of respondents). A small proportion of parents (14%) offered other descriptions (eg 'frustrating').

On this basis, the procedural guide for parents must be regarded as a success. Nevertheless, the fact that quite a number of parents in the

---

16 SENT, *Special Educational Needs Tribunal – How to Appeal* (SENT, 1994).
17 T. Aldridge QC, *The Special Educational Needs Tribunal, Annual Report 1994/95* (SENT, 1995), p 19.

survey also noted that aspects of the procedure at the hearing were rather different from what they had expected (see Chapter 9), suggests that the guidance could be improved to provide a more accurate and more comprehensive picture of how hearings are conducted. At the time of writing, a new edition of the guide is in preparation. The revision of the guide has been necessitated by the changes to procedure introduced in 1995. It is to be hoped that the opportunity will also be taken to effect improvements which will make the guide even more informative.

Voluntary organisations and lawyers were also asked about the guide. Of the 28 who replied, 15 described it as clear and easy to understand and nine said that it contained the right amount of information. However, some were critical: six regarded the guide as too simplistic and five thought it provided insufficient information. One of the voluntary organisations commented: 'I feel it does give the impression that this procedure is rather an uncomplicated one and that experience is somewhat different than the impression [given] of what should occur'.

6.4 TRIBUNAL FORMS AND STANDARD LETTERS

In the course of the research, a number of the forms and standard letters used by the tribunal were examined. These were generally clear and easy for most people to deal with, but the language used in some of the standard letters sent out to appellants could have been intimidating to some.

The following examples are drawn from some of the standard letters to the parties used by the SENT:

Dear [   ]

I am writing in connection with the Notice of Appeal about the special educational needs of ... To allow full consideration I direct you to make available the following additional [information/documents] ... This information will be photocopied and passed to ... on the condition that it is used only for the purposes of the appeal ... This letter constitutes a direction under regulation 21 of the Special Educational Needs Tribunal Regulations 1994. [You/the parents' representative] may apply to vary the direction or set it aside under regulation 20 ...

Yours sincerely
(*President's Direction as to provision of information or documents.*)

Dear [   ]
I am writing to inform you that the Secretary of the Tribunal has received notice from [X LEA] that the Notice of Appeal about [name of child]'s special educational needs is misconceived and applying for the appeal to be struck out. A copy of the notice is attached.

The President has considered this matter and has decided that the Tribunal will hear the LEA's application as a preliminary point of law at a separate hearing in advance of the appeal hearing. This means that a Tribunal will meet shortly to consider whether or not your appeal can be dealt with by the SEN Tribunal.

You may, if you wish, send in your views on why you feel your appeal should be considered by the Tribunal, or you can ask to give your views in person. If you wish to do so, you should send your written comments, or your request to give your views in person, to reach us by [date to be decided by Secretary].

Yours sincerely
(*Letter to parent informing him/her of LEA's application for appeal to be struck out.*)

It is difficult to strike the right balance between a necessary degree of formality in respect of legal proceedings with the informality which a system designed for parents to use without legal assistance demands. Parents are informed that they should seek advice from the SENT office if they are uncertain about anything. Nevertheless, it would be disastrous if the standard forms and letters presented a barrier to access. Fortunately, the overwhelming majority of parents in the survey did not experience very much difficulty with them. However, as we have seen, a majority of these parents were assisted with their appeal.

Voluntary organisations and lawyers were asked specifically about the forms and letters used by SENT. As shown in Table 16 below, most have reacted positively to the documentation, and there were few criticisms.

Table 16

Voluntary organisations' and lawyers' views on the forms and letters used by the SENT

Assessment	Numbers	Percentage
POSITIVE:		
Generally user-friendly	17	51%
Easy to understand	9	32%
Appropriate amount of formality	7	25%
NEGATIVE:		
Off-putting to appellants	3	11%
Difficult to understand	0	0%
Too formal	0	0%
Not formal enough	0	0%

(n=28)

Note: Percentages show the proportion of respondents who agreed with this description; some respondents ticked more than one box, hence the total is more than 100%.

Subsequent to the carrying out of this survey the SENT reviewed its forms and standard letters. A number of *new* forms and letters have been introduced – including some requiring parents who have a preference as regards placement to show that they have secured a place for their child at the chosen school – and improvements to clarity have been made, although the tribunal continues to emphasise that some measure of formality and technicality is necessary in the light of the legal requirements governing appeals, to ensure that a party is informed of the relevant information with as much accuracy as possible.

6.5 PREPARATION BY CHAIRS AND LAY MEMBERS

There are several reasons why it might be expected that chairs and lay members spend a considerable amount of time in preparation for each hearing. For one thing, there is lengthy documentation to be studied, which will generally be sent to the panel members in one bundle. In some cases, the evidence will be conflicting and the tribunal will also be mindful of the President's guidance (formerly contained in a Practice Direction[18]) to the effect that they should decide the issue on the basis of the circumstances prevailing at the time of the hearing rather than when the decision was made initially. Thus, considerable and careful thought will be necessary. The tribunal will also need to apply the law and take account of the Code of Practice. The documentation itself may not necessarily make explicit reference to the relevant paragraphs of the Code or sections of the Act, and it will not necessarily refer to any relevant case law; and the tribunal members may, therefore, have to check the various provisions and law reports.

Tribunal chairs and members will have gained an impression of the workload that was likely to be involved in SENT work from discussions which took place at the time of their recruitment and from the initial training sessions. Nevertheless, in the author's survey of chairs, the majority found the work to be more onerous than they had anticipated on appointment. The results of this part of the survey, which also show that only a minority of lay members found the work unexpectedly onerous, are shown in Table 17 below.

Table 17

Chairs' and lay members' views on whether SENT work has proved more onerous or less onerous than anticipated

Description	Numbers		Percentages	
	Chairs	*Lay members*	*Chairs*	*Lay members*
More onerous	14	12	56%	17%
As onerous	10	55	40%	79%
Less onerous	1	2	4%	3%
No response	0	1	0%	1%

Obviously, the workload derives not only from preparation, but also from the hearing itself and, in the case of chairs, from the writing up of the decision. It may be that the reason why a higher proportion of chairs than members found the work more onerous than anticipated was because of their additional role in writing up. However, a particularly important

---

18 *Special Educational Needs Tribunal – President's Direction*, 15 March 1995 [1995] ELR 335; see further footnote 80 below.

factor must be chairs' relative lack of previous experience of the field of SEN compared with many of the lay members,[19] who would perhaps have anticipated just how much documentation would need to be looked at in each case.

Interestingly, while the majority of chairs and lay members reported that they spent more than two hours in preparation for each hearing, three times as many chairs than lay members said that they spent a shorter time than this. One reason might be that even though chairs may have found that there was more work than they had anticipated, their legal training may have helped them to sift through the information and pick out the relevant issues more quickly, although another explanation is that because many chairs are still in full-time private practice, some, at least, have been unable to devote more time to preparation.

Average preparation times are shown in Table 18 below.

Table 18

Chairs and lay members: amount of time on average spent in preparing each case prior to the hearing

Preparation time	Numbers		Percentages	
	Chairs	Lay members	Chairs	Lay members
Up to one hour	0	1	0%	1%
One hour or more, but less than two hours	9	8	36%	11%
Two hours or more, but less than three hours	12	44	48%	63%
Three hours to a full day	4	9	16%	13%
More than one day	0	2	0%	3%
No response/other	0	6	0%	8%
	(n=25)	(n=70)		

Note: Percentages have been rounded up or down to the nearest whole figure; thus the end column does not add up to 100% exactly.

Chairs and lay members were also invited to give comments on their preparation for tribunal hearings:

---

19 See Chapter 4 at **4.3**.

- 'More onerous than expected in respect of pre-tribunal reading. I read very fast but bundles are often very thick.'
- 'All tribunal work is onerous and on a part-time basis is relatively poorly paid, given the necessary input.'
- 'Cases generate a large amount of documentation, but much of this is irrelevant.'
- 'The papers often include irrelevant or old material.'
- 'I find the amount of time preparing . . . to be more than I anticipated. It is crucial to be well prepared for hearings.'
- 'I hadn't quite expected so much paperwork or such detailed information – often as much as for quite complicated court proceedings.'
- 'The preparation time for each case is very considerable.'
- 'Given the answers to question six (about the amount of time spent in preparation for hearing) it can be seen that a day's fee actually covers two days' work.'
- 'If we take each case seriously and give it as much time as the paperwork submitted (requires), then the preparation time is excessive.'

The last of the above comments was made by a lay member, and the others were made by chairs. It is clear that the amount of work involved in each case has come as something of a shock to quite a number of SENT members, and chairs in particular. The majority of chairs are practising lawyers and a number expressed dissatisfaction with the level of fees paid, given the degree of work involved per case, even though they found the work itself to be very interesting. Some of those who sat in London and normally heard two cases in one day (one before, and one after lunch) found preparation particularly onerous. It is, perhaps, significant that a majority of chairs (60%) had previous experience of acting in an adjudicative capacity, as, for example, a chair of a social security appeal tribunal, a child support appeal tribunal or a rent assessment committee, or via immigrant appeals adjudication. Indeed, seven of the 25 chairs in the survey were current members of such appeal bodies. (Adjudicative experience is also discussed in Chapter 4, at **4.3**.) Several chairs commented that their fees for SENT work[20] were rather less (pro rata) than for most of these other types of adjudication work. It was clear that the onerousness of their task reinforced any dissatisfaction on this point.

---

20 Current fees are cited in Chapter 4 at footnote 19.

6.6 WAITING TIME: LENGTH OF PERIOD BETWEEN LODGING OF APPEAL AND DATE OF HEARING

One of the objectives behind the introduction of the SENT was to establish a more speedy system for the resolution of disputes between LEAs and parents concerning special educational needs and provision. Greater expedition would result, in particular, from replacing the two-tier system which operated in certain cases and by introducing time-limits for various stages of an appeal.[21]

Despite the relatively small number of appeals pursued under the 1981 Act, delays were quite a common occurrence. As noted in Chapter 2, it generally took between 6–12 months for appeals to be determined by the Secretary of State. The consultation document which preceded the establishment of the SENT under the Education Act 1993 acknowledged that the two-stage process for some appeals caused delays and thereby hindered the effectiveness of the system for appellants. A further consultation document[22] suggested that the period from the date of lodging the appeal until being informed of the tribunal's decision should be no more than 130 days (a time target which seems to have been based on all seven days of the week, rather than merely working days). Based on the SENT Regulations and the time-limits laid down for certain stages, the procedural guide offers a time scale of 95 working days.[23] (Provision for extending particular time-limits in exceptional circumstances is, as noted below, made by the regulations.)

The length of time it takes in practice for a case to progress from the initial notice of appeal to the hearing has been much criticised. Naturally, it is parents and/or their advisers who are most concerned about the problem of delay. The principal concern is that delay is detrimental to the interests of the child and prolongs the uncertainty concerning his/her education. However, a number of LEAs commented that delay not only causes problems for parents, it also means that the tribunal will be basing its decision on information some of which (eg evidence deriving from the formal assessment of the child) will by that time not be completely up to date. Although the length of time it took for cases to reach a hearing before a local committee under the Education Act 1981 was not documented,

---

21 See Chapter 2.
22 DFE, *Special Educational Needs Tribunal – Consultation Paper on Draft Regulations and Rules of Procedure* (DFE, 1994) Appendix B.
23 SENT, *Special Educational Needs Tribunal – How to Appeal* (SENT, 1994) pp 18–19.

making comparison with the 1993 Act (now 1996 Act) arrangements difficult, several LEAs commented that in their authority a much shorter timescale had been involved under the earlier legislation; for example:

- '[We] could achieve 1–2 months turnaround, but tribunal cases are running at 4–5 months.'
- 'On this LEA's experiences to date the main criticism would be the length of time before the hearing is arranged. One appeal was lodged with the SENT in July 1995 but not heard until Feb 1996. This is a longer period than that in which the LEA is required to complete the assessment and statementing process!'

The fact that the SENT President's Practice Direction indicated that, when the SENT was considering whether a statement of SEN was appropriate, it should base its decision on the situation at the date of the hearing,[24] was referred to by some LEAs as making the delay in the hearing of the appeal even more problematic. One LEA commented that the President's Direction was 'unhelpful' for this reason and that it would not be necessary for SENTs to adopt such an approach if hearings could be arranged more speedily. One LEA mistakenly believed that LEAs were 'prevented from submitting additional information in the interim period between acceptance of [the] appeal and date of hearing', which made the 'long lead-in time for hearings, usually five months' particularly difficult. In fact, many LEAs did, until the 1995 amendments to the SENT Regs almost completely closed the door on such a practice (see below), submit very late evidence, and indeed this was a particular cause of criticism. For example, the British Dyslexia Association, in evidence to the House of Commons Select Committee, reported that some LEAs had arranged for psychologists to visit children the week before the hearing and produced the evidence at the hearing itself. The Association regarded such a practice as 'unwarranted' and commented further that 'LEAs know the hearing will take place around five months after the appeal has been lodged. There is no excuse for the psychologist not to time his/her visit in plenty of time to discuss the results with parents'.[25]

The Association of County Councils and the Association of Metropolitan

---

24 *Special Educational Needs Tribunal – President's Direction*, 15 March 1995 [1995] ELR 335. As noted in footnote 80 below, this Practice Direction has since been revoked.

25 House of Commons Education Committee, Second Report, 1995–96, *Special Educational Needs: The Working of the Code of Practice and the Tribunal*, HC 205 (HMSO, 1996) Appendix 10.

Authorities also commented on this problem. In their evidence to the House of Commons Select Committee, they noted that 'the time lag between the lodging of an appeal to the tribunal and the actual hearing is now so long that a solution has often been found before the hearing or the advice is so out of date that extensive new advice has to be sought and distributed at the meeting'.[26]

The President has also commented specifically on the problem of delay. His view is that appeals should be dealt with as expeditiously as possible. As he said in his 1994/95 Annual Report: 'Any unnecessary delay needs to be eliminated because it represents an irreplaceable part of the school life of the child concerned. The uncertainty of a pending appeal also creates anxiety for parents which we are keen to keep to a minimum'.[27] At the time that the report was published, the SENT was operating a disposal target period of five months, as noted above. The President acknowledges that there is criticism that this period is too long, and has said that he would like it to be shorter,[28] but he believes that 'fairness demands that time be allowed, as the Regulations provide, for both the parents and the LEA to submit their case and any written evidence to the tribunal'.[29] Another reason for a delay is to ensure that the date of the hearing is convenient for the parties and their witnesses and representatives.[30]

It is widely believed that the delay is as long as it is because the SENT Secretariat is understaffed. The President has acknowledged that a steadily rising workload has imposed strains on the SENT Secretariat and that, in 1994/95, 'it was hard for recruitment to keep pace with the demands'.[31] Despite this difficulty, the President was able to report that the average disposal period during that year was five months and, therefore, the target was achieved. It should be stressed, however, that this target set by the SENT involves a longer period than that which is indicated in the SENT guide.[32] The staffing and organisation of the

---

26 House of Commons Education Committee, Second Report, 1995–96, *Special Educational Needs: The Working of the Code of Practice and the Tribunal*, HC 205 (HMSO, 1996) Appendix 3, para 4.2.

27 T. Aldridge QC, *The Special Educational Needs Tribunal, Annual Report 1994/95* (SENT, 1994), p 9.

28 See footnote 25 above, Minutes of Oral Evidence, Q42.

29 T. Aldridge QC, *The Special Educational Needs Tribunal, Annual Report 1994/95* (SENT, 1994), p 9.

30 Ibid.

31 Ibid, p. 10. See also Chapter 4 at **4.8**.

32 See SENT, *Special Educational Needs Tribunal – How to Appeal* (SENT, 1994) pp 18–19.

SENT have improved over the past 12 months[33] and the average appeal disposal period has been reduced to approximately four-and-a-half months. It is still, arguably, too long, but the improvement is to be welcomed.

The point, noted above, that a delay might be conducive to the settlement of a dispute without a hearing, touches upon an important issue. The spirit of the Code of Practice is indeed that negotiated arrangements on the basis of partnership between parents and schools/LEAs is the best way of resolving any disputes; indeed, some have suggested that settlement during this interlocutory period should be further promoted by having a conciliator.[34] Whilst it is entirely appropriate that settlement should be encouraged, the price should not be unwarranted delay in the date of the hearing. What the ACC/AMA are in fact talking about (see above) is a time period which is so long that the parties, and in particular parents, are simply not prepared to wait for the outcome. This is clearly regrettable, not least because there is a possibility that as word spreads about the tribunal, some parents may be deterred from lodging an appeal, or from seeing an appeal through to its determination by the tribunal, because of the long period of uncertainty which might be involved. A lawyer in the survey commented: '[The] process [is] too lengthy and complicated and as a result LEAs play the system, as parents either do not appeal or are exhausted by the process'. This suggests that delays, if they benefit anyone, are more likely to be to the advantage of the LEA, as they do not cause staff to experience the psychological pressure and the frustration that confront parents when waiting for a hearing.

Parents' perceptions are in many ways rather different from those of anyone else with an involvement in the SENT system. For many of the parents who are in dispute with their LEA, the period between lodging an appeal and the hearing is often perceived as yet another delay on top of the lengthy wait (although not as long as it was before time-limits were introduced following the 1993 Act) for assessment and statementing in respect of their child. In the questionnaire sent to parents, a space was left for general comments. Among their principal concerns, literally dozens of parents included a reference to the length of time it took for an appeal to be heard; for example:

---

33 See Chapter 4.
34 See, House of Commons Education Committee, Second Report, 1995–96, *Special Educational Needs: The Working of the Code of Practice and the Tribunal*, HC 205 (HMSO, 1996), Appendices, Evidence submitted by West Sussex LEA, p 85.

- 'The processing time was long and drawn out ... date of appeal 24/2/95 ... hearing actually took place on 11/8/95, 24 weeks from beginning to end.'
- 'The procedure has taken seven months. Very long winded – seven months to a nine-year-old child is a very, very long time.'
- 'From lodging my appeal to receiving the tribunal's decision took six months and one week. In terms of our child's school life this is far too long. It took far too long to be heard (24 weeks from appeal).'
- 'It takes too long. We waited six months.'
- 'The six-month wait was awful and further lost time in our son's education.'

Parents are naturally particularly dissatisfied if, having experienced such a long wait for a hearing, the outcome of the appeal is that the matter is referred back to the LEA for further consideration. As one parent commented: 'A six-month wait for an indecisive conclusion putting the ball back into the LEA court'. In fact, referrals back to the LEA are infrequent: in 1995/96 referral was the outcome in only nine cases.[35]

6.7   INTERLOCUTORY MATTERS

Between the lodging of an appeal and the hearing before the SENT, a number of procedural steps occur. These are governed by the Special Educational Needs Tribunal Regulations 1995 (the regulations).[36]

Notice of appeal

The appeal commences via a notice of appeal,[37] which must specify, inter alia, the grounds of appeal and, where the parent seeks to change the school named in the statement, the name and address of the proposed new school. The appeal notice must be delivered to the Secretary of the SENT within two months of the parent being informed of the right of the appeal by the LEA. The President may grant an extension of time in exceptional circumstances.[37a] In one case, he refused to exercise this power to assist a parent whose appeal was lodged two days late as a result of her representative's 'dilatoriness and possible ineptitude' (per Tucker J, who held, following a judicial review challenge by the parent, that the

---

35 SENT statistics.
36 SI 1995/3113. For a summary, see S. Oliver and L. Austen, *Special Educational Needs and the Law* (Jordans, 1996), Ch 9.
37 Regulation 7.
37a Regulation 41.

President had not acted unlawfully).[37b] In his affidavit in the proceedings (cited by Tucker J), the President explained that he interpreted his power as requiring him to exercise a discretion and 'only to agree to an extension where there is some reason which is both unusual and bearing strongly on the delay'. Tucker J said: 'I imagine the sort of situation he had in mind was sudden illness or accident, preventing delivery of the notice of appeal ... I see no error of law or any element of perversity being demonstrated in the [President's] approach'.

The parent is entitled to withdraw the appeal at any time before the hearing.[38] There is a high rate of withdrawal: 588 appeals (36% of those registered) in 1995/96 were withdrawn.[39]

Once the appeal is received by the SENT, the Secretary must enter details of it in the records, acknowledge its receipt (giving the correspondence address of the SENT Secretary) and inform the appellant that advice on the appeal may be obtained from the SENT.[40] A new provision, introduced in 1995, empowers the Secretary of the tribunal to correct obvious errors in the notice of appeal.[41] (The explanatory note on the changes to the regulations gave the example of a date of birth stated as 1884 rather than 1984.) The Secretary may also notify the parent of his/her opinion that the appeal is outside the jurisdiction of the tribunal and, if this happens, the appeal will go no further unless the parent notifies the Secretary that he or she wishes to proceed with it.[42] The SENT Secretary must send a copy of the notice of appeal and any accompanying papers to the LEA, indicating the time within which the LEA must reply and the consequences of any failure to do so (see below).[43]

The notice of appeal may state the name, address and profession of any representative of the parent to whom the tribunal should normally send replies or notices concerning the appeal. Failure to do so does not preclude the parent from notifying the Secretary of the tribunal of the name and address of his/her representative at any time before the hearing, provided this is done in writing.[44] Following changes to the regulations in

---

37b *R v Special Educational Needs Tribunal ex parte J* (1996) 13 December, QBD (unreported).

38 Regulation 9.

39 T. Aldridge QC, *The Special Educational Needs Tribunal, Annual Report 1995/96* (SENT, 1996), p 7.

40 Regulation 16(1)(a) and (b).

41 Regulation 16(3).

42 Regulation 16(2) and (4).

43 Regulation 16(1)(c).

44 Regulation 11(1) and (2).

1995, where the representative notifies the tribunal that he or she is no longer acting for the parent, the Secretary is required to notify the parent of that fact and to ensure that any subsequent documents relating to the case are sent to the parent him/herself.[45] At the hearing, the parent will be entitled to represent him/herself during any part of the proceedings.[46]

The LEA's reply

The reply by the LEA must be delivered to the SENT office not later than 20 working days after the date on which the authority received the parent's notice of appeal from the Secretary.[47] It seems that a 'noticeable' number of LEA replies have been lodged with the tribunal outside this time-limit.[48] As with other time-limits in the regulations, an extension may be granted by the President.[49] Quite a number of LEAs have sought extensions of time for replying, although others have not and have missed the deadline. At first, a lenient view of late replies to notices was taken by the President. Then a strict approach, which has continued, was adopted. If the time-limit is exceeded, the case must be referred for a determination.[50]

The LEA's reply must include a statement summarising the facts relating to the disputed decision together with any reasons for the decision and 'all written evidence which the authority wishes to submit to the tribunal'.[51] The parent has 15 working days from receipt of the reply (via the SENT) in which to deliver a response. If the LEA wishes to deliver written evidence or further written evidence it may do so with the permission of the President at any time within 15 working days from the date on which the parent could have delivered his/her response, or with the permission of the tribunal at the hearing itself. Otherwise, any such evidence may not be presented to the tribunal.[52]

Apart from the evidence submitted with his or her notice, the only other way the parent may submit written evidence is in his or her response to the

---

45 Regulation 11(3).
46 Regulation 11(4).
47 Regulation 12(3).
48 President's Statement, *Prompt delivery of replies by local education authorities* [1996] ELR 281.
49 Regulation 41. See also 'Notice of appeal' above.
50 Regulation 14. See President's Statement, *Prompt delivery of replies by local education authorities* [1996] ELR 281. See further Chapter 5 at **5.4**.
51 Regulation 12(2).
52 Regulation 29.

LEA's reply or with the permission of the President, at any time before the hearing, or with the permission of the tribunal at the hearing itself.[53]

The LEA is also entitled, either with the permission of the President at any time before the hearing, or with the permission of the tribunal at the hearing itself, to amend its reply, deliver a supplementary reply or amend a supplementary reply, in 'exceptional cases'.[54] The parent has a similar right in relation to his/her response to the LEA's reply and the submission of amended or supplementary grounds of appeal.[55]

As noted in Chapter 5 (at **5.4**), the regulations in fact now state that if the LEA fails to reply to the notice of appeal within the prescribed time-limit, or if it states in its written reply that it does not oppose the appeal, the SENT must[56] determine the appeal on the basis of the notice without a hearing, or without notifying the LEA hold a hearing at which the authority is not represented.[57]

SENT enquiries

At any stage after the notice of appeal the Secretary of the SENT has the power to make enquiries of the parties with regard to such matters as whether or not they intend to attend the hearing; whether they will be represented and, if so, by whom; whether they wish the hearing to be in public; whether they intend to call witnesses; and the names of the proposed witnesses.[58] Other enquiries may relate to whether the party or a witness will require the assistance of an interpreter and whether the parent wishes any persons (other than his/her witness(es)) to attend the hearing if it is in private, and the name(s) of such persons. Note that when the draft revised regulations were published in 1995, it was proposed that the number of persons whom the parent could bring in addition to witnesses and representatives would be limited to two. Although this was criticised as being unduly restrictive and unfair, the regulations (as amended) impose this limit but enable the President to grant permission, before the hearing, for a greater number to attend; and the tribunal may also grant such permission at the hearing itself.[59]

---

53 Regulation 8(5) and (6). See *Duncan v Bedfordshire CC and SENT* (1996) CO/3062/96 and *Lucy v RB Kensington and Chelsea* (1997) CO/4138/96 (both unreported).
54 Regulation 13(1).
55 Regulation 8(4). See *R v SENT ex parte Lane* (1996) CO/3879/96.
56 Under the 1994 SENT Regs, it had a discretion: see reg 15 of those regulations.
57 SENT Regs 1995, reg 14.
58 Regulation 17
59 Regulation 26(8).

Directions

The President of the SENT has a number of powers to give directions prior to the hearing. Some directions may be given either on the application of a party or at the President's own motion: these are directions requiring a party to provide 'such particulars or supplementary statements as may be reasonably required for the determination of the appeal' and directions with regard to delivery of any document or other material that the tribunal might require either to the tribunal and/or to the other party to the appeal, subject to certain conditions.[60] A party to the appeal may also ask the President to issue a witness summons, which would require the person named to attend a hearing and answer any questions or produce any documents or other material in their custody or control which relate to the subject of the appeal (see below).

If a direction is not complied with, the tribunal may utilise various powers.[61] First, if the direction relates to a parent, the tribunal may dismiss the appeal without a hearing. Secondly, if the LEA is in default of a direction, the tribunal may determine the appeal without a hearing. In some cases, a hearing may be held in the absence of the party who is in default. A failure to comply with a direction relating either to discovery of documents or to attendance at a hearing in order to produce evidence and/or documents, is an offence.[62]

There have been reports of delays in notifying a decision of the President on a direction.[63] If this is true (the SENT has informed the author that it is not aware of any such delays), the result would be increased uncertainty among parents and any advisers who are assisting them in connection with their appeal. Clearly, it would be desirable to minimise any such delays which are occurring.

Witness summonses

The President has referred specifically to the fact that he has received a larger number of requests than expected with regard to summoning of witnesses. In the 1994/95 Annual Report, he expressed surprise at the reluctance of some potential witnesses to assist the parties: 'in the spirit of parent partnership engendered by the Code of Practice I had thought that

---

60 Regulations 20 and 21.
61 Regulation 23.
62 1996 Act, s 336(5).
63 House of Commons Education Committee, Second Report, 1995–96, *Special Educational Needs: The Working of the Code of Practice and the Tribunal*, HC 205 (HMSO, 1996), Appendix 19.

those most closely concerned with the child in question would have no hesitation in coming forward to offer their help'.[64]

It has been particularly difficult for some parents to secure the attendance of their child's teacher at the hearing. The President has confirmed that LEAs are in some cases very unwilling to permit any of their employees, including teachers employed in their schools, to attend and give evidence which supports a parent's case.[65] The President's view, however, is that if the tribunal is to come to an appropriate and balanced decision it is necessary that 'any one with relevant evidence to give should appear as a witness if one of the parties wishes it'.[66] For this reason, he is often willing to issue a witness summons if such a potential witness will not otherwise attend.

The inability of some parents to secure the attendance of a teacher (eg a SENCO) at a hearing was commented on specifically in several of the representations made to the House of Commons Education Select Committee in February 1996. For example, the British Dyslexia Association noted that 'school staff are usually very reluctant to attend the hearings as witnesses for parents. They seem to regard this as speaking against the LEA, who have been known to tell teachers they cannot attend the tribunal'.[67] It would appear that a requirement to attend, under a witness summons, is often helpful to teachers who want to be able to present evidence on the parent's behalf. For example, in its evidence to the Select Committee, the Council for Disabled Children noted that 'witnesses may feel that they need a legal requirement in order to take time out of a busy professional week when their time may be hard to cover and when they could also appear in some instances to be giving evidence against their employers'.[68] A similar comment was made by a representative of the Cheshire Dyslexia Association in oral evidence. He had advised a large number of parents in connection with appeals. In his evidence, he confirmed that:

> 'There is an extreme reluctance among teachers to come to tribunals. They really do not want to be there; because the tribunal is often seen as an

---

64 T. Aldridge QC, *Special Educational Needs Tribunal, Annual Report 1994/95* (SENT, 1995), p 14.

65 Ibid.

66 Ibid.

67 House of Commons Education Committee, Second Report, 1995–96, *Special Educational Needs: The Working of the Code of Practice and the Tribunal*, HC 205 (HMSO, 1996), Appendix 10.

68 Ibid, Appendix 12.

adversarial situation. They do not want to be seen to be . . . not on the side of their employer.'[69]

A representative of IPSEA stated that often SENCOs or headteachers could offer important evidence on the question of whether a particular school has, or does not have, the provision which is required to meet the child's needs. He reported that some authorities appear to have blanket rules prohibiting the attendance of such personnel at tribunals.[70]

One of the parents in the survey confirmed the difficulty which is experienced:

'I was unable to call any useful witnesses (as they all work for the LEA and under their terms of employment they were not allowed to give evidence on my son's behalf) . . . [F]ollowing the hearing I understand that a general directive may be issued allowing LEA staff to appear as witnesses for the child in question without jeopardising their contractual terms of employment.'

This comment in fact highlights the importance of parents receiving advice before a hearing so that they can be made fully aware of their procedural rights (see above), although the procedural guide refers to the President's power to issue a witness summons.

Some of the LEAs in the survey believe that the President tends to favour parents over LEAs in requests for directions. One LEA commented that even though the LEA's observers could be given prior permission to attend a hearing, this was dealt with restrictively by the President, whereas 'it appears that parents can bring a befriender, solicitor (non-participant) and barrister'. In fact, the regulations state that a parent has a right to be represented by only one person; if he or she wishes to be represented by more than one person this can only take place with the President's permission.[71] This is in addition to the restriction on the number of witnesses which either side may normally call (ie two),[72] a rule with which the Council on Tribunals has expressed dissatisfaction.[73] The President

---

69 House of Commons Education Committee, Second Report, 1995–96, *Special Educational Needs: The Working of the Code of Practice and the Tribunal*, HC 205 (HMSO, 1996), Minutes of Oral Evidence, Q27.

70 Ibid, Q28.

71 Regulation 11(4). This is discussed further below.

72 Regulation 29(1) (proviso). Prior to the hearing the President may give permission for more than two witnesses to be called; the tribunal has a comparable discretion at the hearing: ibid.

73 Council on Tribunals, *Annual Report 1995/96* (HMSO, 1996), para 2.50.

supports such a rule as it 'reduces the cost and inconvenience of appeals to the tribunal and helps to focus hearings on the salient points'.[74]

Given the range of witnesses on either side who could, potentially, provide appropriate evidence in a case coming before the SENT, it is necessary to limit the numbers in order to ensure that the proceedings are kept as informal and non-intimidatory as possible and that they are not over-long. (In fact, as shall be shown in Chapter 9, even with this restriction on the number of witnesses present, a fairly large number of people may be in attendance.) On the other hand, although the President's view that often written evidence will be sufficient is valid, it perhaps fails to accord sufficient importance to the psychological impact of oral evidence, not least because the mere presence of a professional as a witness on behalf of a parent can often seem to strengthen the parent's case, because the evidence is more direct and may be given more weight.

A particular down-side to the need to seek the President's permission for additional witnesses is that it, in effect, adds another interlocutory stage, although it will not delay the hearing itself, particularly as the tribunal may give such permission on the day of the hearing, as noted above.[75]

Permission for attendance of solicitors with counsel

In December 1995, the President of the SENT issued a Statement concerning *Attendance of Solicitors with Counsel*.[76] In this, he gave notice that from 1 January 1996 he would no longer automatically give permission for a solicitor to attend with counsel, although he would be willing to entertain applications (made under the regulations) in advance of the hearing for permission in an individual case. It would be necessary, when seeking such permission, to show why, 'in the interests of justice' it should be granted. The Statement explained that it would:

> '*not* normally be sufficient to say that it would be convenient to have a note-taker (which other representatives do not have) nor that counsel is unknown to the lay client (which is frequently the case where counsel is instructed).'

---

74 T. Aldridge QC, *Special Educational Needs Tribunal, Annual Report 1994/95* (SENT, 1995), p 14

75 See footnote 72 above.

76 See [1996] ELR 280. If there are delays in notifying a decision of the President with regard to a direction, which ELAS says (in its evidence to the Select Committee) is sometimes the case, the result would be increased uncertainty among parents and any advisers who are assisting them in connection with their appeal.

The Statement also contained an explanation, by the President, of why he had taken the decision to restrict the attendance of solicitors with counsel. It stated that the restriction was intended to limit the number of people attending hearings in order to create an appropriate atmosphere for an informal tribunal procedure and to meet the concerns expressed by unrepresented parties 'that the experience of facing an opponent represented by a lawyer is made the more intimidating by the presence of a second representative'. He also commented that many other representatives at tribunals, both professional and voluntary, managed to appear on behalf of a party, without a second representative. The Statement has not been withdrawn and applies to both parents and LEAs.

Nevertheless, the Education Law Association (ELAS) has been in correspondence with the President in an effort to reverse this ruling, which does not seem to be mirrored in other judicial or quasi-judicial fora concerned, directly or indirectly, with the welfare of children. The President was pressed to agree to the attendance, on a regular basis, of legal trainees and note-takers for advocates, and he indicated in his 1995/96 Annual Report that he was considering the matter further.[77]

Meanwhile, the Education (Special Educational Needs) Bill, promoted by Lord Campbell of Alloway, was published. The Bill, which, as noted in earlier chapters, is currently before Parliament but does not have Government support, would provide a right for a solicitor to attend a SENT hearing with counsel. Shortly after the committee stage of the Bill in the House of Lords, the President of the SENT announced his conclusions following his review of the Statement. These were set out in a further Statement,[78] which reveals that the President remains unconvinced that it would be right to permit two representatives for a party as a matter of routine. He states that the regulations contemplate one representative as the norm, which is consistent with the aim of maximising informality. Nevertheless, the President explains that in limited circumstances (such as where the case is unusually complex or there is an extraordinary amount of documentary material) permission may be granted for both a solicitor and a barrister to represent. In some cases, parents have built up a close relationship of trust and support with a particular solicitor but wish to be represented by counsel. The President

---

77 T. Aldridge QC, *The Special Educational Needs Tribunal, Annual Report 1995/96* (SENT, 1996), p 6.
78 *Attendance at Hearings – Statement by the President* (16 December 1996).

explains that the solicitor could be permitted to attend as a person nominated by the parent (under reg 17(b) of the SENT Regulations) to accompany him or her. Finally, the Statement explains the President's opposition to the attendance of trainees and parents as observers.

6.8   ASSEMBLING EVIDENCE: INDEPENDENT REPORTS

In some cases, parents will want to obtain a report of an independent assessment of their child's needs. They may feel that such an independent assessment is likely to produce evidence which will contradict some of the views of the LEA as to the child's needs and the provision required to meet them. In the course of the research, there were a number of cases where parents had obtained such evidence and presented it to the tribunal. Such a practice occurred in relation to a whole range of different learning difficulties – not merely dyslexia or dyscalcula, but also those related to behavioural problems, speech and auditory problems, and various other causes of learning difficulty.

In the majority of cases, parents who require such evidence will find that the only way they can obtain it is by paying for it. This obviously puts parents who are less well off at a disadvantage compared to others, unless they can secure a free of charge assessment organised or carried out by a voluntary organisation. Although it has been difficult to monitor this systematically, the firm impression gained when observing tribunal hearings and, in many cases, witnessing the deliberations among the tribunal members afterwards, was that such independent assessment reports were quite influential. Parents and their advisers are therefore quite right to see considerable advantage in arranging for such an assessment to be carried out.

In the survey of 42 parents conducted by IPSEA, 29% had paid for an independent assessment of their child's needs and a further 10% had obtained a free assessment from a voluntary organisation. Of the parents who had paid for the assessment, the average charge was approximately £100; but IPSEA reports that up to six times this amount was paid in some cases.[79] This merely confirms the difficulties which parents on lower incomes would face.

---

79 E. Andrews, *Representing parents at the Special Educational Needs Tribunal: an evaluation of the work of IPSEA's Free Representation Service* (IPSEA, 1996), para 8.7.

There is a danger that, because independent reports are becoming sought on such a wide scale, parents who do not have them may be perceived by tribunals to have a 'weaker' case. Indeed, it is difficult to see how, in some cases at least, parents can mount an effective challenge to the assessment conducted by the LEA unless they obtain an independent assessment. Consideration should therefore be given to the question whether parents should be given the option of a free (perhaps subject to a means-test) independent assessment of their child as a matter of course – which could obviously be very expensive – or whether the tribunal should be empowered to commission an assessment itself if (and only if) it believes there is sufficient doubt about whether the LEA's assessment is accurate. One of the advantages in securing such an independent assessment is that it is likely to be far more up to date than the LEA's assessment. It should be borne in mind that, in accordance with the President's guidance,[80] the appeal should be decided on the basis of what is appropriate for the child at the date of the hearing; thus a recent report of an independent assessment is bound to be of considerable help to a tribunal in reaching its decision. Some LEAs believe that parents often have a tactical advantage where they are able to produce an independent assessment report which is more recent than the evidence which is relied on by the LEA and which is derived from its, generally earlier, assessment.

---

80 This was formerly the subject of a Practice Direction issued by the President in March 1995 [1995] ELR 335. The President subsequently decided that 'procedurally, this was not a subject on which there should be a direction' (T. Aldridge QC, *Special Educational Needs Tribunal, Annual Report 1995/96* (SENT, 1996), p 16 and the Direction was withdrawn (in October 1996). A judicial review challenge to the Direction was dropped.

Chapter 7

TRIBUNAL VENUES AND FACILITIES

7.1 INTRODUCTION

The SENT has a suite of two tribunal rooms at its central London headquarters at Victoria Street. It has no other permanent accommodation and secures the use of conference accommodation at hotels for hearings outside the South-East. There has been considerable comment, much of it negative, about the hotel facilities used for tribunal hearings.

The SENT is, in fact, quite unusual in hiring hotel facilities for tribunal hearings, but there may be arguments in favour of this practice. For example, it may be more economical to pay for facilities as and when they are required, rather than having permanent accommodation which will not always be in use. Given the avowed commitment by the SENT to ensure that appellants do not face a long journey, a large number of tribunal suites would need to be permanently available, were other accommodation not hired on an ad hoc basis.

The Consultation Document said that 'tribunals will sit, as and when required, in places which are easily accessible to both the parents and the LEA'.[1] There has also been an undertaking that, provided suitable accommodation is available, the tribunal will normally expect to sit within a few miles of the parents' home.[2] As noted in Chapter 3, the current tribunal guide states that the hearings will be arranged as near the parent's home as possible, with appeals originating in London and the South-East being heard at Victoria Street, provided the parent lives within a convenient travelling distance.[3] The extent to which the arrangements made in practice have conformed to this pattern is assessed in this chapter.

Also discussed, because of its equal, if not greater, importance, is the suitability of the tribunal room, particularly as regards physical access,

---

1 DFE, *Special Educational Needs Tribunal: Consultation Paper on Draft Regulations and Rules of Procedure* (DFE, 1994), para 21.
2 Ibid.
3 DFE, *Special Educational Needs Tribunal: How to Appeal* (DFE, 1994), p 12.

acoustics and the creation of an appropriate atmosphere. Taking the facilities available at most permanent tribunal premises as the model (while acknowledging that there is considerable variation in the accommodation used by tribunals), consideration is also given to the suitability of the waiting area and the availability of conference facilities (that is, the facilities for the parties to consult their advisers and representatives in a reasonably private environment). Also relevant to the general question of access is the availability of refreshments, on which there were a surprisingly large number of comments.

7.2 TRAVELLING TIME AND DISTANCE TO TRIBUNAL HEARINGS

Based on the information relating to the 40 tribunal hearings which were observed, parents were not required to travel outside the city or area in which they lived. The furthest travelling distance in any of the cases was approximately 20 miles. In most cases, the journey was considerably shorter than this. In a few cases, tribunal venues were on the outskirts of cities and this made them slightly less accessible by public transport. However, this was not a problem in the cases which were observed. Nevertheless, there is evidence from others that venues are not always convenient to the parties; Friel and Hay refer to 'a north Gloucestershire appeal being determined in Reading'.[4]

7.3 PHYSICAL ACCESS TO TRIBUNAL VENUES

Although hotels are, on the whole, problematic as tribunal venues, for reasons discussed below, they do offer good physical access. The fact that hearings are booked for particular venues on an ad hoc basis means that it is possible for the SENT office to arrange for a venue which is accessible via a wheelchair where such access is required. The SENT tribunal suite in Victoria Street is wheelchair accessible via a lift. Most of the hotel venues which were visited in the course of the research appeared to be wheelchair accessible.

Many of the other requirements of disabled people to which the Council on Tribunals refers in its Checklist and Code of Practice are included in the general specification set by the DFEE when booking accommodation

---

4 J. Friel and D. Hay, *Special Educational Needs and the Law* (Sweet & Maxwell, 1996), p 75.

for various purposes.[5] Thus, for example, a hotel would not be used if it had neither toilet facilities nor lifts which could be used by people in wheelchairs (but see below). However, the SENT office does not presently ask parties in advance of hearings whether they or any witnesses or representatives have any disabilities, in order to ascertain any special requirements as regards access. It would be helpful for them to do so. As the Council on Tribunals states in its guidance, 'Procedures should enable [disabled persons'] requirements to be identified in advance of a hearing so that consideration can be given to the provision of appropriate premises or other facilities'.[6]

7.4 OTHER FEATURES OF TRIBUNAL VENUES

A suitable tribunal venue would be one which, as the Council for Disabled Children put it succinctly, 'would provide sufficient privacy and yet be accessible and non-threatening'.[7] How the parent's experience of attending a hearing is affected by the tribunal venue, particularly the facilities and general atmosphere, must carry considerable weight in assessing the general accessibility of the system. The evidence suggests that many parents are extremely anxious when attending SENT hearings.[8] The extent to which tribunal premises contribute to, or ameliorate, this anxiety must be relevant.

Another important element is the degree of confidence on the part of both parties that fair and professional decisions will be reached. Any contribution made by the venue to an impression that the tribunal will not act in a focused, judicial manner, paying serious regard to the issues, would be most unfortunate. A comment attributed to one parent and cited by the Council for Disabled Children – that a 'very busy hotel did not create the kind of atmosphere which was conducive to good decision-making'[9] – clearly raises concerns. The Council reports that it is the out of London venues – the hotels – which parents have been far less satisfied with, rather than the London tribunal rooms. One of the London parents in the survey praised the facilities in Victoria Street, saying that it

---

5 Council on Tribunals, *Access for Disabled People Using Tribunals: Checklist and Code of Practice* (Council on Tribunals, 1993).

6 Ibid, Part 6.

7 House of Commons Education Committee, Second Report, 1995–96, *Special Educational Needs: The Working of the Code of Practice and the Tribunal,* HC 205 (HMSO, 1996), Appendix 13, p 37.

8 See Chapter 9.

9 See footnote 7 above.

had been 'good to have a meeting room beforehand especially as witnesses came some distance', and that there had been a 'non-threatening environment'.

Some of the tribunal members in the survey made adverse comments about tribunal venues. For example, one said: 'I am not sure that the hotel venue idea is as good in practice as in theory. I would have thought that there was a sufficient variety of public sector accommodation available to meet the needs of the tribunal and this could be explored'. Even the London venue did not escape criticism: 'I believe the arrangements for the comfort of both parties – in this stressful situation – to be very important, and not always adequately met. The arrangements for refreshments at London HQ some months ago seemed quite inadequate'. Several parents in the survey also felt that refreshment facilities should have been better, because of the length of time they spent at the tribunal on the day coupled with the travelling time to get there: 'Drinks machine was poor, refreshment facilities could be improved for those travelling long distances'. It should also be borne in mind that, as the Council on Tribunals states, 'Refreshment facilities are particularly important for disabled people because they are likely to have had a more onerous journey'.[10]

Some of the LEAs were also dissatisfied with some of the tribunal venues. Of the 63 LEAs who expressed views on the venues and the facilities which were available, 11 (17.5%) regarded them as unsuitable. Many referred to badly ventilated and, at times, cramped conditions and the lack of separate waiting and conference facilities. Also, two practitioners in the field have criticised 'hastily prepared hotel bedrooms being used for hearings'.[11]

7.5 THE SURVEY OF TRIBUNAL VENUES

A total of 24 tribunal venues were visited by the author or his assistant in the course of conducting observations of 40 individual tribunal hearings as part of the research. The suitability of each of the venues was assessed. The results of the survey are summarised below. It will be seen that some venues, although only a minority, were not ideal and a small number were unsuitable.

---

10 Council on Tribunals, *Access for Disabled People Using Tribunals: Checklist and Code of Practice* (Council on Tribunals, 1993), Part 6.

11 J. Friel and D. Hay, *Special Educational Needs and the Law* (Sweet & Maxwell, 1996), p 75.

Survey of tribunal venues

Venue	Location	Features/suitability
1 Victoria St London	City centre	SENT tribunal suite, comprising two tribunal rooms with separate conference facilities. Suitably furnished and laid out. Acoustics quite good apart from when windows were opened during hot weather and street noise intruded. *Suitable.*
2 X Hotel Manchester	City centre	The room used was noise-free and was suitably furnished and laid out, although the decor was poor. There were no conference facilities, nor separate waiting areas. *Suitable overall.*
3 Y Hotel Manchester	City outskirts	The tribunal room was inappropriately large and background noise was intrusive. No conference facilities, but separate waiting areas. *Not particularly suitable.*

Venue		Location	Features/suitability
4	X Hotel Preston	Some way out of town	The room was of a suitable size, noise-free and offered a pleasant environment. There were no separate conference facilities. Both parties waited in reception, separately. *Suitable.*
5	Y Hotel Preston	Some distance from the city centre	The room was small but well furnished and in a quiet part of the hotel. The acoustics and layout of the room were good. There were no separate conference facilities. Both parties waited in reception. *Suitable.*
6	X Hotel Newcastle upon Tyne	Some way out of the town centre	The room was an appropriate size and quiet and comfortable. The acoustics were quite good. There were no separate conference facilities and both parties waited in reception, separately. *Suitable.*

Venue	Location	Features/suitability
7 Y Hotel Newcastle upon Tyne	A few miles from the city centre	The facilities and layout were good. The room was of an appropriate size, had good acoustics and was well furnished. There were conference facilities. *Suitable.*
8 X Hotel Hull	City centre	The room was of an appropriate size and was very well laid out. It was noise-free. There were no conference facilities and both parties waited in reception, separately. *Suitable.*
9 The Y Centre Hull	A few miles from the city centre	The room was small but adequate in size. The accommodation was basic but was noise-free and comfortable. The centre provided separate conference/waiting rooms. *Suitable.*

Venue	Location	Features/suitability
10 X Hotel Leeds	Outskirts of the city	The room was of an appropriate size, quiet, comfortable and appropriately laid out. No conference facilities. Both parties waited in the bar area, separately. *Suitable, overall.*
11 Y Hotel Leeds	City centre	The room was a hotel bedroom. The air-conditioning was not working. The observation took place on a very hot day. When the windows were opened traffic noise made it very difficult to hear. The door leading out onto the corridor did not close properly. Conditions were cramped. There were no conference facilities and the parties waited together in reception. *Very poor. Unsuitable.*

Venue	Location	Features/suitability
12 X Hotel Barnsley	A few miles outside the town centre	A spacious and quiet room, suitably laid out. Refreshments were available in a conservatory. There were no conference facilities and the parties waited together in reception. *Suitable.*
13 X Hotel Portsmouth	A few miles from the city centre	The room was spacious and quiet, offering comfortable facilities. It was suitably laid out. It was at the top of a flight of stairs which one parent found difficult to climb because of injuries he had suffered in an accident. There were no separate conference facilities and both parties sat separately in the bar area. *Would have been suitable but for the disability of one of the parents.*

Venue	Location	Features/suitability
14 X Hotel Stoke-on-Trent	Central	A very large room which was not very good acoustically, although everyone could be heard. A function was taking place in an adjoining room which was slightly distracting. There were no conference facilities and both parties waited in the general lounge. *Not particularly suitable.*
15 X Hotel Widnes	Fairly isolated position outside the town	The room was of an appropriate size but the acoustics were not good. There was noisy air-conditioning which the chair asked to be turned off in the course of the hearing. The room opened out onto a dining room. There were no conference facilities and the parties waited together in the reception area. The hotel was painted in gaudy colours and the decor was 'tacky'. *Not at all suitable.*

Venue	Location	Features/suitability
16 X Hotel Liverpool	City centre	A large room with good acoustics. Well furnished and laid out. No conference facilities. Parties waited for the hearing in reception area. *Suitable.*
17 X Hotel Chester	One mile from the city centre	The acoustics were good and the room was located in a quiet part of the hotel, although there was some traffic noise and at one point the room's window had to be closed. There were no conference facilities. *Fairly suitable.*
18 Y Hotel Chester	Outside the city centre	The room was an appropriate size and quite well laid out and decorated. The clerk reported that the hotel staff were very unhelpful. The room itself was satisfactory, but the hotel offered an unsuitable environment and the clerk was going to recommend that the hotel should not be used again. *Not particularly suitable.*

Venue	Location	Features/suitability
19 X Hotel Nottingham	A few miles from the city centre	A large room, but not particularly well furnished or laid out, and rather garishly decorated. There was only a small waiting area which both parties had to use. There were no conference facilities. *Unsuitable.*
20 X Hotel Birmingham	A few miles from the city centre	Well furnished and laid out. No background noise from outside. The room was an appropriate size. No separate conference facilities. Both parties waited in the reception area. *Generally suitable.*
21 Y Hotel Birmingham	A few miles from the city centre	A rather small, although quiet, room. Reasonably well laid out, but the hotel was rather seedy. No conference facilities and the parties had to wait with other people in a public area. *Barely adequate.*

Venue	Location	Features/suitability
22 Z Hotel Birmingham	City centre	A small, windowless room was used for the hearing. The layout, acoustics and decor were good. No conference facilities were made available. The parties were required to wait together outside the room. *Just about suitable, certainly not perfect.*
23 X Hotel Stafford	Outside the town	The room was small and in a noisy position. The hotel staff were not very welcoming. The tribunal clerk said he was so unimpressed with the hotel that he was going to suggest having it removed from the list for use. No conference facilities. Parties waited in the reception area with hotel guests. *Unsuitable.*

Venue	Location	Features/suitability
24 X Hotel Crewe	Close to the railway station	The room was about the right size and reasonably well decorated and laid out. There was a fair amount of noise from trains. The location was very convenient. There were no conference facilities and both parties waited in reception, although not seated together. *Suitable, but not particularly good.*

A majority of venues which were surveyed were, therefore, reasonably satisfactory. Most, however, lacked private conference facilities and separate waiting areas. Overall, the survey of tribunal venues confirmed many of the deficiencies reported by LEAs and others, referred to above.

Waiting facilities which involve the parties sitting together in a public lounge area are clearly inappropriate, especially given the anxious state which many parents are in prior to the hearing. The hearing is an ordeal to some parents: indeed, some leave the room very upset or angry at some of the things said in the hearing – particularly points made by the LEA. They need somewhere private in which to calm down and discuss the situation with their adviser or representative, either at the conclusion of the hearing or during an adjournment. They also need somewhere private before the hearing to enable them to consult with their representative, whom they may not have met previously. Tribunals where the hearing is of a similar length to the SENT – notably the industrial tribunal – provide conference facilities; their absence in most SENT venues has been a major drawback to date. On the other hand, the fact that both parties tend to return to a common reception/waiting area after the hearing does provide an opportunity for each side to meet each other and discuss some of the outstanding issues. This was observed to happen on a number of occasions. In some cases, the parents found that the LEA's approach had become more conciliatory than prior to the hearing, so the meeting after the hearing was constructive and fairly amicable.

Another important consideration in evaluating the tribunal venues is the suitability of the environment for any child who may attend. Some parents commented specifically that the facilities (in Manchester) were 'not suitable for parents attending with a child'. In his evidence to the House of Commons Select Committee, the President of the SENT admitted that parents who wish to bring their child also face practical difficulties as a result of there not being a creche or child-minding facilities – which means that parents may have to leave the tribunal room during a part, or parts, of the hearing.[12]

7.6 HOW TO IMPROVE UPON THE TRIBUNAL VENUES USED

The SENT has clearly had a mixed experience with the accommodation which has been used. The author was surprised to discover that due to pressure on staff time the hotels had not been visited by SENT staff with a view to assessing their suitability prior to being booked for the first time for a tribunal hearing. If they had been, the SENT might have discovered, as several parents reported, that some of the hotels were 'difficult to find'! Nevertheless, the SENT has switched from unsuitable hotels in the light of experience, and the suitability of the accommodation used for tribunal hearings can be expected to improve as adjustments are made to the SENT's list. It is to be hoped that the question of provision of refreshments will also be addressed.

An alternative to using hotels for hearings would be to hold them in local public buildings. However, such premises are likely to be owned or managed by local authorities. As such, they will lack hotels' advantage as 'neutral territory'. One of the tribunal chairs in the survey did not regard the use of local authority buildings as problematic, however:

'I am not convinced that we need to sit in hotels in order to give an

---

12 House of Commons Education Committee, Second Report, 1995–96, *Special Educational Needs: The Working of the Code of Practice and the Tribunal*, HC 205 (HMSO, 1996), Minutes of Oral Evidence, Q58.

impression of independence – they often provide inappropriate accommodation and are not always situated at convenient locations for the parties – especially parents dependent on public transport. Planning inspectors often carry out their inquiries at town halls; should the SENT be any different?'

It has to be borne in mind, however, that planning inquiries are public affairs, quite different to private hearings. Using local authority buildings would indeed compromise the tribunal's independence and would worry some parents who are at odds with their LEA. For these reasons the President of the SENT is opposed to the idea.

One way of ensuring that the accommodation is more suitable would be for the SENT to have closer links with the Independent Tribunal Service (ITS), which has permanent accommodation in a wide range of locations. An arrangement could be made between the SENT and ITS for premises to be 'borrowed' for hearings. The problem with that is that the volume of ITS work continues to grow and so rooms will often not be readily available, particularly as they would need to be blocked for half a day for each SENT hearing. Another drawback would be the fact that, although widely dispersed, ITS tribunals are located within a specific number of centres, so the parties to SENT appeals might face a longer journey to the hearing than at present. Nevertheless, the SENT has been exploring the possibility of using ITS accommodation for some of its hearings.

The Council on Tribunals, which has recently referred to the 'unsuitable standard of some of the hearing venues' used by the SENT,[13] has also reminded the SENT Secretariat about the Register of Tribunal Accommodation. This is currently maintained by the Property Advisers to the Civil Estate (PACE), which is an Executive Agency of the Office of Public Service. One of the aims of the Register is to help smaller tribunals 'find hearing venues in a given locality more geared to meeting the occasional needs of the tribunal'.[14] The Council on Tribunals has commented that it continues to 'come across tribunals sitting in entirely inappropriate accommodation when the Register shows that one or more properly equipped tribunal hearing suites is available in the same locality'.[15]

---

13 Council on Tribunals, *Annual Report 1995/96* (HMSO, 1996), para 2.49.
14 Ibid, para 2.133.
15 Ibid.

It is unfortunate that a number of appellants to date have had their appeals heard in unsuitable environments, and it is to be hoped that the SENT will work to eradicate all of the problems.

Chapter 8

REPRESENTATION AT SENT HEARINGS

8.1 INTRODUCTION

Welfare tribunals such as the SENT aim to adopt an informal and inquisitorial approach. The tribunal chair is expected to play an enabling role towards an inexperienced and legally unskilled party by identifying and applying all relevant points of law and challenging evidence presented by the opposing party. Representation of all but the most inarticulate and incapable of parties is, in theory, unnecessary. Nevertheless, the imbalance between the parties, in terms of their generally unequal knowledge and skills in presenting cases, means that the premise that parties, parents in particular, are not disadvantaged by appearing unaided is open to question. Indeed, there is almost universal recognition that representation improves the prospects of success at a hearing. Although it has proved difficult to gather evidence on the influence of representation on success rates at SENTs,[1] evidence from other tribunals shows that appellants are far more likely to succeed if they are represented;[2] and, in any event, there is sufficient evidence to show that representation makes an important contribution to access to justice in SEN hearings, and it requires as much support as can be given to it.

Parents certainly place a high value on representation. As one parent in the author's survey commented, it may be 'essential to have a representative who knows the tribunal procedure and can help you get your points out'. The difficulties which face unrepresented parents were even referred to by some LEAs in the survey. For example, one LEA said:

> '[I]t can be extremely difficult for parents to put their case if they are not assisted. Even when the LEA is not legally represented, it is likely that the representative will be reasonably articulate and more accustomed to the relatively formal setting. Although the chair of the tribunal may make great efforts to assist parents they are still at a disadvantage.'

LEAs have experienced officers representing their case, whereas for most parents this will be their first and/or only appeal. As the National Deaf

---

1 See **8.8**.
2 See, for example, C. Frost and A. Howard, *Representation and Administrative Tribunals* (Routledge and Kegan Paul, 1977); H. Genn and Y. Genn, *The Effectiveness of Representation at Tribunals* (Lord Chancellor's Department, 1989).

Children's Society commented to the author: 'Inevitably the hearing is formal and frightening for many parents. Many need representation . . .'.

Various representatives are used by parents. As shown below, a significant number of parents engage lawyers, but parents are most likely to have arranged for representation by a voluntary organisation.

Both the role and nature of representation in the SENT have been the subject of considerable debate, especially on the value of legal representation. This chapter examines the evidence on this subject, which is important to the whole question of access to justice in SEN cases.[3]

8.2   THE EXTENT OF REPRESENTATION AT SENT HEARINGS

In the first 19 months of the SENT (to the end of April 1996), parents were represented in just over one-third (37%) of cases heard by the tribunal; but the rate was just 26% over the period 1 September 1995–31 August 1996, revealing a marked and so far unexplained decline.[4] In the survey of parents conducted by the author, during the first of these periods, a higher representation rate was discovered (53%).[5] Furthermore, in the hearings which were observed as part of the research, the representation rate was slightly higher again (55%). It is possible that parents who were represented were more likely to return a questionnaire,

---

3 For this purpose, 'representation' refers to attendance at a tribunal to present the parent's or LEA's case. However, it is sometimes difficult to determine whether a layperson who attends with the parent and participates in the presentation of the case is 'assisting' the parent or 'representing' – a distinction made in the SENT Regs, which permit a parent to present his or her case in person, or to do so 'with assistance from one person', or to be represented (see reg 11(4)). The President of the SENT, in a circular to chairs and members, *Befrienders at Hearings* (7 May 1996), advocates a flexible approach to this issue – one which recognises that befrienders who attend with parents may be 'either sharing the advocacy role with the parent, or . . . taking over the presentation of the case as a lawyer generally does'. It would appear that both count as representation for the purposes of SENT statistics on representation. The different roles which befrienders play were also referred to by the President in his oral evidence to the House of Commons Education Committee, Second Report, 1995–96, *Special Educational Needs: The Working of the Code of Practice and the Tribunal*, HC 205 (HMSO, 1996), Minutes of Oral Evidence, QQ54 and 55.

4 SENT statistics supplied to the author.

5 Note that for 80% of parents in the survey who used a representative, it was the same person who had advised them on their appeal.

perhaps because the representative drew their attention to it or reminded them about it, or were more likely to have granted permission for a researcher to attend their hearing.

In any event, these rates of representation are significantly higher than in most other welfare tribunals.[6] The reasons for this are difficult to pin down. For example, unlike most other welfare-related cases, a significant proportion of SEN appellants are middle-class and are thus more accustomed to utilising professional, commercial services (such as lawyers) and are better able to afford them. They also tend to be more assertive in demanding better provision for their child and are, arguably, more likely to have arranged for support from voluntary organisations.[7] Nevertheless, in the author's survey, those parents who may be broadly defined as middle-class were represented in 48% of cases, and working-class parents in 57% of cases. The most probable explanation for the disparity is the fact that middle-class parents were more likely to feel able to cope with the tribunal hearing on their own. Another factor behind the relatively high rate of representation in SENT cases as a whole is the ongoing contact between many parents of children with SEN and voluntary organisations and other support bodies who can offer to represent parents should they appeal or can help the parents to arrange for representation. In many other areas of welfare provision there is not the same level of support, whereas such support had been available to the majority of parents in the survey.

The disparity between the SENT's figures and those resulting from the survey is in fact wider than it might appear, because until very recently the SENT treated a case as involving 'representation' where the appeal documents were prepared by an adviser, even though in a small number of cases there was no actual representation of the parent at the hearing.

---

6 For example, appellants before the social security appeal tribunal were represented in only 30% of cases in December 1995: ITS appeal statistics 1996, supplied to the author. The figures reveal wide regional variations in representation rates. The SENT has not produced a regional breakdown.

7 See S. Riddell, S. Brown and J. Duffield, 'Conflicts of policies and models. The case of specific learning difficulties', in S. Riddell and S. Brown (eds) *Special Educational Needs Policies in the 1990s* (Routledge, 1994), pp 113–139.

8.3 WHO REPRESENTS?

'[I]t had been hoped that tribunals would be "lawyer free zones". They are not.'[8]

The broad picture is that parents are most likely to be represented by a voluntary organisation but that in over one in three of the cases in which parents are represented before the SENT, the representative is a lawyer.[9] The rate of legal representation in all SENT cases (as shown in the SENT's statistics) to the end of April 1996 was 13% of the total number of cases or 36% of all cases involving representation. Not surprisingly, the observations and survey of parents produced similar statistics. In the 40 hearings which were observed, parents were represented in 26 cases (55%) – by lawyers in 8 cases (20% of hearings or 31% of cases in which there was representation) and by lay representatives in 18 cases (45% of hearings or 69% of cases involving representation). A similar rate of legal representation was revealed by the survey of parents: 19 (31%) of the 61 parents who were represented reported that they had used a solicitor or barrister to represent them.

The SENT's latest figures, covering the year from 1 September 1995–31 August 1996, show that lawyers represented in 42% of all represented appeals – an increase compared with the previous year – but that legal representation as a proportion of all cases was down from 15% to 11%, as the overall rate of representation fell. The corresponding figures for lay representation were 58% and 15% (down from 23%).

The SENT's figures do not distinguish between barristers and solicitors. In the survey of parents, a minority said they were represented by counsel (15 out of 61 (25%) parents who reported that they were represented used barristers). Solicitors acted as advocates for 8 (13%) of the parents who were represented, and voluntary organisations (many of which are highly knowledgeable on the law and practice of special educational needs) a further 27 (44%).

---

8 Association of County Councils and Association of Metropolitan Authorities, Evidence submitted to the House of Commons Education Committee, Second Report, 1995–96, *Special Educational Needs: The Code of Practice and the Tribunal*, HC 205 (HMSO, 1996), Appendix 3, p 19.

9 As noted above (in **8.2**), however, the SENT adopted a very idiosyncratic definition of 'representation' when compiling these statistics. Note that middle-class parents are more likely to be legally represented: see *The cost of legal representation* in **8.4** below.

An experienced officer is most likely to represent the LEA, but in some cases LEAs will be legally represented. LEAs' policy on the use of legal representation is discussed below.

8.4 LEGAL REPRESENTATION

Some parents in the survey had formed a clear impression that the SENT's guidance was that solicitors were not necessary to assist with appeals. In evidence to the House of Commons Select Committee, the President of the SENT was keen to deny that what was meant in the guidance was that there were no circumstances when legal representation might help. Rather, the guide was merely attempting to convey the message that it was entirely possible to proceed without using a lawyer:

> '. . . [W]e do not want anybody to feel that a solicitor is necessary in the sense that if you cannot pay for a solicitor you might as well give up now, because that is certainly not the case. On the other hand, we never want to give the impression that a solicitor will not necessarily help you. We are not trying to put them off in either direction . . .'[10]

As noted in Chapter 6, the President has taken steps to restrict the number of lawyers present in tribunals by ruling that he will not normally give his permission for a solicitor to attend with counsel at hearing. The reasons behind this ruling, and the implications of the President's Statement, were discussed in that chapter.

Parents and lay representatives in the survey referred to a small number of cases where the LEA was legally represented when parents were not. Also, in four out of the 40 hearings observed during the research, only the LEA had legal representation. Prior to the establishment of the tribunal, the DFE indicated that the Secretary of State was 'exploring with the local authority associations and the voluntary bodies the possibility of creating a "concordat" whereby LEAs would not normally bring lawyers to tribunal hearings if parents were not legally represented'.[11] Such an arrangement has also been recommended by voluntary organisations, but

---

10 House of Commons Education Committee, Second Report, 1995–96, *Special Educational Needs: The Code of Practice and the Tribunal,* HC 205 (HMSO, 1996), Minutes of Oral Evidence, Q38, Trevor Aldridge QC.

11 DFE, *Consultation Paper on Draft Regulations and Rules of Procedure* (DFE, 1994), para 36.

has not developed, nor has it been further promoted.[12] In any event, most LEAs appear to want the option of using legal representatives in some SENT cases.[13]

The arguments which are presented against the use of legal representation in tribunal proceedings are familiar ones:

- that the presence of lawyers makes the proceedings more formal and adversarial (and that hearings therefore tend to be longer when lawyers are involved[14]);
- that lawyers' involvement in hearings may distance the appellant, because, as the SENT President has said, it may make the proceedings 'more difficult for parents to understand';[15]
- that using lawyers increases the cost to litigants as legal aid is not available; and
- that lawyers may hinder the participation of parents in proceedings – which, given the 'partnership' principle which is supposed to govern the resolution of questions concerning SEN, would be a clear disadvantage.

A counter argument is that the SENT is making decisions which have major long-term consequences for families and where the evidence on which the decisions are based can be highly complex. Furthermore, difficult points of law may, on occasion, arise. Lay representation can, of course, help to redress the balance between parents and experienced LEA representatives, but in some cases a lawyer may be needed. This may be especially true where the LEA has called a number of witnesses, since a legal representative may be particularly skilled at questioning them.

Many of the parents in the survey who used legal representation valued it very highly. Some parents who had not used it felt that, in retrospect, legal representation would have been helpful; they disagreed with the SENT's guide that parents would not need lawyers to represent them. One commented: 'Next time I'll get someone else to do the talking and not listen to the tribunal's advice re: a solicitor not being necessary'. Another parent said that he would have liked to use legal representation but was worried about the cost, given the fact that legal aid is not available for

---

12 See, for example, the memorandum submitted by the British Dyslexia Association to the House of Commons Education Committee (footnote 10 above), Appendix 10, p 31.

13 See Table 19 below.

14 See 'Impact of lawyers on the length of hearings' (below).

15 T. Aldridge QC, *Special Educational Needs Tribunal, Annual Report 1994/95* (SENT, 1995), p 13.

SENT hearings. Other parents were just as insistent that it can be very helpful to be legally represented:

- 'In spite of having been a police officer and a social worker I was still very glad I had taken the decision to be represented by a barrister. I feel all parties should be professionally represented (funds coming from the tribunal) as it is still a very formal procedure and not very parent-friendly atmosphere.'
- 'Get a solicitor to represent you.'
- 'I was very pleased that I had engaged a solicitor to represent me and help me prepare the case.'

In the author's opinion, the advantages of legal representation probably outweigh its drawbacks. Even accepting that it is not necessary for every case, as the SENT President suggests, parents clearly find it helpful and, as a result, will have more confidence in the appeal process as a whole. Given the intensity of the discussion at the tribunal, it is unrealistic to expect that all parents can retain their concentration in a hearing which can last a full day. Several parents in the survey made precisely such a comment. Moreover, if a parent's use of legal representation ensures that more of the issues are covered and results in a more effective challenge to an LEA's case, it is performing an important function and should not be discouraged. Obviously, the arguments outlined above concerning the possible risks of increased formality, confrontation and reduced parental participation do not support such a recommendation. Nevertheless, the Council on Tribunals in its annual report for 1994–95 endorsed the principle of legal representation (supported by legal aid) in more complex or highly contested tribunal cases where a formal approach could be desirable.[16]

The use of legal representation by LEAs

It was noted above that lawyers appear on behalf of LEAs in some cases. In the survey, LEAs were asked about their policy with regard to the use of legal representation in SENT hearings. As shown in Table 19 below, only a minority of LEAs had a policy of not using legal representation for such hearings. A small percentage would always use legal representation,

---

16 Council on Tribunals, *Annual Report 1994/95* (HMSO, 1995), para 1.32.

whilst the overwhelming majority would use it only if the parents were legally represented and/or the case were a complex or difficult one.

Table 19

Surveyed LEAs' policy as regards using legal representation in SENT hearings

Policy on legal representation in the SENT	Numbers of LEAs	Percentage
Never use it for such cases	16	21%
Always use it for such cases	5	6.5%
Use it only if the parents are legally represented	24	31.5%
Use it only if the case is complex or difficult	22	29%
Use it only if the parents are legally represented *and* if the case is complex or difficult	9	12%

(n=76)

Although some LEAs seem to be prepared to use legal representation even if the parents are not legally represented (indeed, this happened in 10% of the hearings which were observed during the research, as noted above), it is possible that in some cases when the LEA alone is legally represented this is because of the parents' failure to have a legal representative on the day, despite giving a contrary indication beforehand. In some such circumstances, especially where the failure of their legal representative to attend comes as a surprise to the parents, it may be necessary for the hearing to be adjourned.[17]

Impact of legal representation on the length of hearings

One of the lay members reported that some of the hearings with which he had been involved were 'lengthy and legalistic, especially where expert witnesses and lawyers are brought in'. Correlating the length of tribunal

---

17 See *Cherrih v Cheshire County Council* (1996) CO/88/96, QBD (unreported) for discussion of adjournments. Here, both the legal representative and, subsequently, a lay representative/witness, could not attend the hearing. But note Dyson J's comments on *Cherrih* in *Lucy v RB Kensington and Chelsea* (1997) CO/4138/96 (unreported).

hearings in the cases observed during the research with the use of legal representation in those cases demonstrated that hearings did tend to be longer where lawyers were involved. Suspicion that this might prove to be the case arose from the very first SENT hearing, in January 1995. It was reported that this case, which was heard in London and in which both parties were represented by counsel, lasted a full day. The longest hearing which was observed during the research lasted well over seven hours. In that case, both parties were legally represented, whereas in each of the other 10 cases where there was legal representation only one of the parties was represented (LEAs in four cases and parents in six cases). The average length of hearings where there was legal representation was 2 hours 35 minutes (this excludes one case where the parents only were legally represented and which was adjourned after 45 minutes – due, amongst other things, to the absence of a witness). In cases where there was no legal representation, the average length of a hearing was 2 hours 18 minutes. Recently, the SENT also investigated this subject and found, from a review of *all* appeal hearings from May–July 1996 (232 cases in all), that while 71% were concluded within three hours, the proportion fell to 62% when cases where the parents were legally represented were looked at in isolation.[18]

It would probably be inappropriate to read too much into this disparity. There are so many variables, such as the complexity of the case, the number of witnesses or the style of chairmanship, which can influence the rate at which a hearing progresses to its conclusion. On the other hand, it is difficult to discount the fact that hearings involving lawyers run, on the basis of the survey findings, an average of approximately 11% longer than others and that, according to the SENT statistics, a smaller proportion of cases will be concluded within the allotted time of three hours when the parents are legally represented. This could suggest that the presence of lawyers does indeed mean that the hearing will be more adversarial (witnesses may be examined and then cross-examined), which could make the hearing longer. But the involvement of lawyers could also mean that evidence is more thoroughly tested and the facts explored more fully. In other words, the additional time for which a hearing runs and where at least one lawyer is involved could be well worth it, depending on whether

---

18 T. Aldridge QC, *The Special Educational Needs Tribunal, Annual Report 1995/96* (SENT, 1996), p 12. A higher proportion of cases were concluded within three hours where both parties were legally represented than where the parent alone had legal representation.

one sees the influence of a lawyer as positive or negative as regards the achievement of justice in a case. Some would argue that lay representation can have a similarly positive influence in many cases. It then becomes necessary to consider the 'added value' of legal representation. There seems to be little doubt that in some cases the added value will manifest itself and thus will be important.

The cost of legal representation

The non-availability of legal aid for SENT hearings means that the parent will generally have to pay for legal representation. Inevitably, this puts lower income parents at a considerable disadvantage. Among the parents in the survey, middle-class parents were more likely to have used legal representation – lawyers represented in 36% of the represented cases brought by middle-class parents compared to 29% of those brought by parents in lower socio-economic groups. Middle-class parents were clearly better able to pay for help. Even so, some parents, including many from lower income groups, undoubtedly made a considerable financial sacrifice in order to have legal representation.

Although the 1995 Green Paper on legal aid[19] discussed the possibility of extending legal aid to more tribunals – with comments on the potential effects of doing so being invited – the proposals in the recent White Paper[20] contemplate no change in the present limitations. Indeed, the costs containment theme in the White Paper makes the possibility of extending legal aid to tribunal representation, even selectively, even more remote, particularly in the light of the likelihood that contracts with advice agencies for the provision of legal services will extend only to advice and assistance, not representation. However, there is surely a strong case for extending legal aid to the more complex SENT cases.

In fact, the absence of legal aid for SENT hearings does not only prevent some parents from being able to hire legal representatives. There is also the cost of providing expert evidence. In some cases, independent expert reports (eg from an educational psychologist) may be paid for under the Green Form scheme. A Green Form extension would be required. There is reference in the White Paper to the Legal Aid Board operating flexible

---

19 The Lord Chancellor, *Legal Aid: Targeting Need* (HMSO, 1995).
20 The Lord Chancellor, *Striking the Balance – The future of legal aid in England and Wales* (HMSO, 1996), Cm 3305. For a review, see T. Goriely, 'The English Legal Aid White Paper and the LAG Conference' (1996) 3(3).

arrangements to pay for expert professional reports.[21] It is possible that this could offer additional help to parents in some SENT cases. At present, most parents seem to pay for an independent assessment of their child's needs, whether they are legally represented or not.[22]

The effectiveness of legal representation

The quality and effectiveness of legal representation are discussed below.[23]

8.5 LAY REPRESENTATION

In two-thirds of cases where there is representation at hearings, it is carried out by voluntary organisations. The SENT does not keep statistics on the actual agencies which provide representation in SEN appeal cases. Nevertheless, it is clear that IPSEA, which offers a Free Representation Service,[24] is particularly active in this field (according to its evidence to the House of Commons Select Committee, it represented in 60 cases in the first year of the tribunal). By July 1996, IPSEA had trained 38 volunteers, 28 of whom had 'passed' the training course and were engaged in tribunal representation.[25] Representation is also provided by the British Dyslexia Association, the National Deaf Children's Society and other bodies concerned with helping children with learning difficulties of various types and their families. It should, however, be noted that the majority of voluntary organisations have had a relatively small amount of contact with the tribunal system, although it is expected that this will increase over time.

It should also be stressed that while such voluntary bodies are providing assistance to the *families* concerned, they tend to see themselves as acting on behalf of the *child* – even though the child is not a party to the appeal before the SENT and his/her interests are not independently represented

---

21 The Lord Chancellor, *Striking the Balance – The future of legal aid in England and Wales* (HMSO, 1996), Cm 3305, para 3.33.
22 See further Chapter 7.
23 See para **8.7**.
24 Members of this Free Representation Service, all volunteers, are either SEN professionals or parents of children with SEN who have experience of the SENT. See IPSEA, 'Finding Support', *Special Children*, September 1995, pp 22–23.
25 Information supplied to the author by IPSEA. Training of representatives is discussed below.

(there is no equivalent arrangement to the guardian ad litem system which operates in the courts under the Children Act 1989: see below).

Whilst there might be concern about the involvement of lawyers as representatives in SENT hearings, there is almost unanimous acknowledgement that other forms of representation can be beneficial in helping parents to put their case forward, in providing guidance and support which helps to put parents at their ease, and in assisting the tribunal by helping it to focus on relevant issues and ascertain all the relevant facts. Parents in the survey who used lay representation valued it highly. Recently, IPSEA conducted a survey of 42 parents who had used its services for appeals to the SENT. Without exception, the parents in this survey also placed a high value on the representation they had received. The IPSEA report concludes that 'the strongest message from the data is how many of the parents felt they could not have gone through the hearing without the support of IPSEA'.[26] Although this was not a truly independent study, a number of the parents in the author's survey had used IPSEA and commented favourably about the quality of the representation provided; indeed, one parent said: 'My own [case] was dealt with by IPSEA and I was represented far better than by a legal person'.

Representation by voluntary sector organisations obviously has resource implications for them;[27] even where volunteers are used there is the cost of training, providing information, supervision of work, correspondence and other contact with clients and the SENT, and so on. Some organisations do not provide representation because they cannot afford the cost of doing so. Those parts of the voluntary sector with a commitment to helping parents of children with SEN secure access to justice continue to campaign for better resources to support their work in this field. The evidence suggests that it would be money well spent.

Not all organisations which accompany parents to hearings in fact 'represent them' as such. Approximately 25% of the organisations in the survey attended the tribunal hearing and provided back up advice and moral support but did not speak on the parents' behalf. This moral

---

26 E. Andrews, *Representing parents at the Special Educational Needs Tribunal: An evaluation of the work of IPSEA's Free Representation Service* (IPSEA, 1996), para 8.3.

27 See ibid, para 10 and House of Commons Education Committee, Second Report 1995–96, *Special Educational Needs: The Working of the Code of Practice and the Tribunal*, HC 205 (HMSO, 1996), Appendix 13, p 38.

support is important to parents and several commented that it helped them to cope with the stress of attending the tribunal. In some cases, parents are accompanied by their 'befrienders' (usually volunteers found by the LEA and/or provided by a voluntary organisation), who may act as advocates on the parents' behalf but are just as likely to provide moral support and/or to prompt the parent. The role of befrienders was discussed earlier.[28]

8.6 SHOULD THE CHILD HAVE SEPARATE REPRESENTATION?

The fact that the child is not a party to the proceedings before the SENT[29] does not weaken the strong argument that, since the case is about the child's education and about achieving the best possible outcome for the child (within the various resource and logistical constraints which apply), the achievement of these objectives requires independent representation of the child's interests in the proceedings. This happens in specific public law proceedings under the Children Act 1989, where the court will generally appoint a guardian ad litem, who adopts a child-focused perspective and in most areas will appoint a solicitor to represent the child.[30] It could be argued that SENT proceedings have the same basic underlying objective as child welfare proceedings under the Children Act and that there is, therefore, an equivalent need to have independent representation for the child, even though the child is not strictly a party to the proceedings.

Such a representative, who would be a person trained and experienced in the field of SEN and child welfare, would be particularly useful in cases where parents have an unrealistic view of their child's educational needs. As one LEA in the survey commented: 'the child is not represented at the hearing – [but] the parents' views are not always in the *child's* best interests'. Furthermore, independent representation of children would help to balance the two sides (ie parents and LEA) in cases where the

---

28 See Chapter 6 at **6.3**.
29 See Chapter 1.
30 Under s 41 of the Children Act 1989, a guardian ad litem must be appointed unless this would not be necessary to safeguard the child's interests. A guardian may also be appointed where the court is considering a residence order in respect of a child in care, and related appeals. For a general discussion of the way that, under the 1989 Act, children's views are presented via representation, see M. Sherwin, 'The Law in Relation to the Wishes and Feelings of the Child', in R. Davie et al, *The Voice of the Child* (Falmer, 1996), pp 15–26.

parents are not represented. Furthermore, independent representation would help to guarantee that the views of the child would be taken into account by the tribunal, another requirement under international law.[31] In any event, there is an argument that international law requires independent representation of the child in proceedings such as these.[32] A crucial question is whether, when Article 12 of the UN Convention on the Rights of the Child states that the child should be heard in person or 'through a representative', that representative needs to be an independent representative of the child. It might be thought that this is not the case, because, presumably, a parent can also be a representative for the purposes of Article 12 in this context. But Bainham argues that 'there must be doubt about whether the lack of independent representation of the child's views in the educational sphere conforms with the spirit, if not the letter of Article [12]'.[33] As Barton and Douglas[34] say, it is significant that the right provided by Article 12, for children to express their views and for those views to be given due weight, is not, unlike the right to freedom, conscience and religion (Article 14), subject to a parental right of guidance.

8.7 THE EFFECTIVENESS OF REPRESENTATION

Assessing the *quality* of representation was incidental to the research rather than a principal objective. The *availability* of representation was the chief concern, although the need for legal, as opposed to lay, representation was another important issue because of the continuing debate over the role of lawyers in SENT hearings (see above and below). Nevertheless, evidence on the quality of representation emerged in the course of the research.

A conclusion to be drawn from the observations of hearings during the research is that much of the representation which is occurring before the SENT is good. Representatives were found to be mostly very well prepared and to be coping well with the large amount of detailed evidence which was generally before the tribunal. There were, however, a small number of cases where lay representatives' over-zealous approach veered

---

31 UN Convention on the Rights of the Child (1989), Art 12.
32 See A. Bainham, with S. Cretney, *Children: The Modern Law* (Jordans, 1993), p 613. See further Chapter 9 at para **9.4** below.
33 Ibid. Article 12 is discussed further in Chapter 9 at **9.4**.
34 C. Barton and G. Douglas, *Law and Parenthood* (Butterworths, 1995), p 42.

on the polemical. Issues such as the treatment by LEAs of children with particular forms of disability or LEAs' reliance on the inadequacy of the resources available as a defence to their decisions were particularly likely to generate a political, campaigning, approach. This, on occasion, antagonised the tribunal and was potentially detrimental to the parent's case. It also tended to lengthen the proceedings, causing chairs to intervene to curtail parts of the presentation. The President of the SENT regards lay representatives as variable 'in the amount of their experience, the quality of their training and their ability to take a full part in hearings'.[35] This variation is, perhaps, only to be expected. The commitment and, in most cases, expertise of lay representatives are nevertheless undeniable. However, clearly the lay representatives' effectiveness as advocates can be improved. Almost all of the voluntary organisations which operate in SENT hearings are conscious of the need to maximise the effectiveness of their representatives, many of whom are volunteers, through training provision (see below).

Legal representation is not always the most effective form of representation in welfare tribunals. Although, as regards the SENT, most parents valued the legal representation they had received very highly, they may not have had any other experience of representation to compare it with – certainly not in this context. In fact, legal representation was of variable quality in the cases which were observed, but was generally competent and, in some cases, excellent. Nevertheless, although lawyers were particularly skilled at questioning the LEAs' witnesses and their evidence as a whole, and, as the SENT President has put it, at 'presenting the parents' case in a focused way',[36] tribunal members in the survey were unhappy with the legalistic and adversarial approach followed by lawyers in some of the cases with which they had been involved. Some also felt that lay representation, or even no representation, was in some cases more effective than the use of a lawyer. For example, one member commented that 'parents . . . have generally presented their appeals in an excellent way – in most cases much better than those few cases where the parents have been legally represented'. The President of the SENT also feels that legal representation, while sometimes helpful to the tribunal, can create too formal an atmosphere.[37]

---

35 T. Aldridge QC, *Special Educational Needs Tribunal, Annual Report 1994/95* (SENT, 1995), p 13.

36 Ibid, p 12.

37 See also his comments to the House of Commons Select Committee, above.

It is to be hoped that the legal profession bear in mind some of the criticisms that have been made about the way some of them practise their art within SENT hearings, and, as they become more familiar with the SENT, modify their approach to make it more appropriate for the kind of informal and inquisitorial hearing which is intended in SEN appeal cases. Some lay representatives will also need to become less adversarial, for the same reason. As one of the lay members in the survey said:

'I feel that the use of legal or self-styled expert fee-charging professional educational advocates, together with advocates from voluntary bodies with national agendas, are very damaging to the real interests of children and parents alike and to the beneficial effects of the tribunal and the law.'

Training is already playing a vital role in improving the effectiveness of representation, even though it is not occurring on a sufficiently wide scale. The Education Law Association (ELAS) has provided information and guidance to its lawyer and lay membership via its Special Needs Group and the London Tribunal Users Group, and has run training sessions. The British Dyslexia Association has developed a range of training materials, including summaries and explanations of the law governing appeals and case studies for analysis. IPSEA includes tribunal training as part of its advocacy sessions for voluntary and employed staff, and it is seen by the organisation as vital to the further development of its Free Representation Service. The National Deaf Children's Society also runs a training programme for representatives.

The Council for Disabled Children has argued that the need for training for lay representatives 'should be more fully recognised'.[38] It is not clear whether this refers to recognition by the organisations themselves or by external providers of funds. The SENT President clearly considers that training of representatives should be encouraged. In his view, training will help to ensure that there will be more 'skilled advocates who are fully familiar with the Tribunal's procedure [which] will help both the parties to the appeals and Tribunal'.[39] He has offered the SENT's assistance with the training of representatives:

'I am anxious that the Tribunal should give as much help as is practical in

---

38 Evidence to the House of Commons Education Committee, Second Report, 1995–96, *Special Educational Needs: The Working of the Code of Practice and the Tribunal*, HC 205 (HMSO, 1996).

39 T. Aldridge QC, *Special Educational Needs Tribunal, Annual Report 1994/95* (SENT, 1995), p 12.

training those who will represent parties before the Tribunal, whether LEAs or parents.'

The President and the Secretary and other members of the SENT Secretariat have attended training sessions and have addressed and taken questions from representatives. They regard such meetings as important opportunities both to encourage a less confrontational and more focused approach to representation and to explain the tribunal's view of its task. Such meetings must surely promote better understanding between the providers and users of this tribunal, which should aid the effectiveness of the system as a whole.

Some would argue that the only performance indicator which matters, so far as the effectiveness of representation is concerned, is the success/ failure rate. Such a view is, however, misplaced. For one thing, there are so many variables which affect the outcome of an appeal and over which the representative may have no control. Thus, most lay representatives and many lawyers will proceed with a case which is fairly weak, because this is what the parents want or, in the case of a defence of a case by an LEA, because so much money is ultimately at stake for the authority. Furthermore, the very high rate of representation at SENT hearings compared with other tribunals makes it difficult to assess the 'value added' factor so far as representation is concerned.

In any event, there are no official statistics which aid assessment of the impact of representation in SENT cases. The SENT does not compile statistics showing the success rates of different representatives, nor figures for represented and non-represented cases respectively.[40] There is simply an overall success rate for parents, which currently stands at 63%.[41] However, IPSEA has published statistics which show that parents were successful in 62% of the cases where it represented.[42] These statistics must, however, be read with caution, as the SENT's figures include cases where an appeal is only partially successful and it is unclear whether IPSEA's success rate is similarly based.

---

40 Statistics produced by other tribunals do, however, prove that representation makes a considerable difference to success rates. In some tribunals the chances of success are more than doubled by having a skilled representative: see H. Genn and Y. Genn, *The Effectiveness of Representation at Tribunals* (Lord Chancellor's Department, 1989).

41 T. Aldridge QC, *Special Educational Needs Tribunal, Annual Report 1995/96* (SENT, 1996), p 13.

42 E. Andrews, *Representing parents at the Special Educational Needs Tribunal: An evaluation of the work of IPSEA's Free Representation Service* (IPSEA, 1996), para 5.3.

Despite the difficulties in drawing sound conclusions from success rates in SEN appeals, it would be helpful to those who regard the role of representation in the SENT to be important (and the President of the SENT seems to be one of their number), if the SENT compiled statistics showing the outcome of cases where different forms of representation were used.

Chapter 9

THE HEARING

9.1 INTRODUCTION

For the parents who have appealed, the day of the tribunal hearing is naturally a very important one. After a wait of some four-and-a-half months (on average) they will finally have an opportunity to bring their dispute before an independent body which will determine which course of action is appropriate for their child, although the outcome may not, of course, necessarily be what the parents want.

Whether or not they are represented, the parents are likely to be attending such a hearing for the first time, whereas the representative of the LEA may well have attended a number of such hearings. Many of the parents in the survey said they had approached the day of the tribunal hearing with some anxiety and trepidation. Thus the tribunal has an important task in ensuring that parents not only perceive it to be a truly independent body, which is free to depart from the professional view of the LEA, but also in creating an atmosphere in which matters are dealt with efficiently and thoroughly, but with an appropriate degree of informality so that parents feel they are able to participate and are not over-awed by the occasion.

Members of the tribunal will have had an opportunity to consider the written evidence in advance of the hearing, and will often refer to some aspect of it as the hearing progresses, as well as giving consideration to it during deliberations. But, above all, the hearing is an opportunity for oral evidence to be presented. Many parents are particularly keen to seize the opportunity to explain their concerns and enlighten the tribunal on various aspects of their child's development and needs – although in the tribunals which were observed during the research, parents' success in communicating their views and relaying relevant information effectively varied considerably.

Some parents also see the hearing as an opportunity to confront the LEA with their grievances, after possibly months of delay and frustration at the LEA's apparent intransigence or its lack of sympathy with their viewpoint. Contrary to the general notion of 'partnership' which is promoted by the Code of Practice on SEN, disputes between parents and LEAs can become inflamed and relations can be somewhat frosty.

Fortunately, however, this is true in only a minority of cases. In the majority of cases there is a genuine, sincere difference of opinion over the course of action which should be taken in relation to the child's special educational needs – largely borne out of the different perspectives from which LEAs and parents are viewing the problem and its potential solution. The task of the tribunal is, of course, not so much to reconcile the differences between the parties but rather to make a decision which best promotes the child's interests, within the constraints which the legislation imposes upon them.

The contribution of the hearing to 'access to justice' is clearly fundamental. As noted above, the tribunal must operate, and be seen to operate, fairly in its procedure and in particular in the way it deals with the issues and the parties. It must also act impartially in its decision-making and yet attempt to ensure that parents are given the best possible opportunity to participate in the proceedings and influence their outcome.

It is considered that these objectives will best be met by creating an informal, non-confrontational atmosphere in which there can be constructive discussion. The procedure followed is actually a matter for the tribunal,[1] and the chair will play a lead role.

9.2   SCHEDULING OF HEARINGS

Tribunal hearings are generally scheduled for half a day. Morning sessions usually start at 9.30 or 10 am and afternoon sessions at 2 pm. Over 70% of the hearings which were observed during the research, and an almost identical proportion of SENT cases as a whole (according to figures supplied to the author by the Secretariat), lasted three hours or less. Chairs and members are often called upon to adjudicate two cases in one day. A number of chairs and lay members in the author's survey felt that this was inappropriate, either because it was too tiring or because the morning session in particular might become a little rushed as the tribunal attempted to conclude its business so as to avoid encroachment on the afternoon session. One tribunal member commented: 'two cases in one day seems not a good idea – rushed, tired, late'. Another said that 'squeezing two hearings into one day is exploiting the tribunal members' goodwill and puts at risk the user-friendly nature of the hearings by putting undue time pressure on chairmen who may pass this on to parents

---

1 SENT Regulations 1995, reg 28: see below.

and witnesses'. However, none of the chairs in the survey commented critically on the scheduling arrangements.

The time constraints did, however, trouble some of the representatives in the survey. For example, one of them said that the fact that a case was listed for morning or afternoon only could mean that they might have to curtail examination of LEA witnesses in order to concentrate on presenting the arguments and facts which they had assembled in support of the parent's case. The fact that quite a number of parents in the survey also felt that their hearing had been rather rushed reinforces the argument that it is not good practice to schedule two cases for one day. Indeed, some parents were well aware that the tribunal had an informal deadline. For example, one parent commented: 'I felt the tribunal was hurried towards the end, almost as if it should be finished in office hours ie 5.30 pm'. Parents were also clearly aware of the scheduling arrangements. For example, one commented: 'two tribunals in one day [is] . . . excessive'. Some parents commented that if a longer period of time had been allowed for each tribunal session, it might have been possible for parents to wait and be given a copy of the tribunal's decision on the day. In fact, the SENT considers that because the outcome of the appeal is not an out and out victory or defeat for the parent, and that what the tribunal has decided needs to be articulated very carefully, it is better for a written decision to be prepared (and checked) and then disseminated.

The pressure arising from the need to complete the hearing within a certain period of time seems to affect the presentation of the parent's case in particular. A number of parents in the survey felt that the LEA had been allocated a disproportionate amount of time so that when it was the parent's turn there was inadequate time available. For example, one parent thought that the LEA took 'the lion's share of the time available' and another reported: 'Time given to LEA and witnesses = three hours. Time given to parents and witness = 45 mins . . .'.

A further problem, which was referred to by some of the tribunal members in the survey, was the late cancellation of some hearings. This is not a scheduling problem and, in any event, it is inevitable that some cancellations will occur. Indeed, it is regarded as a fact of life where tribunals are concerned. Cancellations may be granted at the request of the parties who want a postponement; but they are commonly the result of the withdrawal of an appeal. The present rate of withdrawal of appeals was discussed earlier.[2]

---

2 Chapter 6 at **6.7**, 'Notice of appeal'.

9.3 ATTENDANCE AT TRIBUNAL HEARINGS

The SENT Regulations 1995 (the regulations) specify that the hearing should be in private (unless both parties request otherwise or the President orders that it should be in public) but that individuals falling into specified categories are entitled to attend, along with the parties and their representatives and witnesses. Those categories listed in the regulations, showing persons entitled to be present, comprise:[3]

(i)   any person named by the parent as a person he or she wishes to attend the hearing[4] (although note the restriction on solicitors and trainees imposed by the President, and the other restrictions, referred to in Chapter 6);

(ii)   a parent of the child who is not a party to the appeal;[5]

(iii)   the tribunal's clerk and the SENT Secretary;

(iv)   the President and any chair or lay member of the SENT;

(v)   a member of the Council on Tribunals;[6]

(vi)   any person undergoing training as a chair or lay member or as a clerk to the tribunal;

(vii)   any person acting on behalf of the President in the training or supervision of clerks to tribunals;

(viii) an interpreter.

In addition, the tribunal may permit any other person to attend a private hearing provided the parties or their representatives who are actually present consent.[7]

Note that all hearings to date have been held in private. In the author's survey, several of the chairs and lay members, as well as some of the LEAs, commented that a private hearing was preferable. The President has said that the tribunal aims 'to protect the child's privacy';[8] on this basis, there is unlikely to be a public hearing of the SENT.

The President of the SENT has said that 'an important factor in reducing

---

3 Regulation 26(1) and (2).

4 Note that the parent would have to obtain the permission of the President if he or she wished to have more than two persons in this category present: reg 26(8).

5 That parent is also entitled to address the tribunal on the subject matter of the appeal: reg 26(7).

6 There were several visits by the Council in 1994/95: Trevor Aldridge QC, *Special Educational Needs Tribunal, Annual Report 1994/95* (SENT, 1995), p 22.

7 Regulation 26(3).

8 T. Aldridge QC, *Special Educational Needs Tribunal, Annual Report 1994/95*, (SENT, 1995), p 13.

formality and stopping hearings from being intimidating to those unfamiliar with such proceedings, is limiting the number of persons present'.[9] In addition to the restrictions on those entitled to attend (above), each party is entitled to use only one representative and (unless the President's permission is obtained) a maximum of two witnesses.[10] In the 40 tribunal hearings which were observed in the course of the research, the numbers present ranged between 7 and 13. Table 20 below shows the distribution of numbers attending hearings. It shows that, despite the restrictions imposed by the regulations on the number of persons who should be present at hearings, there are, in the majority of cases, a relatively large number of persons at the hearing. Obviously, these numbers, as shown in the table, included the parent(s) and, if there were any, their representatives and/or witnesses.

Table 20

Numbers in attendance at tribunal hearings which were observed in the course of the research

Numbers present	Number of cases	Percentage*
7	3	7.5%
8	3	7.5%
9	10	25%
10	12	30%
11	10	25%
12	0	0%
13	2	5%

(n=40)

* This column shows the proportion of cases where the particular number of persons was present. Thus, for example, there were 10 people present at the hearing (excluding the researcher), in 30% of the cases which were observed.

One of the potential problems resulting from having so many people present at the hearing is that some parents may feel a little intimidated, at least initially.[11] A further problem is that the amount of time available for

---

9 T. Aldridge QC, *Special Educational Needs Tribunal, Annual Report 1994/95* (SENT, 1995), p 13.

10 See Chapter 6 at para **6.7**, 'SENT enquiries'.

11 One parent commented specifically on the number of persons present at the hearing (13), saying it was one of the 'worst aspects' of the hearing itself.

each person to speak could be rather limited. On the one hand, operating to a time-limit is a good thing, because it means that discussion must be focused carefully on the relevant issues. On the other hand, many parents in the survey reported that they had felt there was insufficient time in the hearing for their views to be heard properly, especially when the LEA presented its case first (as often occurred).

There is no easy solution to this problem other than to schedule cases for longer or to impose further restrictions on the numbers who may be present. The latter could, of course, threaten the quality of justice.

9.4 THE PRESENCE OF THE CHILD AT THE HEARING

As noted in Chapter 4, the child is not a party to the proceedings.[12] If the child attends, he or she will do so either as a witness (whether or not called upon to speak to the tribunal) or, more likely, simply as a person in respect of whom the parent has given notice of his or her attendance at the tribunal.

In fact, the child is rarely in attendance at a hearing before the SENT. In the author's survey of parents, only ten out of 118 (8%) reported that their child had attended the hearing; nine of these ten children gave their views to the tribunal. The low attendance rate among children was confirmed by the tribunal observations. In the 40 hearings which were observed in the research, the child was in attendance in only two of them (5%) (cases A and B below).

> In case A, the child, J, was aged 12 and had severe dyslexia. The parents wanted J, whose needs were the subject of a statement, to attend a private school at the cost of the LEA, but the LEA believed the child's needs could be met in a mainstream school, and at considerably less cost. J was asked for his views by the tribunal and he explained that he wished to attend the private school instead of his present school. He gave evidence for 12 minutes, outlining his difficulties and the reasons why he felt that the private school could meet his needs better than his present school.
>
> Case B concerned D, aged eight. His parents were appealing against

---

12 *S v Special Educational Needs Tribunal and the City of Westminster* [1996] ELR 228 CA.

the LEA's decision not to carry out a formal assessment of his needs. They wanted his needs to become the subject of a statement. The boy's head teacher believed a statement was necessary to ensure that D would obtain the help he needed and so that the classroom teacher could spend more time with the other pupils in D's class who needed her help, instead of having to spend a large amount of time with D. When the head teacher was giving evidence to the tribunal, she directed questions at D about the situation in his classroom. Also, one member of the panel asked D about his occupational therapy.

In another case whose hearing was observed during the research, the parents had obtained permission before the hearing to bring along their seven-year-old daughter, R, although not as a witness. On the day, the panel decided, after careful consideration, that R should not be permitted to sit in on the case because her self-confidence might be undermined as a result of the panel making comments about her academic ability. In fact, R did not attend on the day and so this did not become an issue.

The question of the child's involvement in tribunal hearings received direct consideration from the House of Commons Education Select Committee. The President of the SENT, Trevor Aldridge QC, was asked by the Committee for his comments, in the light of the evidence that children rarely attend SENT hearings and that the child's views tend not to be taken into account. Mr Aldridge said that there were practical difficulties in some cases – because the tribunal was not able to provide creche facilities and so parents might have to leave the room during part of the hearing (as noted in Chapter 7). Furthermore, there was the problem of the child hearing things said about him/her in the hearing which might be psychologically damaging.[13] The latter point is also made by John Friel in his guide to the law and practice of special educational needs[14] and was a factor in the tribunal's decision to refuse permission for child R to attend in one of the cases referred to above. Another reason why it might be undesirable for the child to attend would be that the child might, on the day, appear to be more intellectually capable or well-behaved than the evidence would suggest, and thus the tribunal would not obtain an accurate view of the extent of the child's needs. A further

---

13 House of Commons Education Committee, Second Report, 1995–96, *Special Educational Needs: The Operation of the Code of Practice and the Tribunal*, HC 205 (HMSO, 1996), Minutes of Oral Evidence, Q58.

14 J. Friel, *Children with Special Needs: Assessment, Law and Practice – Caught in the Act* (Jessica Kingsley, 1995), p 124.

problem might arise from the length of most tribunal proceedings – the child may well become bored and restless, thereby adversely affecting the atmosphere in which the hearing is being conducted.

Lawyers and voluntary organisations in the survey were asked specifically to state their reasons for recommending or not recommending that the child be brought to the hearing. Most thought that the advisability of bringing the child would vary from one case to the next and that the child should not attend unless there was a specific need for him or her to be there. Only 6% of those who responded to the survey said they would always advise *against* bringing the child; the other 94% said they would *sometimes* advise that the child should attend, depending on the circumstances. Most would take account of the child's age and understanding, whether the child him/herself was willing to attend, whether the child had sufficient mental ability and whether he or she would be expected to cope with the stress of attending the hearing. Some commented that the decision should be for the parent, as he or she was best able to assess whether the child could cope, although one parent in the survey commented that she 'was given the impression children were *not* allowed'. A number of advisers commented that it was very useful for the child to attend if this were possible, as it was the best way of ensuring that the tribunal had before it, and took proper account of, the child's wishes and feelings.

Those who advocate the attendance of children at SENT hearings believe that, in a situation where the fact that the child is not a party to the proceedings already undermines the child's rights, it is important for the independent interests of the child to be recognised and for tribunals to take full account of the child's wishes and feelings. Reference, in this context, may be made to s 1 of the Children Act 1989, which requires courts in family proceedings to ensure that the child's wishes and feelings are taken into account, having regard to the child's age and under-standing. This particular statutory provision is consistent with Art 12 of the UN Convention on the Rights of the Child. This calls upon State parties to the Convention to ensure that, again subject to the child's age and understanding, the child's views, 'in all matters affecting the child', are heard in any 'judicial and administrative proceedings' which affect him/her (although it also states that the views can be presented via a representative[15]). This is an important principle, which acknowledges the child's independent interests. Furthermore, the Code of Practice requires those making decisions concerning children with special educational

---

15 See Chapter 8 at **8.6**.

needs to take account of the wishes and feelings of the child, in the light of the child's age and understanding.[16] Nevertheless, some argue that the absence of a comparable provision in Part IV of the 1996 Act (formerly, Part III of the 1993 Act) to that in s 1 of the Children Act 1989 (which does not apply to SENT proceedings) is symptomatic of a general failure to give priority to the child's best interests in SEN cases and generally under education law.[17]

Certainly, in the hearings observed during the research, there was a tendency for discussion to get bogged down in questions relating to, for example, the kind of provision that was possible and the availability of resources, rather than confronting directly the interests of the child. Several LEAs and others in the survey argued that there ought to be a specific requirement regarding consideration of the child's interests. As one LEA commented: 'there needs to be more emphasis on what is best for the child, taking into account efficient use of resources and parents' wishes ... [W]hat is best, educationally, for the child is not always the prime factor under consideration'. The impression that the child's interests were only considered indirectly was reinforced by the tribunal's failure, in many cases, to place sufficient emphasis on the child's viewpoint. For example, one parent complained to the author that in the tribunal hearing 'not enough was made of my son's views, feelings and wishes'. Moreover, an LEA said: 'where is the voice of the child/young person heard?', and one of the tribunal members in the survey commented, in similar vein: '[I]t is sometimes very difficult to find the small, individual voice of the child'.

---

16 DFE, *Code of Practice on the Identification and Assessment of Special Educational Needs* (DFE, 1994), eg para 1:3; and see further below. According to Russell, the Code of Practice 'confirms and amplifies ... key messages of the Children Act 1989', including 'the right of children to be heard': P. Russell, 'Listening to Children with Disabilities and Special Educational Needs', in R. Davie et al, *The Voice of the Child* (Falmer, 1996), p 107.

17 See, for example, J. Timms, 'Advocacy 2000 – The Way Forward', and D. King and P. Treseder, 'Why Do I Have to Get into Trouble First?', both in J. Dalrymple and J. Hough, *Having a Voice: An Exploration of Children's Rights and Advocacy* (Venture, 1995), pp 77 and 142. Note that Art 3(1) of the UN Convention on the Rights of the Child states that the best interests of the child should be a 'primary consideration' in decisions taken by, inter alia, public bodies. In its report on the implementation of the Convention in the UK, the Committee on the Rights of the Child commented that this principle did not seem to be reflected in the field of education, amongst other areas: Committee on the Rights of the Child (UN), *Concluding Observations of the Committee on the Rights of the Child: United Kingdom of Great Britain and Northern Ireland* (UN, 1995), p 3.

There are, of course, alternative ways in which children's views can be heard. In a minority of the cases which were observed, the tribunal took evidence (usually from the parent, although in some cases from the teacher) on the child's wishes and experience. The evidence was clearly second-hand, but at least the tribunal was taking seriously the provision in the Code of Practice for the child's wishes to be considered (see below). One of the organisations in the author's survey, Contact a Family, advised that, where it was inadvisable for the child to attend, steps should be taken 'to make representation in *any way* – photographs, video, letter ... [O]f my four hearings, two children sent "letters" to the panel'. In one case, the child, aged 17, had written a letter to the tribunal, setting out his views. In the majority of cases which were observed during the research, however, there was no attempt by the tribunal to ascertain the child's views on his or her needs or on the provision which was being made, or which might be made, to meet them.

The tribunal is, in fact, under no specific statutory obligation to take account of the child's wishes and feelings, although it is required to take account of the provisions of the Code of Practice, which, as noted above, makes reference to the need for the child's wishes and feelings to be taken into account. Nevertheless, it would clearly be better (especially in the light of Article 12 of the UN Convention on the Rights of the Child, referred to above) if tribunals were under a specific statutory obligation. As MENCAP commented in its evidence to the House of Commons Education Select Committee: 'it seems odd that such major decisions about a child's life ... are made without any formal means of ascertaining whether the child has views, and, if (he or she) has, what those views are'.[18]

In cases where there has been a formal assessment of the child, it is possible – perhaps even likely – that the tribunal will have evidence of the child's views, because they ought to have been recorded when the assessment was carried out. The Code of Practice recommends that when assessing a child's needs 'the LEA will wish to establish the views of children and young people themselves on their special educational needs and the way they might be met' and suggests that the LEA should consider 'providing a pupil report form for the purpose', enabling pupils who are able to do so to submit their views on the form.[19] The Code also recommends that the child's views should be recorded separately from

---

18 House of Commons Education Committee (1996), op cit, Memorandum
    submitted by MENCAP, para 2(ii).
19 Op cit, para 3:120.

those of the parent and the professionals, because 'the wishes and feelings of the child have a separate identity'.[20] If this practice is adhered to, there is quite a strong likelihood that the child's views will be considered by the tribunal. In cases where the child's views are *not* recorded and made available to the tribunal, the tribunal should, in the author's opinion, be making more of an effort to ensure that it has this evidence before it.

9.5 PROCEDURE AT THE HEARING

Introduction: an informal approach

There are few rules laid down in the regulations as to the procedure to be followed at the hearing. The regulations give the tribunal a discretion over most procedural matters. The tribunal has a general duty to 'conduct the hearing in such a manner as it considers most suitable for the clarification of the issues and generally to the just handling of the proceedings';[21] and the tribunal itself 'shall determine the order in which the parties are heard and the issues determined'.[22] There is a presumption, however, that SENT hearings are best conducted with the minimum of formality.

When the SENT system was first proposed, it was claimed that the tribunal would operate in an informal and 'user-friendly' manner.[23] The objective is to ensure that, so far as possible, proceedings are conducted in a non-confrontational and non-adversarial manner and one in which parents and LEA alike have a fair opportunity to present their case to the tribunal. It is therefore crucial to the whole question of access to justice, because if the tribunal fails in this objective and parents find it difficult to cope with the proceedings, confidence among parents and their advisers in the tribunal is likely to be weakened. At the same time, the tribunal hearing needs to be structured in a way that ensures that all the relevant evidence is presented (and challenged, where necessary). Thus, a degree of order is necessary and a free-for-all must be avoided at all costs.

The President of the SENT has explained that the tribunal aims to create an atmosphere which is 'that of a business-like meeting where important

---

20 Op cit, para 3:120.
21 Regulation 28(2).
22 Regulation 28(3).
23 For example, the consultation document *Special Educational Needs Tribunal – Consultation Paper on Draft Regulations and Rules of Procedure* (DFE, 1994), para 35 stated: 'the Secretary of State intends that the tribunal's procedures should be as informal as possible'.

issues are addressed and disagreements examined in a non-confrontational atmosphere'.[24] An informal and amicable discussion of the issues is also likely to be conducive to good long-term relations between the LEA and the parents. As the President has explained:

> 'we are conscious that, unlike most courts and other tribunals the parties before this tribunal may have to continue to cooperate for many years in the interests of the child concerned. That makes it important to ensure that the tribunal proceedings do not add rancour to the relation between the parents and the LEA.'[25]

The tribunal, in fact, has a duty under the regulations to 'seek to avoid formality in its proceedings', so far as it appears appropriate.[26] According to the President, 'the tribunal has made considerable efforts to this end'.[27] The layout of the tribunal rooms is intended to promote informality, with the parties and the tribunal seated around a large table (or several separate tables pushed together to form one surface). The most important element, however, is the way in which the hearing is conducted and, in particular, in the approach followed by the chair. This is not simply a matter of who speaks when, although even as regards the running order there have been efforts to maintain flexibility and informality: the President has made it clear that 'it is usually possible to abandon court procedure' and has stressed that 'it is not necessary for one party's case to be put completely followed by the other party's and for witnesses to be first questioned by the party which calls them and . . . then cross examined by the other party'.[28] Perhaps even more significant is the general atmosphere created. An informal environment will, it is believed, help to put parents reasonably at ease in what may be a very stressful situation for them.

In assessing the degree of formality in the proceedings, for the purposes of the research, reliance was placed on the observation of tribunal hearings. In addition, many comments were received from parents, offering their perceptions of the hearing and their assessment of the extent to which they felt able to participate effectively in it. Voluntary organisations and lawyers also commented on the question of formality/informality. The research findings are presented below.

---

24 T. Aldridge QC, *Special Educational Needs Tribunal, Annual Report 1994/95* (SENT, 1995), p 12.
25 Ibid.
26 Regulation 28(2).
27 See footnote 24 above.
28 Ibid.

The conduct of hearings: what the research found

The observations revealed, first, that chairs invariably comply with their duty under the regulations to begin by explaining the order of the proceedings which the tribunal proposes to adopt.[29] Chairs have been instructed to ensure that they introduce the tribunal and the parties to each other and that they explain in relatively straightforward terms how the hearing will proceed. Some chairs will briefly review the nature of the case and highlight the main issues. The purpose of doing this is not only to help to focus the minds of all concerned on the questions under dispute but also to identify any issues about which there is general agreement. For example, there may be agreement about the nature and extent of the child's special educational needs and even about the type of education which the child requires. The dispute may be about the number of hours' special provision or the particular school which the child should attend. In identifying the issues about which there is agreement and distinguishing them from those on which there is dispute, the chair sets out the context and points of focus for the main discussion – although other issues may, of course, arise in the course of the proceedings. Indeed, the latter point is important. There needs to be sufficient scope for flexibility in the proceedings so that new areas of dispute can be dealt with effectively as they arise. The President has stressed that structuring the hearing around the issues rather than adopting the traditional adversarial model under which the parties present all their evidence in turn, may indeed be more suitable.[30] In the 40 cases which were observed during the research, the initial part of the hearing conformed to the anticipated model. Many parents in the survey commented that the chair's introduction helped to put them at ease and reassure them that their case would be dealt with fairly. There is further analysis of the parents' views below.

It is common for chairs to invite the LEA to present its evidence first. There are some advantages to this approach. First, it helps all present to be clear about the LEA's reasons for the decision it has reached. It also enables the LEA to explain any concessions it is prepared to make to the parents. Another advantage to the parents and their representatives is that, when presenting *their* case, they can at the same time respond to and challenge points made by the LEA. Of course, it will often be desirable for the parents and their representatives to respond to these various points as and when the LEA makes them. Practice varies considerably as to whether the parents will be permitted to do this, as it involves interrupting

---

29 Regulation 28(1).
30 See footnote 28 above.

the LEA's presentation and complicating the proceedings somewhat. The presentation of the parents' case will obviously be quite a challenging task if it does involve responding to points made by the LEA as well as presenting the parents' main arguments.

Among those surveyed, there were many expressions of concern about the LEA being invited to speak first. Some argued that the LEA was thereby handed an advantage. For example, one of the parents commented that the LEA had been 'allowed to set the agenda' by being invited to put its case first. This parent felt that the appellant 'should always be invited to put their case first' otherwise he or she would be 'put on the defensive and ha[ve] to prove the LEA wrong'. Similarly, the British Dyslexia Association commented to the author that allowing the LEA to go first 'means that the parents are always answering a point – not posing it the way they would wish'. Another drawback, referred to above,[31] is that if the hearing becomes rushed towards the end (because time is short), it will be the presentation of the parents' case which will be particularly affected. Most parents, however, were unconcerned that the LEA presented its case first. Indeed, one commented that it assisted them 'because we knew immediately how to argue our case when it was our turn'.

As regards the rest of the procedure, the observations of hearings revealed considerable variation in approach adopted by different tribunal chairs, a finding which is confirmed by many of the comments made by voluntary organisations, lawyers, LEAs and lay members of the tribunal. This variation, in turn, contributed to differences in the atmosphere created at the tribunal, discussed below. Many of the voluntary organisations and LEAs commented that some chairs adopted a very formal, judicial approach in which they attempted to exert considerable control over the proceedings – to the extent that they curtailed the presentation of the evidence on occasions if they considered that it had strayed from relevant issues or had become too laboured. This was seen as an effective approach by some participants, because it ensured that the tribunal concentrated only on relevant issues. But it was regarded as a disadvantage by others, because it inhibited the challenging of evidence and witnesses and gave the impression that the hearing was being rushed through. Several chairs commented informally in the survey that unless they kept a tight control over the proceedings, they would never get through all the business in time.

---

31 See **9.2**.

The pressure of time does seem to be a major influence on the way the tribunal is conducted. The Education Law Association (ELAS), in its evidence to the House of Commons Select Committee, commented that 'owing to time pressures the chairs often attempted to rush through their questioning and in this situation it is easy to overlook necessary and important evidence'.[32] ELAS reported that, in its experience, even when a chair determines at the outset of a hearing to deal with the matter on an issue by issue basis, 'the intended structure has broken down during the course of the hearing due to time pressure'.[33] The observations of hearings revealed that the LEA's evidence, including that presented by witnesses on the day, was not always fully challenged by the tribunal. Again, this may well have been a consequence of the pressure felt by chairs to move the matter along, although it may well also be symptomatic of an over-willingness by tribunals to accept LEA evidence at face value and/or of chairs' lack of educational knowledge, which was commented upon by a number of voluntary organisations.

Generally speaking, there were some opportunities for cross-examination of witnesses, although a number of parents referred specifically to the lack of opportunity afforded to them to question the LEA. Furthermore, in the hearings which were observed, some chairs were very interventionist when evidence was being presented – interrupting frequently to ask questions – whilst others would wait until a party or their representative or witness had finished speaking.

There was, at least, some uniformity with regard to the conclusion of proceedings. In almost all of the cases which were observed, the tribunal invited the parties to sum up their case. Typically, each party spoke for approximately 5–10 minutes when doing this.

The inconsistency in the procedure which was followed, was, as noted above, a particular cause of criticism. Both LEAs and the voluntary organisations and lawyers who represent parents felt that their preparation of a case was hindered by not knowing precisely how the matter would proceed after the initial introductions. Some of the chairs and lay members in the survey commented that they would have liked more guidance on procedural matters. There seems to be a strong case for developing a Code of Guidance on procedure at SENT hearings, as has

---

32 House of Commons Education Committee, Second Report, 1995–96, *Special Educational Needs: The Working of the Code of Practice and the Tribunal*, HC 205 (HMSO, 1996), Appendix 19, p 46.
33 Ibid.

been developed for school admission and permanent exclusion appeals by the local authority associations and (in the case of grant-maintained schools) the DFEE. It also seems to be advisable that training of chairs and members should continue to focus on procedural matters.

No matter how informal the tribunal hearing is, the discussion will inevitably become highly technical at times – both in terms of legal issues and relevant psychological or educational development matters. Generally speaking, in the hearings which were observed during the research the major part of the discussion was found to be non-technical. However, perhaps not surprisingly, there was legal argument in the majority of the cases where there was legal representation – including citation of authorities by counsel and analysis of the meaning of particular statutory provisions. There was also, at times, detailed discussion of pupils' disabilities or assessments of their reading, audio and other skills and abilities and so on, which often included highly technical terminology. Unrepresented parents were undoubtedly presented with some difficulties as a result, although this reinforces the case for parents having representation rather than highlighting a weakness in the way the tribunal hearing is conducted.

Despite some of the shortcomings highlighted above, most parents were highly satisfied with the way the hearing was conducted, and were particularly praising of the efforts made to make them feel at ease and to afford them a reasonable opportunity to present their views to the tribunal. Only 3.3% of the parents in the survey said that they had not spoken at the hearing. Most of the parents had had an opportunity to state their case and/or answer questions put to them, although 18% of parents felt that they had not put across their case as well as they would have wished, and 20% said that they had not had an opportunity to say everything that they had wanted. Parents' overall impressions of the hearing were generally very positive, as the results presented in Table 21 below confirm.

Table 21

Parents' views of their hearing before the SENT

Parents' views	Numbers	Percentage
Easy to understand what was happening	70	60%
Procedure was efficient	88	74%
Tribunal helpful	97	82%
Too legalistic	7	6%
Confusing	5	4%
Slow and cumbersome	4	3%
Tribunal unhelpful	4	3%

(n=117)

Note: Many parents subscribed to more than one of these views, hence the totals exceed the numbers of responses; and the percentages, which indicate the proportion of parents who agreed with each of these descriptions as reflecting their views, exceed 100.

Some parents made additional comments about features of the hearing which they felt to be particularly good. The following represent typical views which were expressed:

- 'All aspects of procedure were explained thoroughly.'
- 'We were put at ease and given time to put our point.'
- 'Chairman very helpful, explained what was going on.'
- 'Everything was dealt with very efficiently.'
- 'It was a friendly atmosphere.'
- 'The atmosphere was very relaxed. There was no "slanging" match. Members of the tribunal were approachable.'
- 'The procedure was relatively informal. The chair was helpful and pleasant.'
- 'The chairperson seemed very fair, the atmosphere was as relaxed as it could have been.'
- 'Put at ease. Fair hearing.'

In addition, many parents were reassured by discovering that the tribunal panel knew so much about their case. A large number of parents commented that the panel must have read the papers very thoroughly before the hearing. Above all, they felt that their case had received a good airing and that they had been treated fairly.

There was, however, a significant minority of parents who were dissatisfied with various aspects of the hearing. In some cases, this was related to the cramped conditions and the absence of refreshments (see below). But there were more serious concerns about the handling of some of the evidence, particularly the way that some of the assertions made by the LEAs went unquestioned. Also, several parents made adverse comments about the tape-recording of proceedings. This is discussed below.

9.6 BREAKS AND REFRESHMENTS

As we have seen, tribunal proceedings often run for up to three hours, having been scheduled for just about an entire morning or afternoon. The discussion is very intense and, in some cases, undoubtedly puts a considerable strain on the emotions and concentration of all concerned. Parents, in particular, find the three hours to be particularly straining and demanding. Many of those in the survey commented that they needed a break during the proceedings, especially in the longer cases. Some explained that because there had not been a break they had become mentally dazed and exhausted as the hearing progressed. The following are typical comments:

- 'It was too long a session for one day, particularly with lack of refreshments. I would happily have taken a packed meal and coffee with me ... [I]t started at 10 am and finished at 8.30 pm. We had a 45 minute lunch break and a 10 minute 'comfort' break in the afternoon. It was a long time to go on a few glasses of water! I suffer from low blood sugar and would have taken some food had I known it would have taken so long.'
- 'Time ran out by which time I needed a coffee before I could have tried to consolidate our case.'
- 'During a lengthy ordeal like this, provision of tea/coffee would have been welcome but nothing was offered!'

LEAs were also very critical of the lack of breaks and refreshments. Comments included the following: 'it is unreasonable to have to sit for three hours with no "comfort" break'; 'a bad feature was working through without a break'.

Although breaks can sometimes interrupt the flow of the proceedings and disrupt the concentration of all those concerned, chairs ought, perhaps, to be more concerned to schedule at least one break during the hearing. The SENT office also needs to give consideration, if it is not doing so already, to the possibility that some hearings may continue on beyond the allotted time and that the parties present may need refreshments. Providing coffee and biscuits, for example, would add only marginally to the overall cost of holding a hearing, but could make a positive difference to participants' perceptions, comfort and general state of mind on the day.

9.7 TAPE-RECORDING OF PROCEEDINGS

Proceedings of the SENT are tape-recorded. This ensures that there is a full record of what has been said, which will be helpful should there be any complaint of procedural irregularity or, perhaps, in the rare circumstance where the tribunal is unsure of precisely what was said by a particular party or witness. The tape-recordings are stored after being made and a transcript of a particular hearing may be produced to the court if there is a further appeal. Although a transcript of the proceedings would rarely be needed by a court hearing an appeal,[34] a transcript was made available in one case where bias on the part of the tribunal was alleged.[35]

In a small number of the hearings observed in the course of the research there appear to have been technical problems with the tribunal's recording equipment. In one case, this resulted in a delay of over one hour in the start of the hearing, which, the parent reported, was unsettling as well as prolonging the time as a whole spent at the tribunal. Several parents, in fact, commented that they had been surprised to find that a tape-recording was being made during the hearing and a few found it to be rather off-putting. One parent, however, said that he found it reassuring that the hearing was being tape-recorded, so that there was a proper record of what was said.

It would be desirable if the fact that the proceedings will be tape-recorded could be drawn specifically to the parents' attention prior to the hearing

---

34 Note Carnwath J's comment in *South Glamorgan County Council v L and M* [1996] ELR 400, at 411, that 'it will only be the exceptional case where, on an appeal limited by statute to a point of law, it will be necessary to seek a note of the proceedings from the President. In the normal case the point of law should be apparent from the statement of reasons, or the basic documents in the case such as the notice of appeal and the response'.

35 *Joyce v Dorset County Council*, unreported, 26 January 1996, QBD (soon to be reported in Education Law Reports). This case is discussed in Chapter 10 at **10.3**.

(by now, LEAs can be presumed to be well aware that the proceedings of the SENT are tape-recorded). At the same time, assurances as to the confidentiality of the recording should also be given and the purpose for which the recording will be made should be explained.

As regards the equipment itself, it is trite to say that it should be checked prior to the hearing and should be set up in such a way as to make it as unintimidating to the parties as possible. The SENT Secretary has sought to assure the author that efforts are, in fact, made routinely to do these things.

9.8   MONITORING OF TRIBUNAL HEARINGS

Monitoring of tribunals is an important quality assurance measure. In addition to external visits by the Council on Tribunals, who have already attended an unspecified number of SENT hearings, the President of the SENT has also established a semi-formal monitoring system for the chairs. A monitoring system for the lay members is currently in preparation.

As part of his programme of monitoring in the first year of the tribunal the President attended 'a number' of hearings in London and 'in five other counties throughout England and Wales'.[36] He sees monitoring as an important means of establishing 'consistent standards in a new tribunal'.[37] Monitoring continued in 1995/96.[38] Such monitoring undoubtedly enables the President to offer a more authoritative account of the SENT's work as well as helping to highlight common problems which may require his guidance.

---

36 T. Aldridge QC, *Special Educational Needs Tribunal, Annual Report 1994/95* (SENT, 1995), p 21.

37 Ibid.

38 T. Aldridge QC, *Special Educational Needs Tribunal, Annual Report 1995/96* (SENT, 1996), p 6.

Chapter 10

THE TRIBUNAL'S DECISION AND THE RIGHT OF FURTHER APPEAL

10.1 INTRODUCTION

A high proportion of appeals are decided in favour of the parents. For example, of the 824 appeals on which decisions had been issued by the end of April 1996, 64% had been upheld or part upheld by the tribunal, 2% were remitted to the LEA and 2% were struck out by the tribunal. Only 32% of appeals were dismissed.[1] (There is further discussion of the appeal rates, referring specifically to separate grounds of appeal, under 'the legal framework' below.) Although there are no official records of the outcome of appeals to local appeal committees under the Education Act 1981, it is believed that parents were successful in a far smaller proportion of cases. The introduction of the SENT would, therefore, seem to have provided a considerable boost to the prospects of parents succeeding in overturning LEA decisions concerning the education of their children with learning difficulties.[2] Nevertheless, it has to be appreciated that the grounds of appeal are now wider[3] and the outcome of some appeals might be a referral back to the LEA. Thus the tribunal's decision may go in the parent's favour but could merely result in the matter being put back into the hands of the LEA for further action – as in the case of an appeal against a refusal to assess a child. Overall, however, success rates for parents have improved.

10.2 THE LEGAL FRAMEWORK

Powers of the tribunal

The powers of the SENT when making a decision under the 1996 Act will vary depending on the grounds of appeal, save that in relation to each ground the appeal may simply be dismissed. The alternative options open to the tribunal are as follows:

---

1 SENT statistics.
2 To many LEAs – over one-third in the author's survey – this is the result of tribunals' greater sympathy with parents compared with education appeal committees under the 1981 Act: see Table 24 below.
3 See Chapter 2. See further **10.2** below.

- *Appeal against the LEA's decision not to make a statement* (s 325). Here the parent's appeal arises where the LEA has carried out a formal assessment of the child but decides that it is not necessary to make a statement of special educational needs. If the SENT does not dismiss the appeal, it may order the LEA to maintain a statement or may remit the case to the LEA to consider whether it should make a statement, having regard to the SENT's observations.[4]

- *Appeal where the LEA makes, amends or decides not to amend a statement* (s 326). Here the SENT may, if it does not dismiss the appeal, order the LEA to amend the statement (as far as it describes the child's special educational needs or specifies the special educational provision) and make such other consequential amendments to the statement as the tribunal sees fit; or the tribunal can order the LEA to cease to maintain the statement. Note that if the tribunal wishes to order the LEA to specify the name of a school in the statement, either the parents must have expressed a preference for the school in pursuance of the arrangements laid down in the Act,[5] or, in the proceedings themselves, the parents, the LEA or both, must have proposed the school.[6]

- *Appeal where the LEA decides not to comply with a request by a parent of a child for whom a statement is maintained that the child be further assessed* (s 328). If the tribunal does not dismiss the appeal, it may order the LEA to arrange for a formal assessment of the child to be carried out.[7]

- *Appeal against the LEA's decision not to comply with a request by a parent for the formal assessment of the special educational needs of a child for whom there is no statement* (s 329). Here the tribunal may dismiss the appeal or order the LEA to carry out a formal assessment under s 323.[8]

- *Appeal against the LEA's decision not to comply with a request for the naming of a different school in a statement of special educational needs*

---

4 1996 Act, s 325(3).
5 Ibid, Sch 27.
6 Ibid, s 326(4).
7 Ibid, s 328.
8 Ibid, s 329(3).

(Sch 27, para 8). If the tribunal upholds the appeal, it may order the LEA to comply with the parents' request.[9]

- *Appeal against the LEA's decision to cease to maintain a statement* (Sch 27, para 11). If the LEA decides a statement is no longer 'necessary', and the parents appeal against this, the SENT may dismiss the appeal or order that the LEA continues to maintain the statement in its existing form or in an amended form (ie with amendments to the description of a child's special educational needs or the provision to be made, plus any consequential amendments).

The decision of the tribunal under each of these powers is binding.

The tribunal has no power to grant interim relief. The problems resulting from this were exemplified by the situation in *Re M*.[10] Here the number of hours of additional support provided to a child were being cut by the LEA. An appeal to the SENT was in progress but, because the tribunal could not grant interim relief to restrain the implementation of the cut in provision pending the appeal hearing itself, an injunction had to be sought from the court, in judicial review proceedings. The court refused to grant leave to move for judicial review because the parent's appeal under the statutory appeal system had not run its course.

The Education Law Association (ELAS) has been seeking a change in the law to enable the SENT to make interim orders where a statement is amended or a decision made to cease to maintain a statement. The Education (Special Educational Needs) Bill which is currently before Parliament seeks, in effect, to require an LEA which has given notice that it intends to amend a statement or to cease to maintain a statement to continue with it, where the parent has given notice of appeal, 'until the appeal has been finally disposed of' (cl 2). This would operate as a stay; last year, Dyson J refused to grant such a stay in a case where the LEA had decided to terminate a statement in respect of a girl at the end of the school year in which she turned 16.[11] In such a situation, continuation of existing

---

9 'The issue for the tribunal is whether, in their opinion, the school named is appropriate for the child. If not, they must then go on to consider whether the alternative school named by the parent(s) would be appropriate': *Russell v The Royal Borough of Kingston upon Thames and Hunter* (1996) 6 November, QBD (unreported), per McCullough J (transcript, p 8).

10 [1996] ELR 135.

11 *R v Oxfordshire County Council ex parte Roast* [1996] ELR 381, QBD. For discussion, see A. Bradley and R. Ruebain, 'Interim relief and the Special Educational Needs Tribunal – is there a place for judicial review? (1996) 1(3) *Educational, Public Law and the Individual* 54.

arrangements pending an appeal seems, on the whole, to be highly desirable. As Lady Darcy de Knayth pointed out during the Second Reading debate on the Bill, nearly four-fifths of appeals concerning Parts 2 and 3 of statements are upheld by the tribunal: 'Therefore the education of the children in 78% of cases has been needlessly and pointlessly disrupted for about six months'.[12]

Outcome of appeals

Statistics have been produced by the SENT showing a breakdown of the numbers of appeals upheld, dismissed or remitted to the LEA in respect of the different grounds of appeal (Tables 22A and 22B below). Table 22A relates to the decisions of the SENT in its first year, when 242 decisions were issued. Table 22B shows the outcome of appeals in 1995/96, when there were 908 SENT decisions. The figures for each year are shown in separate tables because the respective annual reports of the SENT present the figures differently, making a true comparison difficult.

Table 22A

Outcome of appeals to the SENT in 1994/95

| Type of appeal | Outcome | | |
	Upheld	Dismissed	Remitted
Refusal to assess	18	31	—
Refusal to make statement	24	27	11
Refusal to change name of school	0	0	—
Decision to cease to maintain			
statement	6	4	—
Failure to name school	1	0	—
Contents of statement			
Parts 2 and 3	23	10	—
Parts 2, 3 and 4	58	8	—
Part 4	9	5	—
TOTAL	139	85	11

Source: *Special Educational Needs Tribunal, Annual Report 1994/95* (SENT, 1995) p 16.
Note: The figures exclude seven appeals which were struck out.

---

12 Hansard, HL, Vol 575, col 1010, 13 November 1996.

Table 22B

Outcome of appeals to the SENT in 1995/96

Type of appeal	Number	Order Upheld	Order Dismiss	Order Remit	Parts 2 and 3 Upheld	Parts 2 and 3 Dismiss	Part 4 Upheld	Part 4 Dismiss
Refusal to assess	176	93	83	9				
Refusal to statement	139	86	44					
Refusal to re-assess	10	7	3					
Cease to maintain	49	29	20					
Contents of statement Parts 2 and 3, not 4	139				117	22		
Total for appeals not including placement	513	215	150	9	117	22		
Refusal to change school named	12						9	3
Contents of statement Parts 2, 3 and 4	294				244	50	137	157
School named in the statement	80						33	47
Failure to name school	5						2	3
Total including placement	391				244	50	181	210

Source: T. Aldridge QC, Special Educational Needs Tribunal, Annual Report 1995–96 (SENT, 1996).

As the SENT President argued in his Annual Report for 1994/95, it is hard to draw firm conclusions from these appeal figures. As he explained, parents commonly appeal against the LEA's decision on a number of individual matters. For example, where the appeal concerns the contents of a statement, the parent may be at variance with the LEA over parts 2, 3 and 4 of the statement, which relate, respectively, to the description of the child's needs, the proposed special educational provision and the name of the school (the 'placement'). The parent may succeed on one or more of these issues, but may fail on the one that matters most to him/her.[13] The figures nevertheless show that appeals against refusal to assess or to make a statement have a good chance of success and that the SENT is quite likely to amend the contents of a statement.

One of the factors which, it is believed by some, has contributed to the parents' high success rate in relation to the school named in the statement, concerns the apparent unwillingness of tribunals to make a decision which would involve moving a child out of an independent school to which the parents have sent/transferred him or her some months prior to the hearing. This issue is discussed below (at **10.3**).

Decision-making and procedure

The SENT Regulations 1995 (the regulations) provide that the decision of the tribunal may, if necessary, be taken by majority; where the tribunal consists of two members only (permission for this may be given by the parties[14]), the chair shall have a second or casting vote.[15] A record of the decision together with, in cases where the decision was other than by consent of both parties, a statement of the reasons (in summary form) for the tribunal's decision, must be prepared and must be signed and dated by the chair.[16] The fact that a decision is by majority is not to be recorded in the formal written decision or reasons, and no minority decision is to be included.[17] The purpose for excluding references to the fact that the decision was by majority is not clear. Presumably, the intention is that the tribunal's decision should appear as authoritative as possible and that confidence in it is not undermined. Furthermore, recording of a minority decision plus reasons could delay further the issuing of a decision. Nevertheless, some tribunals (eg the social security appeal tribunal) do

---

13 T. Aldridge QC, *Special Educational Needs Tribunal, Annual Report 1994/95* (SENT, 1995), p 15.

14 Regulation 28(5).

15 Regulation 30(1).

16 Regulation 30(2).

17 Regulation 30(3).

disclose in the decision papers whether the decision was by majority. It is unfortunate that when an appeal against a decision of the SENT is made to the High Court the court will not be made aware of the basis of a dissenting view by a member of the panel.

The decision of the tribunal may be given orally at the end of the hearing or may be 'reserved'.[18] The consultation document said that 'the chairman will usually give the decision publicly to both parties immediately afterwards', in other words, immediately after the deliberations by the tribunal.[19] But in the cases which were observed during the research, the decision was notified orally in only a couple of cases. The chief problem surrounding oral communication of a decision is that the tribunal may have to deliberate for some considerable time and there may also be difficulty in framing the decision in certain cases. Tribunals prefer to release the parties rather than to have them waiting for an indefinite period. From the tribunal's point of view, reserving the decision also avoids having to give disappointing news in person on the day which could provoke an adverse reaction from some parents. Although many parents face an agonising wait – and, sometimes, an inordinate delay (see below) – it is probably better not to be over-hasty, so that parents can be provided with a written decision with appended reasons and thus might, at least, understand why the tribunal made the decision which it did. On the other hand, there will be a number of cases where an oral decision could be given, with reasons communicated later.

The decision plus reasons must be sent to the parties 'as soon as may be' together with guidance, approved by the President, on right of appeal to the High Court and the procedure to be followed.[20] There is, therefore, no definite time-limit within which the decision must be sent to the parent. Generally, parents will face a wait of at least two weeks, but some have waited longer. Many have complained about the length of the waiting time. This is discussed below. The decision and other documents must also be sent to the parents' representative (if any).

Under the regulations, the decision is treated as being made on the day on which the written record of it is sent to the parent; this would be the case even if the decision were to be communicated orally following the hearing.[21]

---

18 Regulation 30(2).
19 DFE, *Special Educational Needs Tribunal – Consultation Paper on Draft Regulations and Rules of Procedure* (DFE, 1994), para 44.
20 Regulation 30(5).
21 Regulation 30(7).

Reviews

A decision by a special educational needs tribunal may be reviewed on specific grounds – either by the tribunal which heard the case or, if this is not practical, by a tribunal appointed by the President.[22] Either party may apply (in writing, stating the grounds) for a review within ten working days after the date the decision was sent.[23] Also, a tribunal may, of its own motion, review its decision, having given notice to the parties and provided them with an opportunity to attend and be heard.[24]

The grounds on which a decision may be reviewed are:

'(a) the decision was wrongly made as a result of an error on the part of the tribunal staff;

(b) a party, who was entitled to be heard at a hearing but failed to appear or to be represented, had good and sufficient reason for failing to appear;

(c) There was an obvious error in the decision of the tribunal which decided the case; or

(d) the interests of justice require.'

On a review, the tribunal shall 'substitute such decision as it thinks fit or order a re-hearing either before the same or a differently constituted tribunal'.[25]

The President of the SENT has a power to review his decisions[26] on grounds equivalent to those in (a), (c) and (d) above.

The President has issued guidance on *Applications to Review Decisions*.[27] This relates to review of decisions of tribunals, although the President also indicates that the principles set out are also relevant to applications to review a decision of the President. The guidance makes it clear that the scope of a review is more limited than that of an appeal:

'The purpose of a review is generally to reconsider a decision which is technically flawed. It is not a substitute for a right of appeal. Successful applications for a review must demonstrate that there is a flaw either in the decision or in the way it was reached. It is not normally sufficient or relevant to show that the result of the decision is unwanted or undesirable.'

---

22 Regulation 31(1) and (3).
23 Regulation 31(2).
24 Regulation 31(4).
25 Regulation 31(6).
26 Regulation 32.
27 [1996] ELR 278.

A parent or, indeed, an LEA also has a right to appeal against a decision of the tribunal, on a point of law, to the High Court. In a recent appeal, Carnwath J suggested that questions relating to the evidence considered by the tribunal and possibly also the adequacy of the tribunal's reasons might be more appropriately dealt with by the review procedure rather than via an appeal to the court. He felt that such matters could not be said to fall within the scope of errors of law; if the appeal was in respect of a decision said to hinge on a 'radically flawed basis of fact', appeal to the court was not apt, but review was.[28]

To date, there have been at least 74 applications for review.[29] This is a fairly large number relative to the overall number of appeals. The majority of applications made in 1995/96 were refused on the grounds that they had 'no reasonable prospect of success'.[30] The author would like to suggest that the number and grounds of applications should be monitored and the implications assessed.

10.3 BIAS IN DECISION-MAKING

Although there is little direct evidence to support the contention, many working in the field of special educational needs seem to believe that the local appeal committee system under the Education Act 1981 was biased in favour of local education authorities. The basis of their view is that the committees lacked independence because the majority of their members, and very frequently the chair, were local councillors and, as such, tended to be influenced by LEA policy and resource constraints. Many of the respondents to the surveys the author conducted as part of the research opined that the independence of the SENT was one of its most attractive features.

The question of bias is but one issue concerning the overall fairness of the system, but it is an important one. On the face of it, the much greater prospects of success which parents seem to enjoy under the new system suggest that, if anything, the SENT may lean somewhat in favour of parents. Many LEAs in the survey said that they thought that the onus

---

28 *South Glamorgan County Council v L and M* [1996] ELR 400, QBD.
29 'At least', because the SENT office, which supplied this statistic, is not sure that all applications are recorded.
30 T. Aldridge QC, *Special Educational Needs Tribunal, Annual Report 1995/96* (SENT, 1996), p 18; reg 31(3).

had shifted onto them to justify their decisions, whereas in the past the onus had very definitely rested with the parents to show that there was a good reason for departing from what would be presumed to be an appropriate decision by the LEA. If this shift has occurred, it would clearly undermine any claims that the preponderance of past LEA employees among the tribunal members has created an advantage for LEAs when contesting appeals.

Only a couple of parents in the survey believed that the tribunal which had heard their appeal had been biased in favour of the LEA, although some others commented that they thought that the LEA's case had not been fully tested by the tribunal. Ironically, one parent actually commented that 'too many questions were asked of the LEA', but her real complaint was that this had caused the tribunal to run on for an extra 40 minutes.

The strongest views on the question of bias were given by LEAs. Only one LEA in the survey (n = 80) believed that the SENT tended, in general, to favour the LEA above parents. As can be seen from Table 23 below, while a majority of LEAs regarded the tribunal as impartial, almost one-third of authorities considered that the SENT was biased in favour of parents.

Table 23

Views of surveyed LEAs on SENT bias for or against LEAs

| | LEAs perceiving bias | |
Nature of alleged bias by SENT	Numbers	Percentage
Tends to favour parents	26	33%
Tends to favour LEA	1	1%
Is impartial	45	56%
No response/don't know	8	10%

(n=80)

Also investigated were LEAs' perceptions of how the level of any bias shown by the SENT compares with that which might have occurred under the old system. In fact, equal numbers of LEAs believed that the SENT's support for LEAs had increased or decreased, as compared with the level of support under the appeal system under the 1981 Act. Half of the LEAs in fact detected no change as regards bias before and after the introduction of the SENT: see Table 24 below.

Table 24

LEAs' views on changes in bias for/against parents or LEA before and after establishment of SENT

Extent of change	Numbers of LEAs agreeing	Percentage
Under the old system the panel favoured parents more and the LEA less	14	17.5%
Under the old system the panel favoured the parents less and the LEA more	14	17.5%
No difference between old and new systems	40	50%
No response/don't know	12	15%

(n=80)

LEAs were also asked for the evidence which would support their views. Many of those who believed that the SENT tended to be biased in favour of parents referred to the greater number of 'successful' appeals under the new system – one LEA said 'to date we have lost all cases against us'. Some reported that the SENT had a tendency to permit parents to make unsubstantiated comments and that it often avoided direct questioning of parents' evidence. The following are typical comments:

- 'Tends to favour parents – questioning of LEA always more challenging.'
- 'Tends to favour parents – both the results of the appeal hearings and the demeanour of the majority of tribunal members.'
- 'Notable bias in the conduct of tribunal members toward parents'.

As noted above, however, half of the LEAs in the survey considered the tribunal to be impartial. LEAs' comments included:

- 'The hearings have been generally even handed.'
- 'The quality and style of questions from panels indicates neutrality.'
- 'Favours neither side – three cases, all in favour of LEA but felt the SENT was very sensitive to parents' feelings.'

In this connection, it is worth recalling that some members of the SENT in the survey gave as their motive for joining the tribunal a desire to participate in what they perceived to be a fairer, more impartial system.[31]

Bias is a serious matter and tribunals must avoid it at all costs. The rule against bias ('no one may be a judge in their own cause') is one of the rules of natural justice and is based on the principle that if a reasonable person would suspect that there might be bias (potential bias) then doubts would arise as to the fairness of the decision itself.[32] Recently, an allegation of bias on the part of the SENT – at least bias in relation to the conduct of proceedings rather than the substance of the decision – formed part of the basis of an appeal to the High Court: *Joyce v Dorset County Council*.[33] It was alleged that at the end of the SENT's hearing, when the parties were leaving the room to permit the tribunal to deliberate, there was 'an intimate and friendly discussion at considerable length' between a member of the tribunal and a senior officer of Dorset County Council; the two individuals seemed to know each other very well.[34] Members of the parent's party, mindful of the fact that the tribunal had not, at this stage, made its decision, suspected bias. Latham J was not satisfied that there was any real danger or real likelihood of bias on the part of the tribunal member in question; however, he issued a warning to tribunals:

'The procedure at tribunals such as this is intended to be informal. Nonetheless, the issues are serious; and feelings may well run high. In these circumstances, it is easy to see how a perfectly innocuous conversation could be misinterpreted. It would therefore be wise for tribunal members to avoid any discussion or informal contact during the course of the hearing with one party or its witnesses. This may be extremely difficult, bearing in mind that there may be adjournments when social conversation is almost inevitable. Nonetheless, members should try to ensure that they do not act in any way that could be misconstrued.'

One or two parents in the survey remarked that some tribunal members and LEA officers seemed to know each other. This is inevitable given past professional contact and ongoing contact on a regular basis in the tribunal

---

31 See above and Chapter 4.
32 See Wade and Forsyth, *Administrative Law* (7th edn) (Oxford University Press, 1994), chapter 14.
33 Unreported, 26 January 1996, QBD, but due to be reported in *Education Law Reports*.
34 The author has been informed by the SENT Secretariat that the two individuals did not, in fact, know each other and had no recollection of having met on a prior occasion.

and it does not compromise the independence of the tribunal, provided the panel heeds Latham J's remarks and the President's guidance on the need to avoid conduct of the kind which arose in *Joyce* and anything else which would raise suspicions of potential bias.

The research findings as a whole suggest that, where the tribunal is concerned, there is far less frequent acceptance of LEAs' decisions than under the previous system, and it seems fair to conclude that the post-1993 Act system does operate more impartially. Whether the pendulum has swung too far in favour of parents, as some LEAs seem to be suggesting, is doubtful. On the whole, there is no evidence of bias on the part of the SENT. But complacency would be dangerous, and tribunal training should continue to stress the importance of acting, and being seen to be acting, impartially.

One feature of the appeal system that LEAs continue to regard as unfairly skewed against them is the way that placement decisions are made. This is discussed below.

Naming a school in the statement: an example of bias?

A number of LEAs referred specifically to the situation where a parent has moved his or her child to an independent, fee-charging specialist school some months before the tribunal hearing. The LEA refuses to name the school in the child's statement because it believes a suitable place can be found at one of the schools it maintains, and probably at less expense to the authority. It argues that the naming of the independent school in the statement would not be compatible with 'the efficient use of resources'.[35] The tribunal then places considerable emphasis, too much, in the view of many LEAs, on the disadvantage of moving the child from a settled placement, particularly where the child seems to be benefiting from the provision made. Also, the tribunal is likely to consider it necessary, as a result of the President's practice guidance (previously contained in a 1995 Practice Direction[36]), to consider the evidence prevailing in relation to the child at the date of the tribunal hearing. Some LEAs in the survey complained that this emphasis on the current situation means that the tribunal places undue weight on oral evidence presented by the parents on the day, in their view often ignoring formal documentary evidence compiled by the LEA over a period of months or longer.

---

35 1996 Act, Sch 27, para 3.
36 [1995] ELR 335. The Practice Direction was withdrawn in October 1996. See Chapter 6, footnote 80.

Several LEAs made comments on this issue. For example:

- 'The LEAs' decisions are ... not considered as much as the child's current position at the time of appeal. The motive, unsustainable appeals by parents – which cannot be challenged easily – may sway panels rather than the evidence which was gathered at an early date, when the decisions were made.'
- 'We are concerned that parents go to the tribunal after they have placed their child in an independent school.'
- 'The tribunal is hostage to parental representation on the day (and parental dramatics), particularly the emotional pressure of deciding on appropriate placement where the placement has been chosen by the parents in the independent sector and finding in favour of the LEA would mean removal of the child from their present (boarding school).'

The scenario described above, concerning the placement of a child in an independent school, seeking to have that school named in the statement, and appealing against the LEA's decision, was raised specifically when the House of Commons Education Select Committee took evidence in February 1996. Mr Gerry Steinberg, MP said that he disapproved of such action and felt that in a case such as that the tribunal was 'being taken advantage of'.[37] The President of the SENT said that such a case was 'not unique' but that the tribunal was faced with a real 'dilemma'. If the child had made some progress since being moved to the independent school, as would often be the case, then the tribunal could not ignore it. Although it might be patently obvious that, in adopting the said course of action, the parent had engineered the relevant evidence, or 'purchased' it, it did 'not make the evidence any less real, that is to say the child has made progress under that particular regime'.[38]

A related point, again centring on assertions made by some LEAs, is that tribunals are insensitive to the problems facing authorities. In particular, it is argued that tribunals will ignore the difficulties LEAs are facing in trying to ensure that the best use is made of limited resources, even if some parents do not secure quite as good an education for their child as they might otherwise wish for. Some LEAs in the survey referred to the case law,[39] which holds that it is not incumbent on the LEA to provide the best

---

37 House of Commons Education Committee, Second Report, 1995–96, *Special Educational Needs: The Operation of the Code of Practice and the Tribunal*, HC 205 (HMSO, 1996), Minutes of Oral Evidence, 7 February 1996, Q66.
38 Ibid, Q67
39 See, for example, *R v Surrey CC ex parte H* (1984) 83 LGR 219, CA.

possible education for the child, but rather to ensure that provision is suitable.

Reference was made above to the high success rate parents have enjoyed in relation to appeals concerning placement. The fact that parents are often able to have their choice upheld does not mean that some of the claims made by LEAs that the system operates unfairly are well-founded. The SENT is required to decide in accordance with the requirements of the statutory framework. This inevitably means that it tends to focus on what is a reasonable level of expenditure in relation to a particular child, with the impact of its decision on LEA funds as a whole being a somewhat secondary consideration. It should not be supposed that the fact that the SENT tends to focus its decision in this way is indicative of bias against LEAs. Apparent insensitivity on the part of the SENT to LEAs' broader financial concerns is, therefore, not what it seems.

The cases included in the Digest of Decisions prepared by the President of the SENT neither confirm nor negate the idea that some parents act tactically in removing their child to an independent school. The evidence does, however, suggest that parents are genuinely concerned that their child should make progress and are often prepared to dig deeply into their own pockets to pay the necessary school fees. Naturally, such parents would hope that the LEA's responsibility towards the child would mean that it should pay for the child to be educated at an independent school.

Some of the decisions in the President's Digest do confirm the tribunal's unwillingness to name a different school in the statement. For example, in Decision *95/18*, the parents had objected to the LEA's proposal that their child, who had moderate learning difficulties, should be educated at a unit attached to a mainstream comprehensive school. At their own expense, they sent him to a small independent school instead. The tribunal considered that the education that would be provided in a special unit would not be suitable and that the child should remain at a school 'where he was happy and felt secure'. There are other examples of cases where, generally on educational grounds, the SENT ordered that an independent school which the child was attending should be named in the statement (eg Decisions *95/7* and *95/19*). One decision of the tribunal recently went to the High Court, where Collins J upheld the decision.[40] In that case, the child had been placed by her parents at an independent school providing conductive education. The education provided was said

---

40 *Staffordshire County Council v J and J* [1996] ELR 418, QBD.

to offer the child the best possible chance of an early transfer to a mainstream school. The LEA, however, wanted one of its own schools to be named in the child's statement forthwith. It argued that placement at its school would involve a more efficient use of resources. The court found that there had been good reason for leaving the child at the independent school in order to prevent her possible regression and because, in the long run, the benefits of conductive education at that school could result in greater efficiency as the child could be integrated more successfully into mainstream schooling.

These decisions should not be taken to reflect any bias on the part of the SENT. Indeed, some cases have gone the other way. For example, in Decision *95/22*, the SENT decided that the school to be named in the statement should be the maintained school preferred by the LEA, even though the child was already attending an independent school. The report notes that the fact that the child was already attending an independent school 'where she was happy' was not regarded as conclusive by the SENT, although it was a 'relevant consideration'.

The other issue concerns the extent to which the tribunal is sensitive to the question of resources when deciding on placement. The resources argument is not always raised by the LEA in defending appeals before the SENT. Where it is, the tribunal has to balance it against other considerations.[41] The following cases illustrate the approach adopted.

In Decision *95/21*, the LEA proposed that the child should attend one of its schools for pupils with severe learning difficulties, whereas the parents wanted an independent specialist boarding school to be named in the statement. The cost to the LEA in respect of the latter school was several times greater than that of educating the child at the LEA's own school. The tribunal concluded that the child's needs could be met in the LEA's school, but also that educating the child at the independent school would not be an efficient use of the LEA's resources.

In another case, Decision *95/24*, the tribunal considered that both the maintained school in an adjoining borough preferred by the parents and the LEA's own school could meet the child's special educational needs. However, the cost to the LEA of the child's education at the school in the adjoining borough was considerably greater than the cost of educating the child at its own school, and the tribunal considered that the parent's preferred option would not be an efficient use of the LEA's resources and dismissed the appeal.

---

41 *Staffordshire County Council v J and J* [1996] ELR 418, QBD, per Collins J.

In Decision *96/66* the parents disagreed with the LEA's choice of school, but it would have been 178% more expensive to educate the child, who was moving from primary to secondary school, at the school preferred by the parents (which was outside the LEA's area). Other members of the child's class were transferring to that school, but the tribunal concluded that it would not have been an efficient use of resources for the LEA to support his education there. This decision contrasts with that in *96/65*, where the difference in cost between educating the child in the school preferred by the parents (in the USA) as opposed to the school selected by the LEA was not great (because the parents had charitable support). The tribunal found that the school preferred by the parents could meet the child's educational needs satisfactorily and decided that to educate the child there would be an efficient use of the LEA's resources.

The resources argument may also come into consideration in respect of a part-time placement. In Decision *96/13*, the tribunal ordered that the statement should provide for the child to attend a local maintained infants school combined with part-time attendance at a maintained special school. The parents had wanted the part-time placement to be at a school providing conductive education, which the child had attended for the previous 18 months but to which the transport costs would have been several times higher.

The decisions reported in the Digest represent only a very small proportion of the overall number. Nevertheless, they do give a broad indication of the approach being followed by tribunals. Despite parents' high success rate in appeals concerning placements (see above), there is no evidence that tribunals are acting otherwise than in accordance with the statutory requirements and it seems quite clear that they are weighing up the relevant issues in an appropriate manner. If there *is* any bias in favour of parental choice, it is a bias which is built into the legislation (it should be recalled that parental choice was a theme in the White Paper *Choice and Diversity* in 1992[42]) rather than being personal bias, whether 'political' or not, among SENT members.

---

42 DFE/Welsh Office, *Choice and Diversity: A New Framework for Schools* (DFE/Welsh Office, 1992).

10.4   LENGTH OF TIME BETWEEN THE HEARING AND THE ISSUING OF THE WRITTEN DECISION

For quite a number of parents in the survey, the main cause of dissatisfaction was not the hearing itself but the length of time it took before they were notified of the decision of the tribunal. Many commented that the delay in being informed of the tribunal's decision was excessive – frequently more than two weeks (although the SENT guide states that the decision will be posted out to parents and the LEA 'within 10 working days of the hearing'[43]) and in one case over one month. A survey carried out by the British Dyslexia Association produced a similarly high level of dissatisfaction with the waiting time for a decision: 'lengthy delays in relaying decisions to parents, over one month in one instance, are not acceptable'; and 'decisions are taking far too long to reach parents'.[44] Some of the LEAs in the survey were also critical of the delays. One commented that decisions by their local appeal committee under the Education Act 1981 were issued within two days. Another believed that one of the ways in which the new system could be improved would be by the SENT ensuring that decisions were communicated to parents within two weeks in *every* case.

Clearly, decisions have to be worded carefully and checked for errors. The SENT has to produce adequate reasons for decisions.[45] Nevertheless, it has become common practice in social security appeal tribunals for appellants to be given their decision orally on the day, and then sent a written decision, including reasons, thereafter. The arguments for and against giving SENT decisions orally on the day were discussed at some length above and do not require repetition here. The issue is a difficult one, but the author's view is that although deliberations may take some time, and although the precise details of the decision may need to be worked out, it should be possible, in far more cases than at present, for the decision to be given orally, on the day, or by telephone a day or so later.[46] As noted above, the tribunal has the power to communicate its decisions orally.[47]

---

43 SENT, *Special Educational Needs Tribunal – How to Appeal* (SENT, 1994), p 15.
44 Evidence to House of Commons Education Committee, Second Report, 1995–96, *Special Educational Needs: The Operation of the Code of Practice and the Tribunal*, HC 205 (HMSO, 1996), Appendices, p 32.
45 See **10.5**.
46 See also the discussion above at **10.2**, 'Decision-making and procedure'.
47 Regulation 30(2).

The only way of increasing significantly the number of cases in which the decision is issued inside two weeks (or ten working days) is for a time-limit to be included in the regulations. If this is considered undesirable, then the President should increase the pressure on tribunal chairs to expedite matters and should also improve the relevant administrative arrangements. In fact, the President indicated in his annual report for 1995/96 that some improvements were recently made, and he has informed the author that there is a continuing effort to secure further improvement.

10.5 REASONS FOR DECISION

As noted above, the written decision issued by the tribunal must 'contain, or have annexed to it, a statement of the reasons (in summary form) for the tribunal's decision'.[48] There has long been concern about the inadequacy of reasons given by education tribunals;[49] as the SENT is the first education tribunal with a lawyer chair, it would be expected to produce adequate reasons in every case.

Apart from the evidence obtained by the SENT President in the course of monitoring tribunal decisions,[50] which will be at most selectively disclosed, the only evidence currently available on how well tribunals are meeting the legal requirements is derived from the decisions of High Court appeals where the question of adequacy of reasons was raised. These decisions are also important in clarifying the precise nature of the duty to provide reasons and they build on earlier court decisions concerning local education appeal committees.

Of the cases concerning local appeal committees, *Re L*[51] is the most relevant to this discussion. Here the court considered the adequacy of the reasons given by the appeal committee when the parents had challenged the contents of their child's statement of special educational needs. The committee's reasons were set out in five numbered points, each one of which comprised one sentence only. Leggatt LJ said that the appeal committee had complied with its duty to give reasons. The five-point statement, in his view, 'shows that the committee considered the relevant

---

48 Regulation 30(2).
49 See, for example, Council on Tribunals, *Annual Report 1987/88* (HMSO, 1988), para 2.41; see also *Re L* [1994] ELR 16, CA.
50 This evidence can inform tribunal training, which has included sessions on writing up decisions.
51 [1994] ELR 16, CA.

issues and indicates the evidence by reference to which they reached their conclusions'.[52]

The local education appeal committees had, and continue to have, jurisdiction over school admission appeals. Again, there is a duty to give reasons, and some of the guidance given by the courts in relation to such cases is of relevance. In *W (A Minor) v Education Appeal Committee of Lancashire County Council,* Hirst LJ said that 'the depth and elaboration of reasons required in any individual sphere must be considered in the light of the type of committee which is under consideration'.[53] Hirst LJ also said an appeal committee was not required to spell out in detail its assessment of the several grounds put forward by the appellant and weigh them individually and in aggregate against the reasons put forward by the LEA, because that would place 'an undue and unwarrantable burden on this lay committee'.[54] In *R v Lancashire County Council ex parte M,*[55] Popplewell J applied Hirst LJ's dictum in another school admission case. Popplewell J confirmed that:

> 'reasons must be given which are intelligible and enable the party to understand why the court or tribunal has reached the conclusion that it has. It is important for the parties to know why they have won or lost. It is important for any appellate tribunal or court to know the reasons so as to be able to comment on them.'[56]

In these decisions, the courts confirmed that the reasons must indicate, albeit in summary form, how the tribunal reached its conclusion and the principal evidence which it took into account, and perhaps why that evidence was persuasive or conclusive. It will be noted, however, that the court took into account the nature of the appeal concerned. Indeed, while there is a considerable body of judicial review case law which indicates that the duty resting on a judicial body as regards the depth of reasons to be given is fairly onerous, that case law is not wholly applicable to all tribunals. Indeed, in *W,* Hirst LJ said that he did 'not find the citation of other cases concerned with the adequacy of reasons given by other committees or similar bodies in other fields of activity of any great assistance'.[57]

---

52 [1994] ELR 16, CA, at 24.
53 [1994] ELR 530, 538.
54 Ibid.
55 [1994] ELR 478.
56 Ibid, at 483.
57 [1994] ELR 530, at 538.

The paucity of the reasons generally given by lay appeal committees is well known.[58] One of the objectives of having a lawyer chair of the new SENT was to ensure that standards of adjudication, which includes the giving of reasons, would be improved in special educational needs cases. Thus, it could be argued that the statement of reasons to be given by the SENT should go further in indicating the way the tribunal reached its decision than might be expected of a lay local appeal committee. Nevertheless, as noted above, the regulations merely require the statement of reasons to be given by the SENT 'in summary form'.[59] The courts have considered the precise nature of this requirement in a number of recent cases.

In *S v Special Educational Needs Tribunal and the City of Westminster*,[60] Latham J said that a balance had to be struck between:

> 'giving effect to the clear intention of Parliament that the requirement of reasons is to be met by a shortform document, and proper concern that the right of appeal under s 11 of the Tribunals and Inquiries Act 1992 would be emasculated if the document did not at least enable the aggrieved party to identify the basis of the decision with sufficient clarity to be able to determine whether or not the tribunal had gone wrong in law.'

Latham J then proceeded to indicate how that balance might be achieved. He said that the statement of reasons should 'deal, but in shortform, with the substantial issues raised in order that the parties can understand why the decision has been reached'.[61] The extent to which the SENT is required to identify the reasons why some of the evidence presented was given more weight than other evidence, which is an important question on which tribunals needed guidance, was also dealt with. Latham J recognised that, when giving summary reasons, it may not be possible for the tribunal to give precise reasons for accepting the evidence of one witness and rejecting or doubting that of another. He said that in relation to that matter, 'there may have to be the simple assertion of the tribunal's preference'.[62] Nevertheless, the tribunal had to deal with 'all the issues of

---

58 See Chapter 2 at **2.2**.
59 Regulation 30(2).
60 [1996] ELR 102, at 112.
61 Ibid.
62 Ibid.

substance raised by the parties, albeit in a summary way'.[63] He said that that did not mean that the tribunal had to deal with every single point raised in argument on a particular issue. Nevertheless, the tribunal 'should make its conclusions intelligible in relation to the issue itself'.[64] Similar views were expressed by Carnwath J in two more recent cases.[65]

This guidance is clearly very helpful to tribunals. It does seem to go further, in relation to the standard it suggests for the reasons required, than the previous cases on education appeal committees' reasons for decisions. This, apparently higher, standard also makes it more likely that, unless tribunals are particularly careful in their approach to this matter, challenges to the adequacy of reasons given by the tribunal may occur. However, in *South Glamorgan County Council v L and M*,[66] Carnwath J suggested that a party could seek clarification of the tribunal's summary reasons via an application for a review of a decision under the regulations.[67] He said that although the regulations do not provide in express terms for the tribunal to clarify its 'summary' reasons, a request for elaboration of reasons is certainly not precluded. Furthermore, it seemed to Carnwath J 'much more sensible for elaboration of the reasons to be asked for and given at that stage, when the matter was fresh in everyone's mind, than to await the determination of a court some months later'. This guidance is still being considered and it is too early to judge its potential, practical impact. Nevertheless, it seems likely that advisers will recommend that dissatisfied parents seek more detailed reasons from tribunals; the cumulative effect could be increased pressure on tribunals to provide more detailed reasons in the first place, despite the lack of a statutory requirement to do so.

The likelihood that the courts will be resistant to challenges based on inadequacy of reasons given by the SENT was recently confirmed by Collins J in *Staffordshire County Council v J and J*.[68] He said that 'The one thing ... that should not happen in these cases is that a fine toothcomb should be used and a detailed dissection made of the reasons given in order to tease out an apparent error or inconsistency and to try to assert that full reasoning was not given'.

---

63 [1996] ELR 102, at 112.
64 Ibid.
65 *South Glamorgan County Council v L and M* [1996] ELR 400, QBD; *Brophy v Metropolitan Borough of Wirral*, sub nom *Special Educational Needs Tribunal ex parte Brophy* (unreported), 8 May 1996, QBD.
66 *South Glamorgan County Council v L and M* [1996] ELR 400, QBD.
67 Regulation 31, previously reg 32 of the 1994 Regulations.
68 [1996] ELR 418, at 424H, QBD.

Voluntary organisations and lawyers active in this field were asked about the express reasons for decisions in cases with which they had been involved. Most were reasonably satisfied with the reasons provided by the tribunal. One of the lawyers commented: 'they are pleasantly concise – maybe sometimes not dealing with all the issues discussed – but the tribunal should be encouraged to keep decisions concise and intelligible'. However, another lawyer said that the tribunal's reasons tend to be 'too brief, too simple, do not grasp legal issues'. One branch of a large voluntary organisation said it was 'worried about the lack of detail in decisions', such as in several cases where the tribunal held that the school had the capability to meet a child's special educational needs despite evidence to the contrary presented by the parents. Another voluntary organisation informed us that it was 'not satisfied with the decision making' in two cases. The organisation was concerned that it was insufficiently clear that evidence about the child's learning difficulty was given due consideration. That organisation made a general comment that some decisions are 'poorly written and contradictory'.

Thus, despite the general satisfaction with the detail and clarity of decisions of the SENT, it is probable that there are deficiencies in a certain number of cases. Training of tribunal chairs continues to cover writing up of decisions, and hopefully there will be improvements. The provision of more detailed reasons would meet the criticism made by a number of bodies working in this field that parents are sometimes left unsure why their argument and evidence failed to persuade the tribunal in their favour.[69]

10.6 AWARDS OF COSTS AND EXPENSES

The tribunal has a power to make orders relating to costs and expenses.[70] This is unusual for a welfare tribunal intended to provide an informal means of resolving a dispute without the use of lawyers. The regulations in fact seek to ensure that this power will be used in only very exceptional

---

69 Note that currently the Education (Special Educational Needs) Bill which is before Parliament aims to remove the words 'in summary form' from the tribunal's duty to state the reasons for its decisions. The Government does not support this provision (nor the Bill as a whole); it says that a fully argued decision might take up to 25 pages to set out, causing further delays in the issuing of written decisions, and that most parents would not necessarily welcome 'the technical detail entailed' in a lengthy decision: Hansard, HL Vol 575, col 1017, 13 November 1996, per Lord Henley, Under-Secretary of State.

70 Regulation 33.

circumstances. They state that 'The tribunal shall not normally make an order in respect of costs and expenses' but that it 'may' do so in prescribed circumstances and subject to the right of a person against whom the costs and expenses would be awarded to make representations on the subject to the tribunal.[71] Provision is also made for taxation of costs, if required.[72]

Costs may be awarded against a party if, inter alia, the tribunal is of the opinion that she/he 'has acted frivolously or vexatiously or that his conduct in making, pursuing or resisting the appeal was wholly unreasonable'.[73] In one case, costs were awarded against an LEA which, having agreed various matters relating to a child's statement of SEN at the first hearing of the tribunal, subsequently denied such agreement – which led to a reconvening of the tribunal, for a second hearing. The tribunal accepted arguments put forward by counsel for the parents that the LEA had been frivolous or vexatious in its denial that agreement had been reached at the first hearing.[74]

A party may also be required to bear costs if they have failed to attend, or to be represented in their absence, at a hearing of which they have been duly notified.[75] Costs may also be awarded against an LEA only,[76] if it has 'not delivered a written reply' to the notice of appeal[77] or if the tribunal 'considers that the disputed decision was wholly unreasonable'.

The procedural guide advises parents that they will 'not normally have to pay any costs' but that 'in very exceptional circumstances, if the tribunal thinks that either you or the LEA have acted unreasonably, or deliberately wasted the tribunal's time, you or they may have to pay the costs'.[78] It is entirely appropriate that parents should be warned of the circumstances in which costs might be awarded against them. Furthermore, the guide does make it clear that any such award would be very exceptional. On the other hand, it is possible that this reassurance could actually operate to raise, inadvertently, some parents' anxiety and could deter some potential appellants. People often fail to appeal to tribunals, even where they have good grounds for an appeal, because they do not want to cause any

---

71 Regulation 33(1)–(3).
72 Regulation 33(4) and (5). Essentially, this involves independent scrutiny of the costs.
73 Regulation 33(1)(a).
74 President's Digest of Decisions, Decision *96/74*.
75 Regulation 33(1)(b).
76 Ibid, paras (c) and (d).
77 Presumably, a failure here means a failure to deliver the reply within the deadline of 20 working days set by reg 12.
78 SENT, *Special Educational Needs Tribunal – How to appeal* (SENT, 1994).

trouble or because they feel they might be wasting the tribunal's time. The disadvantages of any disincentive to appeal provided by the reference to the rule on costs in the guide probably outweigh the advantages of the rule itself.

10.7   PUBLICATION OF TRIBUNAL DECISIONS

Decisions of the SENT are sent to the parties and the parent's representative but are not published or reported other than in the President's Digest. The Digest contains summaries of a selection of decisions. It is designed 'to illustrate approaches taken by individual panels towards particular issues which are likely to arise in a number of cases throughout the tribunal's jurisdiction'.[79] The President believes that 'a common basis of shared information will help to get a useful degree of national consistency in approaching special needs problems'.[80] The President has, however, stressed that the cases reported in the Digest have no precedent value, as a tribunal is not bound to follow an earlier decision, and he considers that it would be inappropriate for representatives to cite previous SENT decisions before tribunals.

At the time of writing, six Digests have been published, summarising a total of 117 decisions. The President has indicated that issues of the Digest will be published on a regular basis – every three or four months. Copies of the Digest are circulated free to members of the tribunal and other interested parties. They are also published in the *Education Law Reports*.[81] The Digest achieves its purpose, but the necessarily brief account of the facts and other details makes objective evaluation of individual decisions impossible.

10.8   IMPLEMENTATION OF TRIBUNAL DECISIONS

Some parents have succeeded with their appeal only to find that there is intransigence on the part of the LEA with regard to implementation of the tribunal's decision. Some of these parents have complained to the

---

79 Senior Editor's note, approved by the President, preceding each Digest published in the *Education Law Reports*.
80 T. Aldridge QC, *Special Educational Needs Tribunal, Annual Report 1994/95* (SENT, 1995) p 20.
81 Published by Jordans.

SENT office about this, but the matter lies outside the jurisdiction of the tribunal. In the author's survey of parents, several respondents expressed disappointment at the slow response by the LEA, or the lack of one, to the tribunal's decision. One parent had to make a complaint to the Secretary of State under s 99 of the Education Act 1944 (now s 497 of the Education Act 1996) before the LEA acted. It is clearly unacceptable that a parent should, in effect, be forced to invoke the remedy of a direction under the Secretary of State's default jurisdiction in order to enforce a judicial decision. It is true that in some SENT cases the matter may have been referred back to the LEA for assessment and so on. It is also the case that the LEA may need time to put in place the arrangements contemplated by the tribunal. Nevertheless, some parents feel that the credibility of the SENT system is being put at risk if tribunals' decisions can be simply ignored by LEAs. One parent commented:

> 'In my experience, even if the decision is in your favour the LEAs appear to ignore the judgment. Then the tribunal inform you they cannot comment further on whether or how the LEA are complying with the decision.'

If parents lose confidence in the SENT because its judgments are sometimes failing to be acted upon by LEAs, some may decide not to appeal in the first place, which would be most unfortunate. Arguably, consideration ought to be given to the adoption of a more effective means of ensuring that tribunal decisions are acted upon by the LEA.[82] If s 497 decisions could be taken more speedily, that would undoubtedly help.

Special educational needs problems feature very prominently in the caseload of the local government ombudsman. This is obviously one route to redress which parents may wish to utilise,[83] despite its limitations (eg establishing that there has been maladministration causing injustice will be necessary and, in any event, may only result in a relatively small award of compensation).

The risk of civil litigation should damage result from negligence on the part of the LEA, following the decisions in the education cases reported with *X v Bedfordshire County Council*,[84] may well already be precipitating

---

82 Note that judicial review seeking an order of mandamus in the High Court is a possible way of enforcing the duty resting with the LEA to make the special educational provision specified in a statement, as noted by A. Bradley and D. Ruebain, 'Interim relief and the Special Educational Needs Tribunal – is there any place for judicial review?' (1996) 1(3) *Education, Public Law and the Individual* 54.

83 See further S. Oliver and L. Austen, *Special Educational Needs and the Law* (Jordans, 1996), pp 164–165.

84 [1995] 3 WLR 153; [1995] 3 All ER 353; [1995] ELR 404, HL.

a more punctilious response by LEAs to SENT decisions. The court upheld the right to bring common law negligence claims in respect of damage resulting from a failure properly to identify and respond to certain special educational needs. Both that decision and the recently reported launch of the civil claims in respect of damage resulting from poor educational provision[85] suggest that LEAs would be wise to implement SENT decisions quickly.

10.9   APPEALS TO THE HIGH COURT

Number and outcome of appeals to date

Section 11 of the Tribunals and Inquiries Act 1992, as amended,[86] enables appeals to be brought against decisions of the SENT to the High Court, on a point of law.[87] An appeal may be brought under Ord 55 (originating motion) or Ord 56 (case stated) of the Rules of the Supreme Court.[88] As at 13 January 1997 there had been 72 appeals, 64 brought by parents and eight by LEAs.[89] The decisions in the appeals disposed of by that date (47 in total) show that if it upholds the appeal the court is most likely to remit the matter to be re-heard by a tribunal; this is perhaps to be expected where an appeal lies on a point of law in a field in which the merits of appeals have been considered by Parliament to be most suitably assessed by a specialist tribunal. A breakdown of the outcome of the appeals to the High Court is shown in Table 25 below.

---

85 See J. O'Leary, 'Education chiefs call for laws to prevent pupils suing schools', (1996) *The Times*, 2 December.
86 By s 181(2) of the 1993 Act.
87 The meaning of 'error of law' for the purpose of deciding whether a challenge to the decision of a tribunal lies within the province of the statutory right of appeal was considered in *South Glamorgan County Council v L and M* [1996] ELR 400, QBD. The jurisdiction of the court in SEN appeal cases was recently described by McCullough J thus: '[T]he court must ask whether the tribunal, in making its decision, applied the correct principles of law, whether it failed to take into account any material factor, whether it took into account any immaterial factor and whether it reached a decision which was irrational, in other words one which no tribunal could reasonably have reached': *Russell v The Royal Borough of Kingston upon Thames and Hunter* (1996) 6 November, QBD (unreported), transcript p 9.
88 As to the choice of proceeding under Ord 55 or 56, see below.
89 SENT statistics supplied by the Secretariat.

Table 25

Appeals to the High Court against decisions of the SENT to 13 January 1997

Appeals disposed of, and outcome		Live (unresolved) appeals
Dismissed	15	
Withdrawn by LEA	3	
Withdrawn by parent (by consent in 4 cases)	14	
Remitted for re-hearing (by consent in 1 case)	6	
Tribunal conceded	3	
Other (procedural matters, eg time extensions granted or refused)	6	
TOTAL	47	25

Source: SENT statistics supplied to author.

Effect of appeal procedure on access to judicial review

Appeal to the High Court has inevitably taken the place of judicial review challenge in SEN cases. Indeed, in *R v Special Educational Needs Tribunal ex parte F*,[90] Popplewell J said that, on the basis of various authorities concerning the effect of statutory appeal mechanisms, 'the present law is that if there is a statutory right of appeal it is to be exercised and, save in exceptional circumstances, judicial review will not be granted where the statutory right of appeal exists and has not be exercised'.[91] In this case, the tribunal in fact applied to have the court's earlier leave to apply for judicial review struck out on the grounds that statutory appeal should have been brought under Ord 55. Popplewell J granted the application and set aside the leave. The courts, relying on established judicial review authorities such as *Swati*[92] and *Preston*,[93] have in fact followed a consistent line on this point in a number of cases.[94]

---

90 [1996] ELR 213, QBD.
91 Ibid, at 217.
92 *R v Secretary of State for the Home Department ex parte Swati* [1986] 1 WLR 1; [1986] 1 All ER 164, CA.
93 *R v Inland Revenue Commissioners ex parte Preston* [1985] 1 AC 835, HL.
94 See, for example, *R v Special Educational Needs Tribunal ex parte South Glamorgan County Council* [1996] ELR 326; *Re M* [1996] ELR 135; *R v Barnet ex parte Barnett* (unreported), 27 November 1995.

The tribunal as respondent to the appeal

The court in *R v Special Educational Needs Tribunal ex parte F* (above) also decided that the tribunal was not a proper respondent to the appeal, applying the dictum of Latham J in *S v Special Educational Needs Tribunal and the City of Westminster*.[95] The chair of the tribunal is the correct respondent[96] even though, as Oliver and Austen point out,[97] he or she does not have an automatic right to appear and be heard.

Parties to the appeal

As noted elsewhere in this book,[98] the parents and the LEA are the parties to the appeal.[99] The case of *S v Special Educational Needs Tribunal and the City of Westminster*[100] confirmed that the child is not a party to the proceedings (a view upheld by the Court of Appeal in that case[101]). This view was supported by the Court of Appeal in *R v Special Educational Needs Tribunal ex parte South Glamorgan County Council*.[102] In that case, however, the court felt that the exceptional circumstances which had arisen justified a direction that the child be present and represented at the hearing. More recently, in *Council of the City of Sunderland v P and C*,[103] Brooke J held that the power of the court under Ord 15, r 6, which enables a court to order that certain persons be added as parties to proceedings, could not be utilised in the context of an appeal against a decision of the SENT. This was, in fact, the first reported case involving an appeal by a local education authority against a decision of the SENT. The decision closed off another opportunity to a child's challenge.[104]

As noted in Chapter 1 (at **1.1**), the Education (Special Educational

---

95 [1996] ELR 102, QBD.

96 *S and C v Special Educational Needs Tribunal* (unreported), 7 November 1995, QBD. This case is summarised in the SENT President's Digest of Court Decisions (No 3) prepared for tribunal chairs.

97 S. Oliver and L. Austen, *Special Educational Needs and the Law* (Jordans, 1996) p 158.

98 See eg Chapter 1 at **1.1** and Chapter 6, footnote 3.

99 As noted in Chapter 1 (at footnote 12), in *Fairpo v Humberside County Council* [1997] 1 All ER 183, QBD, Laws J held that 'parent' included a local authority foster parent for this purpose.

100 [1996] ELR 102, QBD.

101 [1996] ELR 228, CA.

102 [1996] ELR 326, CA.

103 [1996] ELR 283, QBD.

104 As noted earlier, the significance of the child not being a party to the proceedings lies in the fact that he or she will not qualify for legal aid – with the result that the parents may have to pay legal expenses in bringing the appeal themselves (see 'Access and legal aid', below).

Needs) Bill, which is presently before Parliament but does not have the Government's support, aims to enable the child to be an appellant before the SENT. He or she could thus be a party to an appeal to the High Court.

RSC Ord 55 or Ord 56?

The question of which of the two procedures – originating motion under Ord 55 or case stated under Ord 56 – is appropriate for an appeal against the decision of the SENT was considered by Latham J in *S v Special Educational Needs Tribunal and the City of Westminster*.[105] The judge said that the appeal could be made in either form, and he explained:

> '[I]t is clear[106] that an appeal under Ord 55 is appropriate in relation to a decision of the tribunal, but that the tribunal may of its own motion or at the request of either party state a case on any question of law arising in the course of the proceedings.'[107]

In *Brophy v Metropolitan Borough of Wirral*,[108] Carnwath J confirmed that where an appeal is in respect of a final decision of the SENT, it should be brought under Ord 55 rather than by case stated under Ord 56, which was 'confined to matters which arise in the course of the proceedings'.[109] There is a time-limit specified by Ord 55 for bringing appeals, yet there is no time-limit where the appeal is by case stated, although as Carnwath J said, because the request for a case stated must arise in the course of proceedings 'that imposes a time limitation in any event'.[110] Clearly, appeal via Ord 55 will be the more commonly used procedure in SEN cases.

Access and legal aid

The utility to parents of the right of appeal to the High Court will depend not only on the approach taken by the court on the substantive issues argued before it, but also on the accessibility of this avenue of redress. Although litigants can prepare appeals and appear in person, legal help will probably be crucial. As the child will not be a party to the proceedings,

---

105 [1996] ELR 102.
106 This was on the basis of a reading of Ord 94, rr 8 and 9, which lays down the rules governing appeals under s 11 of the Tribunals and Inquiries Act 1992.
107 [1996] ELR 102, at 107B.
108 *Sub nom R v Special Educational Needs Tribunal ex parte Brophy* (unreported), 8 May 1996, QBD. This case will shortly be reported in ELR.
109 Approved transcript, p 15.
110 Ibid.

any access to legal aid will depend on the income and other financial circumstances of the parents (in addition, of course, to satisfaction of the legal aid 'merits' test). Very few parents will qualify for free legal aid. For the majority, a contribution will be payable – often quite a sizeable one. The Education Law Association has suggested that, as a result, 'appeals on points of law are largely inaccessible to parents'.[111] Judicial review proceedings, which were commonly pursued in SEN cases prior to the introduction of the new statutory appeal mechanism, can be brought in the name of the child. Usually, the child has few or no resources of his or her own and so qualifies for full legal aid. The legal aid situation where statutory appeals against decisions of the SENT are brought has, because of the fact that the child is not a party to the appeal (a situation which, as noted above, Lord Campbell's Bill is, at the time of writing, seeking to remedy), been described as an 'anomaly' by the House of Commons Select Committee.[112] It seems absurd that, on the one hand, legally aided court challenges to other education decisions can be brought by children,[113] whereas, on the other hand, pursuit of legal challenges concerned with special educational needs will generally have to proceed without such assistance.

---

111 House of Commons Education Committee, Second Report, 1995–96, *Special Educational Needs: The Working of the Code of Practice and the Tribunal*, Appendix 19, p 47.

112 Ibid, para 15.

113 Subject of course to the exclusivity principle – a statutory remedy generally provides an exclusive remedy, precluding judicial review challenge: see N. Harris, 'Education By Right? Breach of the Duty to Provide "Sufficient" Schools' (1990) 53 MLR 525 and see above.

Chapter 11

CONCLUSION

Almost everyone who has had any involvement with the Special Educational Needs Tribunal believes that it represents a considerable improvement on the appeals arrangements which it replaced. The evidence presented in the preceding chapters reveals that there are flaws in the system, but confirms that, overall, the general level of confidence that has built up in it is well-grounded. Whether the continuing role of local appeal committees in two other areas – school admissions and exclusion appeals – should be reconsidered further[1] in the light of the SENT's record to date is surely to be answered in the affirmative, although further research into their operation is undoubtedly needed before a final judgement is made.

Overall, the SENT is making an important contribution to enabling many more parents and (although only indirectly, as we have seen) their children than before to secure access to justice in respect of disputes over SEN issues. The tribunal membership offers an appropriate blend of specialist knowledge and experience and legal skills. The SENT's independence, enhanced by operating on a national basis under a President, is a considerable strength, as is the tribunal's general openness of approach – exemplified by the President's publication of Digests of Decisions of the tribunal. The President and his staff have taken a number of steps to improve the operation of the tribunal and to develop both the skills and knowledge of panel members through training programmes. They have also taken very seriously their mission of providing an accessible, 'user-friendly' system, although the formality of some of the procedural arrangements and documentation which they have employed have undermined their own efforts at times, whilst also tending to emphasise that, in a basically adversarial situation, where impartiality is essential, and where the issues are often complex, a degree of impersonality and judicial detachment is necessary, even if off-putting to some.

It was clear even before the SENT received its first appeal that the kind of procedural regime under which it would operate – with rules on discovery

---

1 As noted in Chapter 2, the Council on Tribunals already considers that school exclusion appeals jurisdiction should be transferred to the SENT.

of documents, witness summonses and so on – could present some parents with considerable difficulty. The evidence from the research suggests that many parents have experienced problems in coping with the whole process of appealing to the SENT. The procedural guide has helped but needs to be improved by, for example, showing parents more clearly what to expect when they bring their appeal to the tribunal. For example, some parents in the author's survey were, as noted in Chapter 9, quite taken aback by the tape-recording of the proceedings. It would be simple enough to inform parents in advance about tape-recording and perhaps also explain why it is considered necessary. Variations in the way that hearings are conducted make it difficult to give definitive guidance in advance to parents. However, this would become more feasible if there were greater uniformity and consistency of approach among tribunal chairs, something which the SENT ought perhaps to be taking even greater steps to ensure.

Many parents have sought, and have come to value, either legal help (despite the arguably unjustifiable absence of legal aid for SEN appeals to the tribunal) or the assistance of voluntary organisations. Often specialist assistance is needed to build up a case for presentation to the tribunal. The adviser might help by, for example, ensuring that there is an independent specialist report for the tribunal to consider (although such reports can be expensive to obtain, putting parents who are on low incomes at a disadvantage) or by arranging for witnesses to attend, albeit that some (particularly teachers) have been reluctant to do so.[2] Although advice on the particular kind of learning difficulties from which the child suffers is often available, specialist advice on appeals may have to be sought from one of relatively few expert sources.

Hearings have generally been conducted with as much informality as the circumstances permit. As we saw in Chapter 9, most parents in the author's survey felt that the tribunal had done its best to make them feel at ease and to make the environment as relaxed as possible, despite the underlying tension on both sides. Nevertheless, once the hearing is underway there has to be a degree of formality and order. In these circumstances, many parents find representation at the hearing to be invaluable. There is a considerable amount of documentation and oral evidence to be worked through and, in some cases, legal or other technical points to be made. Specialist representation can, at this stage, hold the key to effective access to justice; it will be particularly important when, as is

---

2 See Chapter 6 at **6.7**.

sometimes the case, the tribunal is insufficiently challenging of the LEA's case.

However, the effectiveness of representation before the SENT has been variable. As discussed in Chapter 8, some lay representatives have, for example, been over-zealous or have sought to make political points. Furthermore, legal representation has tended to make proceedings slightly more formal, adversarial and longer, although it has also been very useful in helping the tribunal to focus on the relevant issues. There are some cases where the LEA will be legally represented but the parents will not; in a situation where the parties are already unevenly matched, the use of a lawyer by the LEA alone must give rise to considerable concern. Perhaps the President should have the power to deny the LEA the opportunity to be legally represented in such cases unless the LEA can show good reason.

Overall, the research confirms the benefits of representation for parents at tribunal hearings. Nevertheless, the effectiveness of such representation could be improved, and the continuing dialogue on this subject between the President and voluntary organisations is likely to be very useful.

There are two groups whose access to the tribunal seems to be limited. Ethnic minorities appear to be seriously under-represented among appellants (and also among the tribunal membership, as noted in Chapter 4). This might well reflect a general reluctance on the part of some ethnic minorities to utilise legal processes,[3] and is matter which the President ought to investigate, if he is not doing so already, through discussions with relevant bodies, including the Commission for Racial Equality. The other group has no direct access to the appeal system at all – children. The arguments relating to the fact that children are not parties to appeals (including appeals from the SENT to the High Court), nor are likely to be called as witnesses or asked for their views, were discussed at various points throughout this book.[4] It was surprising, during the observations of

---

3 See, for example, the comments of Professor Sally Tomlinson on the legal action relating to the closure of Hackney Downs School in December 1995: 'a number of black pupils and parents, who felt similarly, declined to attend the court proceedings, indicating some cynicism about the whole legal process': 'Closure judgment must not be the last word', letter published in the *Times Educational Supplement*, 24 November 1995.

4 As noted in previous chapters, at the time of writing, Lord Campbell's private member's Bill, the Education (Special Educational Needs) Bill, aims to enable children to be parties to appeals. It has completed its committee stage in the House of Lords, but it does not have Government support and therefore may not have particularly good prospects of becoming law.

hearings, to find that the child was in attendance in so few cases. At the very least, the tribunal ought to take greater account of the recommendation of the Code of Practice[5] that the views of children are important and should be considered in the light of their age and understanding. Indeed, the ascertainment of those views ought to become a standard feature of SENT procedure. If the views were presented in writing, however, there would be doubts about whether they truly were the child's own. It might be necessary, therefore, for those views to be recorded by or in the presence of the 'named person',[6] but it would be even better if there was a person acting in an equivalent role to that of the guardian ad litem in Children Act 1989 proceedings who could represent the child's interests independently, which does not happen at present.

Most of the problems with the SENT are amenable to practical resolution, although in some cases additional resources may be needed. The length of the period between lodging an appeal and a hearing before the tribunal has been over six months in some cases and the average period between registration of an appeal and the decision has exceeded five months, although is now four to four-and-a-half months. The reduction in the average waiting period which faces the parents and the child is to be welcomed, but even this improved waiting time can be problematic when the child's educational provision has already been in doubt for a considerable time. The new 'default' mechanism has put LEAs under greater pressure to meet the statutory time-limits, but further reductions in time will require additional administrative efforts. Staffing levels in the SENT office have, however, improved of late and administrative changes have been made with a view to achieving greater expedition. Similarly, better listing arrangements for appeals, so that a particular chair does not hear two cases in one day,[7] might result in a higher proportion of appeal decisions being issued to the parties within the target time of ten working days. It would also help to prevent some hearings being 'rushed', with a chair keen to finish a morning session promptly because he or she is hearing another case after lunch. It might in turn mean that there is a greater likelihood of breaks in the proceedings – where they are not detrimental to the flow of the proceedings and the

---

5 DFE, *Code of Practice on the Identification and Assessment of Special Educational Needs* (DFE, 1994), para 1:3.

6 See Chapter 6 at **6.3**.

7 The SENT Secretariat's view of this suggestion is that it would have 'serious resource implications' because, inter alia, it would increase the overall cost of meeting members' travel and subsistence expenses and would require more members and chairs to be appointed (and trained).

presentation of evidence. The absence of breaks for refreshments was a particular concern of many parents.

Problems with tribunal venues and the lack of refreshments can also be overcome. Various suggestions were made in Chapter 7 about alternatives to the present arrangements under which, outside the London/South-East area, hearings take place in hotels. Even though their use means that hearings can be held in locations which are convenient to parents, hotels are not the ideal venues for quasi-judicial hearings and better accommodation can surely be found.

As far as can reasonably be ascertained, the SENT operates impartially, despite claims by a number of LEAs that under the new system there is a degree of bias in favour of parents. Indeed, the establishment of the SENT has redressed some of the imbalance of power between LEAs and parents in SEN disputes. The introduction of the SENT has in fact had an impact on LEAs in a number of ways. LEAs admit to now being under greater pressure to produce more evidence to justify their decisions, which in turn has meant a greater workload, especially in view of the reduced likelihood that a dispute will be settled without a hearing.[8] Nevertheless, many LEAs have not increased staffing to necessary levels, have provided insufficient staff training, and have not made more suitable administrative arrangements for appeals work. Consequently, some LEAs' case-work has been poor and the slowness of their response is contributing to the delays in the waiting time for a hearing, exacerbating the uncertainty for parents and children caused by many LEAs' failure to achieve their target times for statements of SEN.

Some LEAs believe that the new appeal system results in decisions which, while of benefit to the individual children concerned, place an undue financial burden on the LEA and may skew its allocation of resources by diverting a disproportionate amount to the education of children for whom there have been successful appeals, leaving less for special educational provision as a whole. There is, however, no good evidence that tribunals are acting other than fairly within the range of their powers and the statutory framework. There is, in fact, a case for extending those powers to enable interim orders to be made to avoid reduction in provision pending the outcome of an appeal.

The SENT received almost universal, if at times qualified, support when plans for its introduction were first announced. The evidence to date suggests that, while some aspects of its operation have been problematic,

---

8 See Chapter 5.

the SENT has met many of the positive expectations which were held prior to its introduction. Nevertheless, improvements will need to be made to increase its accessibility and build on its strengths. The author hopes that this book has helped to highlight those strengths and also the weaknesses of the new system in a way which will be of use to those who are committed to ensuring the maximum effectiveness, which includes accessibility, of any redress mechanism concerned with the education of children who face particular difficulty in learning.

BIBLIOGRAPHY

Aldridge, T., QC, *The Special Educational Needs Tribunal, Annual Report 1994/95* (SENT, 1995)

Aldridge, T., QC, *The Special Educational Needs Tribunal, Annual Report 1995/96* (SENT, 1996)

Andrews, E., *Representing parents at the Special Educational Needs Tribunal: An evaluation of the work of IPSEA's Free Representation Service* (IPSEA, 1996)

Audit Commission, *Local Authority Performance Indicators 1994/95* (HMSO, 1996), Vol 1, p 12

Audit Commission/HMI, *Getting In On the Act – Provision for Pupils with Special Educational Needs – The National Picture* (HMSO, 1992)

Bainham, A. with Cretney, S., *Children: The Modern Law* (Jordans, 1993)

Bainham, A., 'Sex education: a family lawyer's perspective', in N. Harris (ed) *Children, Sex Education and the Law* (National Children's Bureau, 1996)

Baldwin, J., Wikeley, N. and Young, R., *Judging Social Security* (Clarendon Press, 1992)

Barton, C. and Douglas, G., *Law and Parenthood* (Butterworths, 1995)

Bell, K., *Research Study on Supplementary Benefit Appeal Tribunals. Review of Main Findings: Conclusions: Recommendations* (HMSO, 1975)

Berthoud, R. and Bryson, A., 'Social security appeals: what do claimants want' (1997) 4(1) *Journal of Social Security Law* 17

Bradley, A. and Ruebain, D., 'Interim relief and the Special Educational Needs Tribunal – is there any place for judicial review?' (1996) 1(3) *Education, Public Law and the Individual* 54

Brooke Ross, R., 'New Training Initiatives 1995/96' (1996) 3(2) *Tribunals* 15

Budge, D. 'Huge gender gap in special needs revealed', (1997) *Times Educational Supplement*, 24 January

Commission for Local Administration in England, *Local Government Ombudsman Annual Report 1995/96* (CLE, 1996)

Committee on the Rights of the Child (UN), *Concluding Observations of the Committee on the Rights of the Child: United Kingdom of Great Britain and Northern Ireland* (UN, 1995)

Council on Tribunals, *Access for Disabled People Using Tribunals: Checklist and Code of Practice* (Council on Tribunals, 1993)

Council on Tribunals, *Annual Report 1986/87* (HMSO, 1987)

Council on Tribunals, *Annual Report 1987/88* (HMSO, 1988)

Council on Tribunals, *Annual Report 1992/93* (HMSO, 1993)

Council on Tribunals, *Annual Report 1994/95* (HMSO, 1995)

Council on Tribunals, *Annual Report 1995/96* (HMSO, 1996)

Department for Education, *Special Educational Needs: Access to the System – A Consulation Paper* (DFE, 1992)

Department for Education, *Code of Practice on the Identification and Assessment of Special Educational Needs* (DFE, 1994)

Department for Education, *Special Educational Needs Tribunal – Consultation Paper on Draft Regulations and Rules of Procedure* (DFE, 1994)

Department for Education/Welsh Office, *Choice and Diversity: A New Framework for Schools* (DFE/Welsh Office, 1992)

Evans, J. and Lunt, I., 'Special Educational Provision after LMS' (1993) 20 *British Journal of Special Education* 59

Franks, Lord (chair), *Report of the Committee on Administrative Tribunals and Enquiries*, Cmnd 218 (HMSO, 1957)

Friel, J., *Children with Special Needs: Assessment, Law and Practice – Caught in the Act* (Jessica Kingsley, 1995)

Friel, J. and Hay, D., *Special Educational Needs and the Law* (Sweet & Maxwell, 1996)

Frost, C. and Howard, A., *Representation and Administrative Tribunals* (Routledge and Kegan Paul, 1977)

Gardiner, J., 'Rise in special needs drains council funds' (1997) *Times Educational Supplement* 17 January

Genn, H. and Genn, Y., *The Effectiveness of Representation at Tribunals* (The Lord Chancellor's Department, 1989)

Goriely, T., 'The English legal aid White Paper and the LAG Conference' (1996) 3(3) *International Journal of the Legal Profession* 353

Hannon, V., 'The Education Act 1981: New Rights and Duties in Special Education' (1982) *Journal of Social Welfare Law* 275

Harris, N., 'Education By Right? Breach of the Duty to Provide "Sufficient" Schools' (1990) 53 *Modern Law Review* 525

Harris, N., *Quality and Effectiveness in Welfare Benefits and Related Work in Solicitors' Offices*, Research Study No 9 (The Law Society, 1991)

Harris, N., *Law and Education: Regulation, Consumerism and the Education System* (Sweet & Maxwell, 1993)

House of Commons Education Committee, Third Report, 1992–93, *Meeting of Special Educational Needs and Provision*, HC 287–I (HMSO, 1993)

House of Commons Education Committee, Second Report, 1995–96, *Special Educational Needs: The Working of the Code of Practice and the Tribunal*, HC 205 (HMSO, 1996)

House of Commons Education, Science and the Arts Committee, Third Report, 1986–87, *Special Educational Needs: Implementation of the Education Act 1981*, Vol 1, HC 201–I (HMSO, 1987)

IPSEA, 'Finding Support', *Special Children*, September 1995

Kempson, E., *Legal Advice and Assistance* (Policy Studies Institute, 1989)

Khan, A.N., 'Provision for Special Educational Needs in Britain' (1995) 6(3) *Journal of Education and the Law* (Canada) 301

King, D. and Treseder, P., 'Why Do I Have to Get into Trouble First?', in Dalrymple, J., and Hough, J., *Having a Voice: an Exploration of Children's Rights and Advocacy* (Venture Press, 1995)

Knill, B. and Humphreys, K., 'Parental preference and its impact upon a market force approach to special education' (1996) 23(1) *British Journal of Special Education* 30

Lister, R., *Justice for the Claimant*, Poverty Research Series No 4 (Child Poverty Action Group, 1974)

Lord Chancellor, The, *Legal Aid: Targeting Need* (HMSO, 1995)

Lord Chancellor, The, *Striking the Balance – The future of legal aid in England and Wales* (HMSO, 1996)

O'Leary, J., 'Education chiefs call for laws to prevent pupils suing schools' (1996) *The Times*, 2 December

Oliver, S. and Austen, L., *Special Educational Needs and the Law* (Jordans, 1996)

Rabinowicz, J. and Friel, J., 'The New Tribunal. First Responses' (1994) 21(1) *British Journal of Special Education* 27

Riddell, S., Brown, S. and Duffield, J., 'Conflicts of policies and models – the case of specific learning difficulties', in Riddell, S. and Brown, S. (eds), *Special Educational Needs Policy in the 1990s* (Routledge, 1994)

Robinson, J., 'Special educational needs, the code and the new tribunal' (1996) 8(1) *Journal of Education and the Law* 39

Russell, P., *Developing the role of the 'named person': some implications for policy and practice* (Council for Disabled Children, 1995)

Russell, P., 'Listening to Children with Disabilities and Special Educational Needs', in Davie, R., Upton, G. and Varma, V., *The Voice of the Child* (Falmer, 1996)

Sainsbury, R., Hirst, M. and Lawton, D., *Evaluation of Disability Living Allowance and Attendance Allowance*, DSS Research Report No 41 (HMSO, 1995)

SENT, *Special Educational Needs Tribunal – How to Appeal* (SENT, 1994)

Sherwin, M., 'The Law in Relation to the Wishes and Feelings of the Child', in Davie, R., Upton, G. and Varma, V., *The Voice of the Child* (Falmer, 1996)

Steele, J. and Bull, G., *Fast, Friendly and Expert?* (Policy Studies Institute, 1996)

Timms, J., 'Advocacy 2000 – The Way Forward', in Dalrymple, J. and Hough, J., *Having a Voice: An Exploration of Children's Rights and Advocacy* (Venture Press, 1995)

Timms, J., *Children's Representation. A Practitioner's Guide* (Sweet & Maxwell, 1995)

Wade, H.W.R. and Forsyth, C.F., *Administrative Law* (7th edn) (Oxford University Press, 1994)

Warnock, M. (chair), *Special Educational Needs* Cmnd 7212 (HMSO, 1978)

Wolfendale, S., 'Policy and provision for children with special educational needs in the early years', in S. Riddell and S. Brown, *Special Educational Needs Policy in the 1990s* (Routledge, 1994) 51

INDEX

References in the right-hand columns are to page numbers.